JOSEPH CONRAD AND HIS CIRCLE

RICHARD, PETER AND PHILIP KORZENIOWSKI

JOSEPH CONRAD
AND HIS CIRCLE

by

JESSIE CONRAD

Second Edition

WITH

A HANDLIST

of the various books, pamphlets, prefaces, notes, reviews and letters written about Joseph Conrad by Richard Curle

PORT WASHINGTON, N. Y. 1964
KENNIKAT PRESS, INC.

TO

PHILIP, RICHARD AND PETER CONRAD

THE THREE SMALL GRANDSONS OF JOSEPH CONRAD
THESE PAGES ARE AFFECTIONATELY DEDICATED BY
THEIR GRANDMOTHER, JESSIE CONRAD

". . . But the dwarf answered: 'No, something human is dearer to me than the wealth of all the world.'"

(*Grimm's Tales.*)

JOSEPH CONRAD AND HIS CIRCLE

This edition published in 1964 by Kennikat Press by arrangement with J.M. Dent and Sons, Ltd.

Manufactured in the United States of America

Library of Congress Catalog Card No: 64-24449

LIST OF ILLUSTRATIONS

JOSEPH CONRAD AND HIS CIRCLE

JOSEPH CONRAD AND HIS CIRCLE

CHAPTER ONE

MY first meetings with Joseph Conrad, sandwiched as they were between his last two voyages as Chief Officer of the sailing-ship *Torrens,* were most casual and, I am certain, could have held little significance for him beyond the recollection of a pleasant half-hour or so. We were introduced by a friend of his. I was not a little awed at those first meetings. His strangeness was very noticeable, almost oriental in its extravagance, both in gesture and speech. He was the first foreigner I had met and in my youth and ignorance I must have appeared very unsophisticated and somewhat raw. The fifteen years that separated his entry into the world from mine appeared a very wide stretch of time just then.

The ceremonious courtesy and exaggerated politeness, so characteristic of Joseph Conrad, was entirely new to me and rather took my breath away. In later years I have seen the same effect produced, over and over again, but in the beginning I was completely out of my depth. I felt unduly important and yet, funnily enough, at times absolutely nonplussed—all my natural cheek seemed to desert me. Indeed I owe much to my calm placid temperament, that was in the end such a sound foundation for our future understanding. I watched the exchange of friendliness between him and his two most intimate friends with interest. One, being a German, perhaps came nearer the true appreciation, or rather, understanding of his nature than the other; but what their friendship lacked in common was plainly made up in intensity. Those three men were staunch friends.

My acquaintance with Joseph Conrad and these two great friends who, together with their wives and families, welcomed me with so much sympathy and understanding began at the end of 1893, and was resumed in 1894. I must confess to a very lively interest in this stranger from the first. I had now and then some news of him from one acquaintance or another, but he remained for a long time an elusive figure, a man met by chance for a few hours, and I never had any idea when I might see him again.

To be exact I heard afterwards that he had made two short voyages after our first introduction and may have completely forgotten me for a time. Then out of the blue and just as I had concluded that this was to me no more than a passing friendship, a box of beautiful flowers arrived addressed to me at my home. The handwriting was strange to me. Greatly puzzled and excited I drew the small visiting card from beneath the spray.

"Konrad Korzeniowski"; that name was utterly new to me. I turned the tiny piece of paste-board over and read the closely written intimation that the sender hoped to give himself the pleasure of calling and paying his respects to my mother and myself, when next in London.

I was at a loss to recall to my mind who this could be, till I suddenly recollected hearing Mrs. Hope say that the Captain Conrad I had met was in truth a foreigner, and I remembered seeing the two gilt initials K. K. in the inside crown of his hat.

This curious habit of signing his letters as Konrad Korzeniowski or Joseph Conrad, or even a third and fourth form of signature persisted through all his life. I became in time, of course, familiar with this, but just at first I was frankly puzzled.

Weeks, months, passed before that call—it was in fact almost a complete year before I saw him the second time. From different sources I heard that his proposed stay in London had been cut short by a sudden hasty call to the death-bed of his much loved Uncle Thaddeus Bobrowski. This visit to his native country he subsequently forgot, and declared that when we went to Poland in 1914, he had not been there for over forty years.

I had quite decided that his promised call was forgotten, and because I was the least bit piqued, I was extremely anxious that no reference should be made, in my family circle, to his forgetfulness. But early one Saturday afternoon when I was sitting in the drawing-room window at work and taking a gloomy interest in the numerous funerals following each other to the big cemetery at the end of the road, the cheerful tinkle of a hansom-cab bell fell on my ear. Hansom cabs were rare at that time in the day. The long suburban road was flanked both sides by discreet villas, whose residents lived, and, one might almost say died, according to an established routine. I dropped my work in my lap and craned my neck to watch the unusual phenomenon so early in the afternoon.

I stared curiously at the cab drawn by a tall bay horse, as it proceeded at a slow trot up one side of the road and down the other. Then I saw the trap in the roof pushed up and an impatient order given. The animal was pulled up abruptly on its haunches just outside our gate, and a faultlessly dressed figure leapt swiftly to the ground almost before the vehicle had ceased to move. The swing of the square shoulders became instantly familiar to me and I watched fascinated the rapid passage up the long front path and hurried climb of the steep stone steps. Joseph Conrad—at last. I decided in the fleeting moments of his rapid approach to address him as Captain Conrad, Konrad Korzeniowski seemed to me then impossible to pronounce.

I remember thinking to myself as I watched him that there

appeared a very definite purpose in his quick movements—something fixed and final. I reached the door before he had time to ring, and by the time my mother appeared, I had recovered my equanimity, and was able to perform the ceremony of the introduction without undue concern. I managed to cloak my surprise at his unexpected appearance and eagerly seconded his invitation for us both to go with him out to dinner that evening. My mother made me smile by her slight show of resistance, when he almost demanded her acceptance. We were to dine at Overtons, near Victoria Station, a restaurant that was destined to see each stage of our later acquaintance. It has many pleasant memories for me even after this lapse of time.

On this the first evening after such a long interval I found little to say. The swiftness with which everything was arranged for that meal rather overpowered my mother. I suspected that it had been ordered in the morning before he had paid his promised visit, but to my mother, a perfect stranger, it must have been very disconcerting. However, she professed to have enjoyed herself—a profession I could not help taking with a certain reserve. I was thankful that while she was certainly a good deal puzzled she forbore to make any comment so I held my peace.

This was the first of many very pleasant times we, Joseph Conrad and I, passed together. A young sister, a model of tact and discretion at the age of thirteen, became a willing third in our subsequent jaunts. She was too young to be exacting and too generous by nature to mind being at times overlooked. She became a great favourite with the strange, impetuous foreigner, and we had many grateful recollections of that small girl's mature understanding. Good old "Ethelinda," as she was re-named by the man who ultimately became her affectionate brother-in-law.

It was soon after this that I was presented with a copy of *Almayer's Folly*, and one of my first Conradian treats was being asked to read aloud from the manuscript of the second book, *The Outcast of the Islands*.

I can never forget that evening, my consternation and nervous anxiety to acquit myself well. Alas ! I had not reckoned on the exacting irritability of my listener. He sat biting the tips of his fingers and wagging his foot with the most disconcerting rapidity. A few moments passed and he drew the papers none too gently from my hand and, turning a few pages quickly, handed them back again with an exasperated gesture. "Disregard those corrections, that passage is not going to stand. Never mind. Start three lines lower down, now over leaf, over leaf."

And then, "Oh, do speak distinctly. If you're tired, say so. Don't eat your words. You English are all alike ; you make the same sound for every letter."

I was nearly reduced to tears by this time although I knew that I had deserved his displeasure. He sat for a few moments with his head in his hands, an attitude with which I was to get extremely familiar later on.

Presently he roused himself, flinging out his arms with a wide gesture, and rather roughly he snatched the manuscript again, saying: "Poor little Chica, let us put all this 'paperas' away. Come out and let us get something to eat."

It must have been some months later when we met at Victoria Station. I knew by the way he received me that some unusual excitement had him in its power. First of all, he found fault with my hat, my dress and with my general appearance. Why hadn't I more colour? I was beginning to feel rather sorry I had accepted his invitation that morning. As if he could read my thoughts he gave a short laugh, squeezed my arm and drew me to the edge of the kerb, then beckoning a passing hansom he hurried me into it and got in after me. I glanced at his face when we were seated and was startled by the expression of gloomy determination on it. He had not spoken a word since he had directed the cabman to drive to the National Picture Gallery. Arrived there he handed me out with his usual punctilious politeness, paid the man and, with a characteristic swing of his shoulders, slowly mounted the steps by my side.

He paused at the top and muttered something uncomplimentary as to our English climate, then passing his hand through my arm he steered me through the various rooms, scarcely giving me time to even glance at anything, and abruptly guided me to a seat. He glanced round to see that we were alone and without any preamble began:

"Look here, my dear, we had better get married and out of this. Look at the weather. We will get married at once and get over to France. How soon can you be ready? In a week—a fortnight?"

I do not pretend that I was altogether surprised, or that his haste disturbed me. In fact, I felt that the sooner the better if at all. Certainly I had some few qualms a few moments later when I thought of my people at home. The idea of marriage would be new to them I was quite sure. I managed to voice this opinion with some anxiety at last. But even that little show of opposition seemed to make my future lord and master the more set upon this affair being settled out of hand and with the greatest speed. All the points in favour of haste he put forward, such as the weather, his health, his work. He even urged as a further inducement that he would not live long. This rather appalled me. I was young enough to be startled at the prospect of an early widowhood, and I did not know him then well enough to discount such statements or make allowances for his curious habit of exaggeration.

I had heard from several of his friends how nearly he had died from dysentery while being carried to the coast when he left the Congo. Of the many months he had lain between life and death in the German Hospital in London. I knew also that he had been lately staying at Champel in Geneva under medical treatment, and that he suffered from gout—but as to what particular form of illness this might be I was entirely ignorant.

After his proposal—surely one of the strangest ever made—we moved about gazing at the pictures we did not see, and it was nearly three in the afternoon when we remembered we had not lunched. At this discovery he became quite gay ; the tension grew less and we went to a small café and there proceeded to eat something that, whatever it was, in combination with our sentimental adventure, or as a result of picture gazing, proved our undoing. We had got as far as the park after lunch when we stopped short and glanced at each other in consternation. Violent pains had seized us both and each exclaimed at the deadly pallor that had come over the other's face. What was it ? Hastily Joseph Conrad called a cab and almost swooning we were driven to my home. Neither of us said more than a few words during that agonized drive, that seemed as if it would never end. Huddled in our respective corners of that vehicle, as far apart as we were able to get, intent upon our own sufferings, that seventy-five minutes passed at last. After an almost inarticulate farewell and a mumbled promise to write, he scrambled back into the hansom and I watched it disappear down the street.

We must have been poisoned with some part of that lunch. I was desperately ill for days. Meanwhile no word or sign had come to me from my fellow-sufferer. I had been filled by considerable remorse at having allowed him to take that return drive alone, my motherly instincts were aroused, although it had seemed impossible to do more at the time than endeavour to hide my own pain and acute discomfort from the man who had made that strange proposal. Was this sudden illness a preliminary to our great adventure together ?

I said nothing of what might be going to happen to my people at home, and as the time passed without the promised letter, I tried to convince myself that I must have dreamt most of what had happened. Then a few days later a rather peremptory wire came asking that my mother and I should go that very evening to Victoria for dinner.

After much silent commune I decided even then to say nothing about the possible change that might lie before me. It might well be that he would say no more about the matter that had filled my thoughts to the exclusion of nearly everything else. I had a very guilty feeling every time I looked at my mother; indeed it was a hard matter to hold my peace when she began to tell me her plans for our immediate future. I wondered how she would take it if I were suddenly to turn round and say: "I think of getting married in a week or so. . . ."

I was extremely solicitous for her comfort that evening and myself dressed her with great care for our dinner invitation. For a few moments she seemed disinclined to accept the somewhat terse expression of Joseph Conrad's desire for her company. Short notice, the trouble of dressing and a thousand other objections were advanced, all of which I overcame by a quiet determination.

I saw our host waiting for us under the big clock long before we reached his side. I found myself contemplating him from quite a different standpoint. He was no doubt the same, but in every small detail he seemed altered somehow. As he stood waiting, peering eagerly at each passer-by in his short-sighted fashion, I seemed to sense the fact that his wild proposition to get married out of hand was no dream, but a fixed and stern reality. The light from the big station lamps fell full upon him, showing up the brilliant flash of his perfect white teeth as he smiled his welcome. Here was no ordinary man, to be seen in dozens in London anyway. He came quickly, or rather, he swung, towards us, his brown haverlock resembling a long kilt, more than any kind of overcoat.

My mother caught my arm as we came abreast and murmured somewhat breathlessly, "Oh, dear; one could never take him for an Englishman, and he doesn't look French, either, I . . ."

She surrendered her gloved hand to his eager grasp and he raised it to his lips with his usual military click of the heels, my greeting was much less impressive but I felt in that moment that my fate was sealed. There was a curious air of possession in the hand he laid upon my arm as we turned to leave the platform where he had awaited us.

I followed the two figures, my mother and my prospective husband in silence, the two figures became a trifle blurred as I began to realize the importance of this meeting. I could utter no word of warning to my unsuspecting parent, who could have no notion of what was to be sprung upon her. Never before had I failed to tell her of any interest in me that might have been shown by one of my many friends, and even if she had sensed anything out of the ordinary she would put the idea aside because of my unusual reticence.

This time it was very plain that we were expected and our repast ordered in advance, except for the choice of the wine. The red shades over the lights mercifully hid my sudden confusion as I took my seat between them. I felt terribly nervous and self-conscious. But the dinner proceeded without any delay and until the coffee appeared the conversation was general and not of any very special interest. My nervousness increased.

Suddenly with his usual disregard of any form of preliminary introduction Joseph Conrad began to speak, the words tumbling out one after the other rapidly. My mother, surprised and greatly disconcerted, turned to look reproachfully at me. I swallowed hard and patted her hand that lay on the table. I was beyond speech. She smiled a little ruefully when he began to explain that one of his chief reasons for haste was that he hadn't very long to live and further that there would be no family. He ended up with a demand for a very short engagement and declared his intention of taking me abroad at once—indefinitely.

After this speech he sat back with an air of finality, lit a cigarette and turned to me with a brilliant flash of his teeth in a wide smile.

The matter was settled as far as he was concerned, but my mother had not yet recovered herself and was frankly puzzled. No family. Then why want to get married ? And what was the trouble that was going to cut short a life that to outward appearances was as normal as that of most other men.

She was still mystified when we reached home. The parting between the two arbitrators of my fate was almost silent. A quick hand-shake, a profound bow and a wide sweep of his hat, and my future husband walked away from the railway carriage without a backward glance. I sat waiting for the storm to burst, feeling rather remorseful for my seeming want of confidence, for I could see endless difficulties in the way of explanations. As it was, my mother, although slightly flushed, made no reference to the fact of my engagement until we reached home. Then she made the dramatic announcement to the rest of my family in these few words:

"Jessie has engaged herself to Captain Conrad, the foreign sailor—and . . . will be married in six weeks' time. Let me get to bed."

Once again the unreality of the situation took firm hold of me. The family's surprise was as complete as my mother's had been, but my part of it seemed outside their reception of the news. My eldest sister turned away leading my mother upstairs and the younger ones were silent. I made my escape feeling too great an emotion to say anything and longing to be alone.

What with the prospect of an early death depriving me of a husband and the knowledge of his determination not to have a family, it took several days to reconcile my mother to the idea of my marriage. At last I had a chance to explain that the idea of an early death existed in imagination only, and had no other significance than the fact of his having nearly died when he was being carried to the coast from the Congo.

My mother accepted this explanation and became somewhat more reconciled to the idea, even although she had a strong prejudice against a foreigner. This, in 1896, was much more common than it is now. My six weeks' engagement was rather a troublous time, a time that needed much tact and endurance. My desertion of the nest was not at all approved of. Many were the pin-pricks administered with no little dexterity and I found myself longing desperately for the end of that engagement and the fulfilment of my destiny. There was a golden prospect of journeying into a remote unknown. I had no regrets, and our many meetings during these weeks only cemented the tie between this aloof foreigner and myself. In a very short time all my maternal instincts were centred upon the man I was to marry, he became to me as much a son as a husband. And this state of accord lasted all our married life.

By this time I had made the acquaintance of several close friends who had known Joseph Conrad for all the time he had been in England, a few longer than the rest, but it was easy to see that all of them regarded him with deep affection. Among the earliest of these were Mr. and Mrs. Hope and their family of small children; Mr. and Mrs. Edward Garnett and David, who became my friends at once. Mr. John Galsworthy and Mr. E. L. Sanderson. These last two friends had been passengers on board the sailing-ship *Torrens*, which was the last but one on which Joseph Conrad served during his sea-going days.

I felt that I knew my future husband very much more intimately after meeting these dear people. But I must not forget Mr. and Mrs. Krieger. They accepted me at once without any reserve, as did the dear Hopes and those two passengers of the *Torrens*. From them I heard several interesting stories of that momentous voyage.

I think it was some time during the passage home that these two young men shared a cabin and frequently caused a great stir on board because of their habit of leaving their port-hole open. A miscellaneous collection of clothes, books, etc. would float out every now and then through the open port and bob saucily on the surface of the water in the wake of the vessel. But apparently no loss served as a warning, and time after time the open port-hole allowed the sea to flood the cabin and take liberties with their personal belongings.

One tragic happening on board was the suicide of the doctor who was suffering from some internal complaint; he had taken an over-dose of some sleeping draught, regardless of the large

JOSÉF TEADOR KONRAD KORZENIOWSKI AND JESSIE, HIS WIFE, IN 1896

LANNION, CÔTES-DU-NORD, BRITTANY, IN 1896
Where the honeymoon was spent.

number of invalid passengers under his care. Mr. Sanderson sat by his berth all through the long night unaware that the poor spirit had already flown.

Joseph Conrad told me of a rather amusing incident that happened during one voyage. In this case two elderly and modest spinsters had carelessly hung a bag of soiled linen too near the cabin lamp, with the result that it caught fire. They were greatly incensed when too smooth-faced middies were ordered into the privacy of their cabin to extinguish the flames. The two ladies reproached the officer of the watch bitterly. If he had been unable himself to be the intruder, in deference to their sex an older person should have been sent instead of these beardless youths. My husband was very fond of telling this story against the mock-modesty of my sex. I always laughed because he invariably concluded with one about the tactful plumber who, finding himself in a bathroom in which a lady was taking her bath, had the presence of mind to retire with a "I beg your pardon, *sir*."

It was also during this voyage that the manuscript of *Almayer's Folly* was begun, and because of the encouragement of those two passengers and one other (who was a very sick man), that the finished book was later on submitted to Mr. Edward Garnett, who was then reader for Mr. T. Fisher Unwin. Mr. Edward Garnett was the only one of Joseph Conrad's early friends who was doubtful as to the wisdom of marriage for the creator of that Eastern story.

His objections, I learned afterwards, were not at all personal to me, but he had formed a very just and complete understanding of the strange character who sought to bind himself in the bonds of matrimony to a woman not even of his own race and so many years younger. But I am thankful to know he modified his opinion after he had grown to know me and further than that, he agreed that I was the one woman possible to be the wife of his gifted friend. How great a compliment he paid me I was not at the time fully aware, but since then it has come home to me as a truth. For Joseph Conrad has endorsed that friend's early opinion many, many times. And thus I have my one remaining consolation after eleven years of widowhood.

I take some credit to myself even from the first, for I entered into that compact with the full determination that I would leave my husband virtually as free as if no symbol of a wedding-ring had passed between us. It came as a kind of intuition that this man would find any demand upon his liberty both irksome and galling, and because of my understanding I was able to hold his interest and fidelity to the end. His reaction to this rule I had made differed according to his mood. Sometimes he was absent for only a few hours and would bombard me with long and anxious telegrams, at others he took refuge in his "liberty" and refused to let me know even where he was or when he might return.

Once, two years after we were married, he left the house early one morning to take leave of a young friend who was starting that day on the first stage of his journey to America. I had expected him back again within a couple of hours. Imagine my concern when lunch-time passed and he had not returned. In the early afternoon, full of anxiety, I made my way to the little railway station and put a few tentative questions to the single porter.

The man performed the usual laconic aids to memory, pushing his cap back and scratching his head, before he volunteered full information as to the disappearance of my lord and master. "Oh, yes, mum, I see Mr. Conrad this morning, 'long of Mrs. Hope and the young gentleman. Went to town, he did with 'em."

Before our six weeks' engagement had come to an end my future husband had sprung upon me yet another surprise. He found it hard to leave the sea, and his imagination had been fired and his old desires renewed when he heard that in Grangemouth there was a wooden barque lying waiting for a purchaser. Nothing would satisfy him but that I should accompany him and his friend Mr. Hope there and then to inspect this vessel.

Once more our little chaperon was annexed and we made the journey up the East Coast in the S.S. *Forth*. I for one thoroughly enjoyed the trip, my first of such a length by steamer, and so did the small girl. Joseph Conrad and "Ethelinda" were by this time fast friends and they could be seen arm in arm parading to and fro. I made one of four at whist each evening with the ship's captain, Mr. Hope and another unlucky captain who was going North to attend an enquiry as to the loss of his ship.

This voyage made a very pleasant interlude and gave me a jolly week's holiday into the bargain, and my nerves were beginning to get a little frayed trying to mask my anxiety for the great wedding-day to arrive.

When we reached Grangemouth in the short sunlight of a February afternoon our spirits sank. The ship lay close to the quay with a large number of sea-gulls sitting on her mast-heads. These birds flew round us angrily resenting our approach, evidently possession was nine points of the law. Mr. Hope shook his head, pointing dramatically at the masts and its feathered proprietors. "I don't like the look of it, my dear chap. She must have been lying here a long time for those sea-gulls to be so firmly established."

Aboard there was desolation everywhere. The saloon presented a picture of cruel and wanton destruction. The big settee running nearly the full length of the saloon had been ripped open, wooden bunks torn from their positions, and hinges of the port-holes forced off. In fact, there was a brooding air of ill-omen about the ship. Something fateful and sinister that we all felt. It seemed only a fulfilment of that grim destiny when we heard, some four years later, that the wooden barque *Windermere* had been lost off Dover with all hands.

Only three days after our return the wedding-day arrived. My modest trousseau was ready and packed away in two trunks bearing my new initials. (I knew nothing of the rice that was to betray me at the Custom House.) The great day dawned without a cloud in the sky.

Here, again, Joseph Conrad took refuge in the most matter-of-fact attitude. To begin with, he kept me waiting to be married just half an hour, and even when his two friends, Mr. Hope and Mr. Krieger, did persuade him to make a move, he delayed still further in some futile argument with the cab-driver. I was feeling physically sick at this delay and rejoiced when the ceremony was over and we were on our way to a little café in Victoria, where we five lunched. My mother was the only one of my vast family in attendance, and I was touched to see her pitiful attempts to keep calm. Still, lunch over and Joseph Conrad having duly signed his will which his two friends witnessed, they departed. Mr. Krieger had presented me with a beautiful bouquet of early roses, red and white, the Polish colours. These I had reluctantly to relinquish for my husband flatly refused to allow me to carry them to my home, where we were due for the purpose of cutting the wedding-cake and bidding my family farewell.

I have thought many times with amusement of the comic distress displayed by my husband on the day of our wedding when the whole of my many brothers and sisters raised their voices in loud lament when the time came for us to leave.

"Good Heavens, if I had known this would happen, I—well, I would never have married you," he muttered, turning away with an expression of utter disgust.

We dined that night at Overtons, and then we walked the short distance to the bachelor rooms that Joseph Conrad had retained for our last night in town. First of all I tackled a huge heap of masculine garments that had somehow to be included in my trunks which had been sent there the day before. I managed very well on the whole and the trunks swallowed the last pair of socks without a strain. Surreptitiously I shook out a quantity of the tell-tale rice in the process.

This done, I seated myself at the table and took my share of the heap of correspondence that had to be disposed of before we could leave England. A great deal of it I found was nothing less than our two photographs and a curiously formal and grandiloquent announcement of the day's proceedings. My awe increased and I felt shy and a little disconcerted. Still he gave me no time to think much of my personal feelings, but pushed the pile of envelopes towards me and called my attention to a list of addresses in his note-book. It was thirsty work licking the stamps, but at last this task was finished and the tearful landlady appeared with a welcome tray with tea.

After this my strange husband insisted upon going out to post the batch that night. He took no heed of my protest that it was then nearly two in the morning and they might well wait until a little later in the day. Just as he closed the street-door, the curtain-pole fell to the ground and our brilliantly lighted windows faced the street uncovered. An unkind stroke of fate —with the dawn yet some few hours distant.

The next morning, or rather, some seven hours later we were ready to start on the first stage of our big adventure. My mother had elected to come to us for lunch and to see us off at Waterloo. I had received the strictest orders that there should be no tears or display of emotion on my part. I was rather concerned because I knew that this restraint would be a lasting reproach in the eyes of my parent. She stood at the door of the railway-carriage, and behind the back of my new husband I raised my handkerchief effectively to my eyes as the train steamed out of the station, then I turned to him dry-eyed and quite composed. This little deception may, I hope, be forgiven me.

One incident disturbed me greatly during that run to Southampton. We were passing through a long tunnel, there was no light in the carriage and we were sitting opposite each other in the most decorous fashion. Without the least warning there was a terrific detonation somewhere very close at hand and the carriage was momentarily filled by a blinding flash. I was startled and for a second a sickening fear held me dumb. It was then that I realized how great an adventure it was on which I had so lightheartedly embarked, and how little I really knew of the man I had married. Suppose he turned out to be a member of some secret society ? The flash and explosion had seemed to be in the very compartment, and he had made no sound since. I held my breath as the train cleared the tunnel and the welcome daylight filled the carriage. He smiled across at me, evidently quite undisturbed. I was ashamed to tell him the reason of my sudden fright, but I suppose my face betrayed me. I explained as best I could. " Silly little donkey, it was only a fog signal they were using as a warning to the men at work on the line."

My relief was almost painful, but I decided not to give a complete explanation. Instinct somehow showed me that I might be misunderstood. He might think I distrusted him, and anyhow, my feeling was too indefinite, too unreal for me to give it expression—least of all to him.

For the rest of the journey he came out of his preoccupation and was the charming companion he knew so well how to be. I remember his laughing heartily at my modest request for a little French money. This he gave me at once and jokingly asked if I would like to have my own ticket ?

The next few hours were too full of novelty and excitement for me to worry much as to my rather disturbing experience on the train. It was an entirely new adventure upon which I had embarked. There was the first sight of the dock gates in Southampton, and our leisurely dinner in the hotel. I was desperately hungry and refused to take advice in my choice of food. Certainly that dinner was, to say the least of it, highly injudicious. Weather-wise, my companion cast anxious looks out to sea and almost, I firmly believe, decided to wait a bit in Southampton for the prospect of a calmer crossing. I believe it was my rather teasing remark that decided him that we would keep to our original plan, and accordingly about midnight we went aboard.

"Dirty night, sir," remarked the captain on his way to the bridge, "we shall run into it directly we get outside." My new husband looked at me with a comic air of dismay and we continued our way to our cabin, which opened on to the deck.

Already the few passengers were making their way to their berths in haste. One very fat man amused me greatly when we started. He leaned over the rail in the throes of seasickness and then distrusting his legs to perform their legitimate function dropped on all fours and crawled into his lair. The second stage of my adventure had begun not too propitiously. I turned at the door of our cabin to look for the last time at the shores of my native country as they receded, lost in the mist of rain and darkness.

CHAPTER TWO

I WAS not to see those cliffs again for over six months. The night we left, as I stood beside Joseph Conrad, I had no misgivings, but I must confess to a certain feeling of awe. The man by my side was even more concerned. He had already lived half his normal life and, as he said, he had no notion how to look after a wife. The first time he heard me called by the title of "Mrs. Conrad," he asked impatiently: "to whom are they referring?" I have a feeling of tender gratitude, however, when I recall his solicitude for my comfort that night, our second married night, aboard the steamer, that pitched and tossed, rolled and wallowed. The night was appalling in its raging fury of wind and rain; and only the day before the weather had been perfect.

Our private cabin for some reason was not within the care of the stewardess. I soon knew the horrors of sea-sickness, and it added much to my consternation to find my sailor husband afflicted in the same manner. Long before we sighted St. Malo, where we arrived just twelve hours late, I had decided that nothing should induce me to cross the water again, family or no family. It was impossible to stand to clothe myself; in a dressing-gown and slippers and my hair hanging down my back I must have presented a very woebegone appearance. Enough, as my new husband later told me, "to inspire a dead man with distrust." At the moment my indifference was complete and my terrible nausea at the mere mention of food rather alarmed him. From long acquaintance with the sea, his sickness had left him some time ago. I shuddered to see him devour some thick sandwiches and put out of sight two huge cups of broth. His next move astonished me not a little. Barely were we clear of the Customs and I had managed to hang a few more conventional garments around me than he insisted we should go at once to a queer block of hut-like structures which advertised themselves as bath-houses. This was surely the most primitive place, just two big square tanks in two little cubicles. These were filled with a most unpleasant steam. They were situated in rather closer proximity than my modesty would have chosen, but this turned out to be a blessing. Being plump and feeling like nothing on earth, I carelessly neglected to let some of the water out. The next moment I was gasping and spluttering and calling loudly for help, having had my head under water twice!

It was nearly six o'clock when we were once more dressed and seated near the ramparts looking at the sea. It was then I voiced my need of some sustenance. My voice sounded even in my own ears very tearful. "I am so hungry, I have had nothing to eat since last night."

The effect of my lament was laughable. My poor man's compunction was out of all proportion. I was filled with remorse for having mentioned my hunger, his distress was so great. I did not then, as I have said, know his habit of exaggeration of word and gesture. I remember he got me a pot of tea and some biscuits, and, what was to my English mind a trifle shocking, a big bottle of rum in place of milk on the same tray.

An hour or so later we dined and after another short walk round the battlements, retired, and slept soundly till the entrance of a man in his baize apron to transport our luggage to the 'bus, roused us to quick activity. As it was, I had perforce to conclude my toilet in the 'bus, and my new husband obligingly laced up my long boots during the short drive to the station.

It took us the best part of the day to get to our destination, Lannion, a quaint little French village at the head of a tidal river on the coast of Brittany. Here we proposed to stay until we found a furnished peasant house where we could spread ourselves out and begin work on a new book in earnest.

A few weeks before we were married we had been included in the English Census and two days after our arrival in the picturesque little French hotel in Lannion we were included in the French. Joseph Conrad's face was a picture of comic dismay when the papers were handed to him ; he half refused to sign, fuming inwardly when the matter was pressed. Then a bright smile illuminated his face and he spoke rapidly in French. I had not understood all that was said, but I caught sufficient to comprehend that this new husband of mine had indulged in a little white lie, for some reason or other. He had declared that we had been married some months. My protest was received with the usual shrug of the shoulders and a quick retort : "Well, my dear, to me it seems years."

I did not quite know how to take this statement, and turned it over and over in my mind in some concern. It hardly sounded complimentary, yet it could hardly have been intended otherwise.

"Hôtel de France, Lannion," was typical of its size and type. Many business men, electricians, lawyers and a few idle Frenchmen (bachelors) took their meals in the big sanded dining-room at the same long table. We were soon on friendly terms with most of those who were regular clients, and one in particular used always to sit by my side. I had noticed his extreme politeness, but I was too uncertain of my French to take much part in the conversations or arguments he carried on with my husband, sitting as usual on my left. We lived in the hotel about a fortnight, taking a daily drive in search of our modest El Dorado (in the shape of a peasant's cottage). These drives were a source of a great deal of amusement at first, but as our wealth steadily diminished it became rather a more anxious business. Joseph Conrad was anxious to begin his work without further delay. One day we discovered a tiny place adjoining a very primitive hotel; a perfect example of the simple life, without a single luxury, and many glaring inconveniences. Knowing my fastidious partner, I was a bit dubious as to my power to make him sufficiently comfortable. We had four rooms. One big bed-sitting-room with two four-poster beds (only one equipped with the conventional needs as regards blankets, etc.), a big round table in the centre of the room, a tiny wash-hand stand with the most minute toilet set on its blistered and painted top. A chest of rickety drawers surmounted by a cupboard with glass doors, which would serve either for books or superfluous china. The coarse linen sheets had a seam down the centre very like the low stone walls round the fields on the island. The big kitchen below had a bedplace under the stairs for the maid, a tiny slip of a room with a table and three chairs completed the furnishing, and a corresponding garret above provided me with a place to do the typewriting. Here the sole furniture was a small iron bedstead, a rickety table and a bottomless cane chair.

Still, what would you have. I was satisfied and greatly intrigued by the strangeness of the situation. A big loft above allowed me a wide view of the sea on all four sides. We clinched the arrangement in a very short time, engaged a niece of our prospective landlady as general maid and returned to the mainland and our hotel to collect our belongings.

It was just lunch time when we arrived and I went hastily to my room to smooth my hair. Thus I arrived in the dining-room a little after my husband and just in time to see him greet my table neighbour with what struck me as an excess of politeness and formality. The next moment I was startled by an expression of ferocity and anger, and listened aghast to the rapid stream of words Joseph Conrad hurled at the surprised Frenchman. I looked on amazed till I caught the words, uttered with concentrated fury: "This lady, sir, is my wife, not my daughter."

It was the most uncomfortable meal I ever remember eating in my life. I did not know what had happened or why I was shepherded into a chair with my irate husband between me and my usual neighbour. Neither of the two men uttered a word all through the meal and my well-meant attempts to start a conversation fell flat. Luncheon ended at last then with a profound obeisance to me on the part of the tall Frenchman, who then inclined his head haughtily in the direction of my husband, and turning abruptly on his heel, left the room, and the hotel knew him no more.

It was not until we were in our own room that I heard the cause of the commotion, and I had decided to let the storm blow over before I made any reference to it. We had packed most of our wearing apparel into the trunks and I had seated myself for a few moments' rest when, with the usual little short laugh that heralded something untoward, my husband came abruptly to my side and muttered: "Dam' cheek. What do you think the fellow said, Jess.? Asked my permission to pay his addresses to my daughter." I laughed and crept closer to him, laying my hand affectionately on his arm. He made an impatient movement. "That comes of your looking such a kid," he said with a profound sigh.

That afternoon we finished our preparations, bought large stores of tea and coffee, biscuits and not a few "swineries" as Joseph Conrad called them, and with our luggage piled high and our purchases stacked beside us, we withdrew from the friendly circle in the little hotel, promising to return often for a meal, or when we wished to forsake our tiny island home for a few days.

When we arrived at this new home the preparations for our first evening meal were in full swing. I gasped in horror when the huge pile of big round sausages appeared. I had not quite understood. The meal had not been intended for our consumption only. We were expected to pay our footing on that island by providing a feed for most of the inhabitants. This explained the monumental pile of sausages and the long lengths of bread, mound of butter and cheese. Not to speak of the drink that each expected to get at the hotel bar at our expense. My relief was comical, if my consternation as to the cost excusable. We became very fast friends with the inhabitants, who were mostly stone cutters. Most of them had enormous families and more than one father petitioned that we should pay the rent of his potato field. Their arguments in favour of our philanthropy were various and lengthy if not always convincing. However, I soon discovered that my husband was excessively generous and disliked the trouble of refusing any request within his power to grant. Our neighbours also speedily discovered that my mission in life was to protect the peace and privacy of my man, and I found my patience sorely tried when young infants were placed in dangerous places at the top of our flight of steps, left there to howl until I removed them, and pacified them with gifts of biscuits or sweets. Still our honeymoon remains a time that is a joy to recall, and I don't think there ever appeared a rift in the lute, outside illness which was beyond our control.

One of our early visitors to the island was a dear old man, a Capitaine le Bras, and the day he paid his first visit he brought the small boat we were hiring from him for the length of our stay, round the coast. After lunch we went to see her lying at anchor. This little craft was to be our toy and provide our recreation when we had earned it.

It was surely an unkind stroke of fate that, the night when we returned from our first short sail after the dear old man had departed, my husband should develop an intense fever. Full of concern, I got him hot tea and did my best to stop the violent shivering fits. It was my first experience of malaria, although I knew he had suffered considerably from this complaint before we were married. By degrees he became more and more incoherent and rambling in his speech, and the shivering fits increased. I became seriously alarmed and sought the aid of my friendly landlady. I could not have been away from him more than a quarter of an hour, but when I returned with the good woman in tow, my husband had gone to bed, fully dressed even to his overcoat—the thick haverlock. Now he raved in grim earnest, speaking only in his native tongue and betraying no knowledge of who I might be. For hours I remained by his side watching the feverish glitter of his eyes that seemed fixed on some object outside my vision, and listening to the meaningless phrases and lengthy speeches, not a word of which I could understand.

Here was a plight indeed. It seemed a terrible long time before my messenger returned with a doctor, a dear old man, who had driven the nine odd miles to my aid. I was at great pains to follow his directions and I had no help. Delirium was almost unknown to me, and I felt horribly alone, and now, to add the culminating stroke of ill luck, a violent attack of gout developed in one wrist and ankle. My resources were well-nigh exhausted by the next morning and I welcomed the good old doctor tearfully. He was a real friend in need. He insisted that I should go and lie down for an hour or so and leave my patient to his care. When I returned I found that the painful wrist and ankle had been neatly bandaged and a sling improvised out of an old pillow-case to sustain the poor arm. But he could not induce my sick husband to part with a shred of his clothes. Then, when he turned to leave the room, the old fellow threw out his hands, remarking that it would be well if I could get some heat in the room.

All that night Joseph Conrad continued to rave in Polish, a habit he kept up every time any illness had him in its grip. Some of the, to me, outlandish sounds became sufficiently intelligible for me to follow, at least to the extent of giving him a drink or smoothing his pillow. But he resisted fiercely any attempt I made to get him to let me remove even his socks or overcoat. He made a striking picture in that French four-poster with its white curtains draping all but one side, his fierce looks, dark pointed beard and gleaming teeth.

Towards the morning of the fourth day the fever seemed to leave him somewhat and I woke from a doze to see him resting on the elbow of his sound arm, and staring at me in a very disconcerting fashion. I made as if to rise and approach the bed, but sinking back he waved me back. Then he said distinctly: "I must tell you what the doctor said about you." There followed such a stream of disjointed accusations as to my moral and spiritual character that speedily reduced me to tears. Not being wise enough to guess that he was still in a state of delirium my fortitude forsook me entirely and I burst into hysterical tears and rushed from the room. My distress must have penetrated his muddled consciousness for he called me several times, but I had to regain my self-control and I did not venture for over half an hour to come back to his side.

Then I stole softly across the room and seated myself in my chair facing the bed. He slept, not fitfully as he had done for the last few days and nights, but calmly and restfully. Two hours slipped away and I must have slept a little, too, then rousing myself I got ready as dainty a little meal on the tray as I could manage with my very limited resources. When he woke he appeared quite rational and ate with a relish. It was many days before I asked him why he had not defended me from the unkind attack made upon me by the doctor. He denied all knowledge of everything, declaring that I had been dreaming. So—it rested at that, but I always felt a little distrustful of the old doctor, a feeling I could not shake myself clear of.

Altogether the illness lasted well over a fortnight and as soon as he recovered somewhat he set to work with frantic haste. Something had to be finished and sent to his publisher in London. He could not afford to loaf in this fashion. We conned carefully over our financial position and found no immediate cause for anxiety. But the fact remained that only a fortnight before we married, Joseph Conrad had, through the failure of some gold-mining company, lost all but a few hundred pounds of his modest capital. Indeed he had felt some misgiving as to the advisability of our marriage adventure with such a small sum behind us. We anxiously discussed the matter, but I am thankful that in the end we decided to risk the possible consequences and take the plunge. We kept our financial misfortune to ourselves. I have thought since that his courage was greater than mine. He knew more of life because of the difference in our ages, certainly, but what remained of his capital seemed quite a good sum to my inexperienced mind.

But with the advent of a warm spring and the interest of the little sailing boat as a reward for our labours we got along fairly well. I had mastered my erratic elderly typewriter well enough to keep pace with his activities. The first pages of the *Rescue* were to me a pure delight, although my early efforts lacked finish, and my machine refused to line and space every now and then. Any abrupt or clumsy movement would bring about disaster without fail. The bar had a nasty habit of releasing itself from the carriage, and the whole of the type in a moment became scattered over the floor. Putting those in order again was a nightmare. To begin with every letter was separate, all had to fit into the slot in the bar upside down, and I have been as much as two days putting it in order.

The day the first batch of manuscript was sent from Ile Grande was a " festa " and we had made our plans well in advance of the day for a jaunt. It was a curious coincidence that on the night the *Drummond Castle* went down off Ushant, we should have been at sea in our little boat, barely twenty miles away. The gold mine director was a passenger in the *Drummond Castle*; he would have had news for us. The weather that day was most promising and we were feeling very virtuous and bent on enjoying our first little holiday trip of any distance along the coast. We provisioned our boat for a week with dry stores, intending to get what fresh provisions we might need where we spent each night. I had given the maid a few days holiday. Accompanied by the old French seaman who did duty as crew we embarked that sunny morning light-heartedly enough. There was no cloud in the serene blue sky, no premonition of anything untoward in our minds. We stowed ourselves and our provisions comfortably aboard, and sat patiently awaiting the flow of the tide when our boat would float and we could begin our cruise. I must here explain that we had two wooden legs, one each side of the boat, to keep her upright when the water receded, as it did for a great distance, leaving her high and dry. Our anchorage was very far away from the shore end of the sands and it meant an exercise of patience, unless we used the dinghy. Usually we walked across the stretch of sand and boarded the boat dry-shod and waited for the tide. This morning was no exception to the rule and neither of us minded waiting.

Joseph Conrad had been sitting smoking silently, his eyes on the distant horizon. Suddenly he turned to me, tossing the cigarette-end over the side, where it fell in the water with a slight hiss. I looked across at him, wondering what this man of moods had been thinking of. He answered my smile with a slight shake of his head and said :

" You remember old Furley, Jess, the Gold-mining Company's solicitor." I nodded my head and waited. " Well, the principal Director is due home in England the end of this week, so the old fellow tells me in his letter this morning. He seems to think that there may be something saved out of the fire after all. He's coming home in the *Drummond Castle*. Strange, isn't it? She should be off Finisterre some time to-night, about twenty miles away. She will have a fine passage by the look of the weather. I confess I should be glad if old Furley turns out right and even a little is saved."

It was almost the first reference he had made to the loss of his money since the night we decided to risk everything and get married. I had not known that he had any English mail that morning before we started. I answered as hopefully as I could and begged him to put it out of his mind for the time being. "You may have news when we get back on Sunday. That would just give time for a letter to reach us here, wouldn't it?"

Just then we floated and he sprang to his feet, sacrificing almost a whole cigarette this time. "Haul away," he commanded the old seaman, while he grasped the tiller. As soon as the anchor was clear and the mainsail set he handed me the tiller with instructions to keep her close to the wind, what there was of it. We had cleared the last rock and were standing well out to sea before he answered my question with an impatient shrug of his shoulders and in a rather exasperated tone.

"Barely, by Sunday. But let's forget the blamed thing just now. Happy?"

I assured him I was thoroughly enjoying every moment and called his attention to the wide expanse of clear water and we remarked how calm and serene was the outlook on every side. There was no premonition of evil, of death or disaster. Later on in the afternoon when we had finished our lunch we began to feel a bit sleepy, for our start had been an early one, even the old seaman was nodding over his pipe. We decided to heave-to, and when Joseph Conrad had made all snug and hauled the sails aback, there being no wind, we settled ourselves and closed our eyes in complete security. Joseph Conrad himself undertook to keep half an eye open for a time and old Milo was to relieve him in an hour.

But evidently we must all have slept soundly for some little time longer for it was past seven when a startled exclamation from the old sailor awoke us with a start. I heard a smothered curse from my husband, more forcible than elegant, and I sat up quickly, rubbing my eyes incredulously. All around, and over us, lay a thick blanket of white fog. Not a sound seemed to penetrate it, not a glimmer of light to enable us to guess our whereabouts. We had been out of sight of land when we closed our eyes, as the coast just at that point was very low-lying.

Joseph Conrad's first act was to let go the anchor. I watched his face anxiously. " We are drifting, Jess," he muttered, " our cable's too short to hold. What the devil . . . ? "

He stood up cupping his ear with his hand, listening intently for a few seconds. Then as no sound came, he instructed the man by a gesture to haul up the anchor.

" Where do you think we are ? " he asked tersely, and nodded in agreement when the old fellow shook his head helplessly. My husband swung round in a desperate hurry. " Take an oar," he said, seizing one himself. For a few seconds there was nothing further said as the two men bent to their task. " No good," he announced, " we're simply turning her round and round, in a circle. Here's a pretty go, Jess, we may be run down any minute—or hit one of those blasted rocks before we know where we are—can't see a blamed thing."

I had seated myself philosophically in the stern sheets on the tiny cabin roof, out of the way, but the next moment I raised my head and said, quietly, pointing the way we were slowly drifting, " I can hear the tinkle of a cow-bell over there."

We listened anxiously, and my husband shook his head.

" I heard it then, monsieur," old Milo jerked out. " Mainland's over there."

Quickly the two men began to furl the sails which just then began to flap against the mast as the first breath of wind made itself felt. Tense moments passed, our little craft was drifting slowly but surely towards the sound of the cow-bell that came now in regular rhythm. Our luck was in after all, we ran aground on the shelving sand, and soon after we let down the two wooden legs to keep her upright, and Milo volunteered to get assistance and disappeared abruptly over the side into the thick mist. We heard a few hallos and then fainter and much farther off an answering shout. We sat silently holding hands, both too thankful to speak.

It must have been fully an hour later when we heard voices and shouted ourselves to guide the three burly Bretons towards us. Their grotesque shapes loomed up in the fog and friendly hands assisted us over the side of the boat, and on to the soft sand on which we had had the luck to beach our boat. We left one man with the old seaman to get a grip with the anchor, and helped by the other two natives we made our difficult way up the steep beach, and found ourselves at last in the sanded bar of a big rambling hotel.

Our adventure caused a great deal of excitement, and listening to the talk we made out that we had indeed had a lucky escape. The wind now began to blow quite fresh from the sea. " There are some ugly rocks a bit to windward of this hotel, that stretch some two miles or more out to sea. Your boat wouldn't have stood much buffeting against them in this wind, and the water is very deep round them," remarked one man.

At ten o'clock we decided to leave Milo in charge of the boat with instructions to sail her back on the morrow to the island if the weather cleared. Then, Joseph Conrad having secured the services of a young Breton who agreed to drive us home over the sands for a sum that appeared fair to us, we started in the dark sitting side by side in the high cart. I was in the middle. It struck me as a trifle rash, but knowing my husband better by now, I said nothing. The cart had no lights and I had a lively dread of the rocks that quite likely would obstruct our way. However, as the young driver declared he knew the road over the sands and where to make a detour to avoid any rocks, I hoped for the best. We sat silently thankful for our escape. Beyond clicking his tongue from time to time, to encourage his steed, the Breton was as mute as ourselves. The drive seemed endless over those sands, for we could proceed only at a walking pace. About halfway the animal came to a sudden and determined standstill. Even a sharp cut with the whip and a jumble of words uttered in, to me, meaningless phrases, failed to move him and our Jehu, with the reins in his hand, descended heavily from his perch beside me on to the sand. In the dark he stooped down by the head of the horse and we heard a surprised whistle, then the sound of a hoarse voice protesting drunkenly, and our driver's short laugh.

"Only a drunken man fairly curled round the horse's fore feet," my husband translated for my benefit. The Breton spoke very indifferent French, but this much my husband had understood. Still laughing grimly the driver hauled the helpless bundle out of the way and we left him mumbling curses in his thick throaty voice. The rest of the journey was without incident and we arrived at the door of our home in the dark and without a key.

It took some time to rouse our landlady, who could not be persuaded it was really her tenants who were thus disturbing her heavy slumbers. But convinced at last and voluble in her sympathy, she attired herself hurriedly and descended, and what was more stayed to make some hot coffee for us before she left us.

The next morning we had the dreadful news that during that disastrous fog, that so easily might have ended our honeymoon, the *Drummond Castle* had run on to a reef and sunk, drowning all aboard but one man. The fog had enveloped the doomed vessel just as it had us in an unexpected sinister pall, impenetrable and dense. And this was the last we ever head of any possible change in our fortunes, the Director had been aboard and the old solicitor Furley's optimistic hopes were at an end. He himself died before our return to England, somewhat suddenly.

For some weeks we worked, my husband feverishly and dissatisfied with his progress, and even more so with what he managed to write. These days were difficult and I fear I was not very helpful. My inexperience alarmed me and made me over-anxious.

Then our stone-cutter friend arrived one evening carrying a metal explorer's trunk, which he had received from a diligence plying between Lannion and our little island. It was the trunk that had accompanied Joseph Conrad on his journey to the Congo. We had carefully packed in it some batches of papers, a pair of sea-boots, a tall standard paraffin oil lamp and sundry small objects connected with his bachelor days. At first he cursed roundly at the stupidity of those people who had undertaken to house the trunk for us during our absence. It would mean so much more unnecessary luggage to take back. He flung the rolls of paper into the big empty grate, the sea-boots into the furthest corner of the big kitchen. I had visions of the lamp following suit, but fortunately the stone-cutter claimed his attention by admiring the trunk, which was fire-proof and which appeared to have greatly interested him. The short respite enabled me to remove the lamp, etc., to a place of safety.

CHAPTER THREE

AS so often happens the unexpected brings some benefit in its train, the appearance of that big lamp had exasperated my husband, but when I had got it filled and trimmed he was very thankful to have it. He was able to work by its light in greater comfort and it also provided no little warmth, which was welcome. We had no fires, other than the wood fire in the kitchen, and the evenings in May and early June were very chilly on that island, exposed to every wind that blew.

Just at that time there was a lull in material for me to type and it seemed advisable for me to keep as much out of sight during the early morning as possible. At the same time I was afraid to leave the house as my husband was still sufficiently at the honeymoon stage when he would feel bound to accompany me. I exhausted the little store of books, my work-box held nothing of interest, and I felt that my letters were inclined to reflect perhaps too clearly the strain we were feeling, because of the difficulty with the work of creation.

It was then that I bethought myself of those rolls of paper which I had rescued from the grate and transported to my "play-room" in the big loft. Here was something that could claim my interest. Armed with some stout pins and a pencil I retired noiselessly every morning when I had ascertained for certain my services with the ancient machine would not be required. Here I patiently sorted out the complete manuscripts of *Almayer's Folly* and *The Outcast of the Islands*, fastening each page in place with a stout pin on the box-spring mattress which also provided me with a comfortable seat. Here I spent hours on end. Whenever I heard a movement below I would stop and listen intently, I grew almost guilty in my desire to keep my whereabouts a secret. I had a positive dread of seeing my neat little piles of manuscript swept forcibly from my care, and without doubt destroyed. By this time I had nearly completed the *Almayer's Folly*. *The Outcast,* being carefully numbered, would be a much easier task. I had secreted some stout paper and strong string. I had a narrow escape once for I had become absorbed in my task and had not noticed a sudden movement in the room below. I held my breath while I listened to him descending the uncarpeted stairs to the kitchen and his impatient voice demanding my whereabouts from Suzanne the maid. But just as he turned to remount the postman appeared at the kitchen door and his attention was held just long enough for me to make a somewhat hurried appearance. Then I was lucky for the post drew his further attention from me and he did not ask where I had been for the last three hours.

Two days later I had finished my self-imposed task to my entire satisfaction and hidden the thick manuscripts in the bottom of my special trunk. Some twenty years later these very manuscripts formed a considerable part of those that were sold in America, having been bought by Mr. John Quinn from us, for about £2000, and resold by Mr. Quinn for £24,000. Of that, more later.

My next care was lavished upon the private papers, family and business, that had accompanied their owner in his various wanderings. Soaked with sea-water, frayed and torn by frequent handling, they had won through to become whole under my care, and by the aid of transparent adhesive tape, once more readable and tidy. For this service I received very grateful thanks and my industry was rewarded by a trip to the mainland and a liberal number of francs to spend as I wished. Little remembrances for the different members of my family began to accumulate in readiness for our return some day.

A few days later enough of the new book was written to make it possible to dispatch a fat batch to London and we felt that we could reasonably enjoy another nautical adventure. This was to be an attempt to reach Roscoff and the failure in this case was due to my native obstinacy. We had spent the night in our favourite little hotel in Lannion, and I refused to leave before the day's mail was in, only to draw blank. For this reason we lost the tide. Full of dismay, I lowered my miserable head and did not attempt to defend myself in the face of my husband's exasperation.

"I knew perfectly well there would be no post this morning, my dear," he said at last. "But you women," a shrug expressive of the deepest disgust seemed to emphasize his words and then he continued quietly: "Sunday we seldom get anything if you please to remember. We are here now to boil in the sun till the next tide, too late to do anything, damn."

We had made only a short start down the long river from Lannion leading to the open sea. Stuck firmly in the mud the boat refused to budge an inch, while there was still enough water in the narrow channel to float her. The sun blazed down upon us and we bid fair to spend the next twelve hours held firmly upright in the mud, just too far away from the bank to get ashore. I was overwhelmed with useless regret and held my tongue. But the fates after all were kind to us in this respect. A shallow boat drawing much less water than ours passed at that moment and the three or four Frenchmen, bent on a fishing expedition, gave us a friendly hail. We responded thankfully and accepted their invitation to board their boat and get a passage to the hotel at the mouth of the river, leaving old Milo to bring ours down on the next tide.

On the whole that Sunday stays in my mind as a pleasant remembrance. We lunched with the Frenchmen, who sat at the table with bare feet and with their trousers turned up to their knees. They talked a lot and as soon as they had finished the last mouthful pushed the knives and forks, dirty plates and glasses on one side and rolled back the cloth. Each one then produced a brown closed basket full of croaking frogs which they proceeded to sever across the middle, drawing the skin off the hind legs by the same movement. These resembled limp male nether undergarments in miniature. I was taken by surprise and in spite of my determination not to be squeamish I was forced to seek sanctuary at the further end of the sanded room until the operation was over.

I was told that these frogs were a great delicacy and ate like tender chicken. Ugh!

On the first flow of the tide old Milo appeared with our little craft and amid a shower of *bon soirs* we boarded her and headed once more for our original destination, Roscoff. There was still some hours of daylight to count upon and there was a promise of some wind. For the first two hours we made steady progress and talked hopefully of reaching Roscoff before dark.

The wind by this time had freshened almost to a gale and unfortunately was set off shore. We made practically no progress for the next three hours and my husband peered under his hand ahead anxiously. Then he shook his head.

"No use, Jess. Better try another day, looks foxy to me. I believe there's a change coming." A sudden squall decided him and we wore round and headed for the low line of rocks which marked the coast of our island on that side. Our sails were reefed down as close as possible, but the wind came from all sides at once and we were soon forced to creep slowly forward under the least possible spread of canvas.

It was the first time I had been at sea in such rough weather and entirely ignorant of any risk, I was enjoying myself. The old Frenchman sang out a warning and we turned our heads to watch an object bobbing along in our wake. It looked more like a miniature lighthouse than anything else. On it came, apparently following us with the most determined purpose. Then as abruptly it altered its course in the most erratic manner and headed for a point of land just short of our destination. As we passed it, firmly wedged between two high rocks, we discovered that it was a large vertical buoy, from Roscoff, and had been, as it were, chasing us home. It must have broken loose from its moorings and drifted some miles on the incoming tide.

We were wet to the skin and shivering with the cold when at last we managed to wade ashore from the boat. Milo had to remain behind until he could let down the legs and make her fast for the night. Tired and hungry and not a little depressed we toiled over the rock-strewn shore till we reached a point where we managed to climb up on to the roadway that led us home. And we had not been to Roscoff.

Joseph Conrad flatly refused to repeat the adventure the next day and for many more we worked soberly without using the boat. Old Milo, who had attached himself firmly to us, mooched about morosely, hanging over the little gate in front of the house every evening till long after sunset. I used to watch him from my window upstairs, waiting motionless till, exasperated at last, he would send a long stream of saliva and tobacco juice far into the road beyond, before he turned disconsolately away for the night. I felt that the failure of our enterprise was entirely my fault and I waited my lord's pleasure, never hinting at a desire to make another attempt to reach that elusive place Roscoff.

During those months on the island not the least of our pleasures were the letters we received from our friends at home. Edward Garnett would write long encouraging letters to the new author, letters that were of the greatest help in the construction and mastery of a language that was too entirely foreign for my husband to master. I have often thought how wonderfully tenacious this man to whom I was married must have been. I think tenacious is the right word to use because he managed to combine with his set purpose a certain indolence, that made it impossible to call him determined.

Then the letters from John Galsworthy and E. L. Sanderson were full of friendly interest in his work and our general well-being. I came in for my share of their goodwill and I am truly grateful for their ready understanding and approval of the way I was trying to fulfil my undertaking. I think our honeymoon, or rather the way we spent those months, brought us closer to each other than we should have been if we had indulged in a regulation honeymoon of a month say, and had attempted to begin a life together under more everyday circumstances. By the time we settled down to a routine we knew each other well enough to make allowances for one another. I could also claim a much wider knowledge of the strange being who was to be my constant care for all the rest of our married life. That understanding was the secret of the success of our big adventure.

My home letters were full of affection, but I do not think my attitude was quite understood or approved of. I can understand that from their point of view I might have justly been accused of being too wrapped up in my new life, but at the same time it would have been impossible to have attempted an explanation, and I was pledged to make a success of this marriage at all costs.

It was during our drives on the mainland that we came across the idiots, who became the subject of one of the short stories written on the spot. It was not usual for my husband to use material so close to hand and at the time of finding it, spread out as it were before him. In his story, *The Idiots*, which has sufficient relation to actual truth to need no explanation by me, he has not given quite the full number of unfortunates. I pointed out to him that there were two more at least and was quite startled by his unexpected violence: "Good God, my dear, I've put enough horror into that story in all conscience. Two more! More than enough of them without, to my mind."

It was indeed a dismal spectacle to see those creatures meandering up and down that narrow lane, shuffling aimlessly in the deep ditches or lying in the long grass bordering the road, their staring eyes fixed and a silly grin on their formless mouths. One only, I think the second in age, a youth of about seventeen, had sufficient intelligence to smile when he saw me, but even that smile would become a fixed grin if you happened to look back after you had driven past his motionless figure. Many times we have had to make a wide detour, even going on the grass the other side of the road, to avoid knocking one of these poor things down. Our coachman would start cracking his whip and shouting as soon as we turned into the lane if he caught sight of them. "The Idiots," he would declare, pointing at them with his whip.

At the end of another week, just six since our attempt to reach Roscoff, we decided to try again. Old Milo's face was wreathed in smiles when we summoned him and directed him to get the boat ready for an early start the next day. I was pleasurably excited and determined to do my part and cause no delay this time, post or no post. We got a good supply of provisions together and early the next morning prepared to embark with the first of the tide.

This time we were to make our start straight from our island. The Breton stone-cutter, the most wealthy man on the island, insisted upon carrying our portmanteau to the landing-stage, a rough stone jetty to which Milo had made the boat fast. The tiny dinghy bobbed saucily astern as if aware that we were bound on an adventure once more. No cloud appeared in the bright sky that showed a uniform arch of heavenly blue over the horizon. Joseph Conrad was jubilant and in fine form. "A perfect day, Jess. We shall make Roscoff this time without any trouble, come along, don't let us waste the tide." So saying, he shook hands heartily with the rich man, who would take no sort of gratuity, but who would have been terribly hurt if we had omitted this formality. It always meant a vigorous rubbing of his horny palm on the skirt of his long blue blouse before he grasped our hands with a grip that made me wince.

We had started at last, and I was feeling that the ill-luck was broken. I enjoyed steering more than anything and the two men, my husband and the old shellback, busied themselves in making a good stowage in case the wind freshened later on. The tiny covered cabin boasted of no window or porthole, but we seldom sought its shelter, preferring to get wet to being in such a confined space. I don't believe it was ever used except by old Milo, who had slept in there once or twice.

At midday the sun had got very hot and blazed down on the little craft, and instead of freshening the wind died down entirely. A slight swell on the oily sea soon made me decidedly uncomfortable and I began to feel an inclination to return the lunch I had so much enjoyed an hour or so before. My husband glanced anxiously at me from time to time, and I could give him only a very faint smile in answer. "I warned you, my dear, against that red wine," he said at last as he tucked a cushion under my aching head. I turned an appealing glance at him as I edged feebly a little nearer the side of the boat.

By this time the wind had altogether deserted us and we could not even keep steerage way on the boat. Both my husband and the old seaman looked a greeny yellow and glanced round under the shade of their hands. Was it possible to run ashore anywhere along that sun-baked coast. As far as the eye could reach no human habitation showed on the shore-line. The swell increased and the boat turned round and round in sickening evolutions, impossible to control. Prone on the deck and feeling like nothing on earth, I watched the green water, cold shivers running down my back at each heave and roll. We had drifted off our course and only the glistening, rolling water showed on every side. By and by a noisy little steamer loomed up within hail, and in answer to my husband's request one of the crew threw us a heavy coil of rope. I had managed by slow and painful degrees to haul myself into a sitting position on the roof of the tiny cabin, and sat, too miserable to care, leaning my head on my hand. The coil of rope flew with a heavy thud right over my head on to the cabin roof, I was lassooed : I was indifferent in my misery, till I caught sight of my poor husband's face. Fortunately for me the main boom, motionless just above my knees, bore the force of the thud, which must otherwise have broken both my legs. I hastened to reassure them that I was all right and they made fast, quickly towing us as close as they dared towards the shelving shore. Then casting off they accepted a gratuity which Milo had tied in an old rag and fastened to the end of the tow-rope.

As soon as we were far enough in, willing hands helped me over the side and I crawled painfully up the steep beach till the road became level enough for me to stand upright. Thankfully I tottered into the little hotel on the top of that stony beach. That afternoon, or rather early evening, was a nightmare. I refused all food and only asked to sleep, unable to raise my aching head from my pillow. The sun beat on the wooden walls of the little shanty, dignified by the name of an hotel, with a terrific heat. It was stifling in the little bedroom. How I longed for a cup of English tea. A welcome rain poured down all night and in the morning I was sufficiently refreshed and free from pain and I enjoyed my coffee and roll.

When I had dressed leisurely and found my way once more down the steep stairs to the sanded bar-parlour, which was the principal room of the inn, I found that the good dame had prepared quite a nice little lunch for us before we left. With a sneaking relief I heard that old Milo had already been dispatched with the boat for our island, and Joseph Conrad had secured a trap to drive us to the station in Morlaix, the nearest railway station to the tiny village. The man paid his official visit to the authorities for his permit to drive the strangers to the station and then appeared before the hotel seated in the two-wheel cart drawn by a wicked-looking chestnut mare. I eyed both the vehicle and the animal with a certain distrust. I suppose this must have appeared in my face, for the good man hastened to assure us that she was perfectly quiet and the only thing she objected to was a bicycle. This was a very unlikely thing for us to meet, he continued, one chance in a hundred, but still, I felt, a chance.

We climbed into the cart and started three abreast down the steep descent into the town; the chestnut had a long loping stride, very uncomfortable in a two-wheeled cart, as well as a nasty habit of putting on a sudden spurt now and then.

Of course, half-way down the hill, on the steepest part and on a bend, an elderly man appeared mounted on a brand-new bicycle.

Forewarned is forearmed to a certain extent, and I am confident that nothing but our tight grasp on the back of the cart saved us from the instant disaster of being flung into the road. As it was, the mare came to a decided stop, for one second, snorting defiance at her pet abomination, then let out a vicious kick as the machine came abreast, that all but forced us to release our hold of the seat.

There was a startled exclamation as the rider of the cycle left his saddle and landed unhurt in a pile of soft mud by the side of the road, a rattle of bicycle spokes as the horse's heels hit the overturned machine, and then my mind lost interest in the hapless cyclist and concentrated on what might be going to happen to us.

As soon as we were well clear of the cause of her fright, the mare came to a standstill, her sides heaving and covered with lather. We were both glad to forgo the last few yards of our transport and hurriedly descended from the cart and walked the short distance to the station.

It was on the return drive from Lannion the next day that I saw again the whole of the family of idiots together, and noted to my surprise that one was a girl. In repose her face was exceedingly pretty, but catching a glimpse of our driver a most diabolical expression came over the young child's face, she yelled and shouted abuse till she was forced to stop to draw breath. The man retaliated by making violent show with his whip and aiming a slash at the slim figure as we passed. The girl was dressed exactly like the boys, in long black shapeless garments, from the bottom of which their lean shanks protruded a few inches. They usually had their hands thrust into the loose sleeves and their bare feet in wooden sabots. These sturdy youths and the well-grown girl were the children of a small farmer, or peasant retainer, of a Marquis who owned a considerable property, and the parents were employed, we were told, in the fabrication of the famous Camembert cheese. They had a certain allowance from the State to keep these children out of an Institution.

There were other unfortunates, men and boys mostly, misshapen in mind and body, who inhabited those lanes, shuffling sideways in the deep ditches under the hedges, sometimes almost out of sight, by the side of the road.

One heard almost unbelievable stories of hardship and injustice done to these creatures due to family greed.

Drink also provided a good deal of the misfortune and not a little amusement to the casual observer, because the drunken objects were for the most part ridiculously dignified. Such incidents generally ended in some droll and laughable situation. One day a tall Breton with his red kerchief knotted round his lean brown throat, his round black hat rammed low over his forehead, and his long arms waving like a grotesque semaphore, stopped right in the fairway and obstructed our progress while he wished us a drunken "Bon jour." Prijean, the coachman, made a playful lunge at him with his whip. The man, then gravely apologetic, turned at right angles, and pitched head first into a deep hole. There he stayed for a few seconds on his head with his legs in the air, until we managed to haul him out and plant him, dazed and very nearly sobered, in a sitting position on the bank close by.

Many are the times when I have longed to revisit those scenes, even now when I am alone. I am sure there are not many people who can have happier recollections of their honeymoon, and

JESSIE CONRAD THREE YEARS BEFORE HER WEDDING

BERDICZEW
The house where " Joseph Conrad " was born.

I truly believe that one of the secrets for those happy memories is the fact that we mixed most judiciously work and play, and because of my ability to make myself useful—he was good enough to say indispensable—and without undue conceit I accept his commendation.

The summer drew to an end and we were half inclined to stay on the Continent indefinitely. He had the idea of going to the Basque country. I should have made no objection, I was out for adventure, no matter where. But when fate in the shape of a stranger-tourist came accidently to our island, directed there by the gossip he had heard on the mainland of some foreigner and an English wife living the simple life on the lonely island, our plans were altered in a very short time.

The man was middle-aged and appeared to be of the schoolmaster type, very intelligent and well read. He displayed considerable medical knowledge, and once the talk had drifted to the subject, my husband immediately began to discourse at length on his recent attack of gout and fever. The stranger was interested at once and remarked that the winter in that house, exposed to the four winds of heaven, was scarcely an ideal spot for anyone subject to sudden illness. And again he pointed out that a man who depended on his pen for his livelihood would need more congenial conditions to work under. Without scruple he concluded with a bald statement of fact which I was surprised my husband received so tolerantly.

"You see, sir, this is how it strikes me. You are a younger author than you are a man, and although you must have ample material to draw upon, it has got to be written. I should not consider your health good enough to risk the chance of making yourself sufficiently comfortable in out-of-the-way places. That is if I may offer you my opinion?"

It was impossible to misunderstand the friendly interest that led this man, a complete stranger, to proffer his advice with such sincerity. We thanked him, and after a substantial meal that he accepted in our house we walked with him across the sands to the mainland. We parted with hearty expressions of goodwill and the promise to renew the acquaintance at some future occasion. But when he had waved his last good-bye, we discovered that we had neither his initials, nor address.

For several days nothing more was said about our proposed removal to the Pyrenees, and I was hardly surprised when he decided to follow the stranger's advice and return to seek a home in England. And two short weeks afterwards saw us on our way back to St. Malo, bound for home.

This crossing I enjoyed greatly, and we had a fine passage, arriving at Southampton on Sunday morning in good time and quite unruffled. There followed some few days in town and then began a frantic search for the home. My husband inclined greatly to some little place in Essex near his friends, the Hopes. Accordingly we went to their hospitable house and began to look round in earnest. The first house in Stanford-le-Hope was not too fortunate. He felt the urge to get settled at once, and the best thing we could find was a brand-new twin villa at the end of a road running from the railway station. May the fates ever preserve me from another like experience. The other semi-detached house shared our drainage and water system, and one night the lady there sent in to beg the loan of my husband to unstop her drain: a job quite outside his knowledge or ability, as I pointed out rather impatiently.

This first semi-detached villa was the one and only of its kind. I was rather apprehensive from the first, it was so terribly new and the entrance gate not even hung. Still, what young girl is not thrilled by the prospect of her own home, a place where her family can visit her, and, perhaps, envy her? The furnishing of this little place held from the first every element of humour and no little anxiety. To begin with, my strange husband had given me a quite inadequate sum to expend upon the necessities in the way of furniture. Fifty pounds. Looking back, I am not sure that this demand upon my good will and ingenuity was not after all the greatest he ever made.

It is fair to add that he had undertaken to procure the cutlery and china, and needless to say his expenditure upon these things far exceeded the amount I was to stretch to cover everything else. It was a very real evidence of his unreasonableness. But I even then did not know him well enough to protest, but set about my task with troubled energy.

I recall my expeditions, accompanied by my long-suffering mother, in search of the impossible. At last my scratch collection was complete, that is to say, the last shilling had been expended, and the day came when they were delivered at the Villa. I had, through the good offices of dear Mrs. Hope, secured a very good and efficient maid.

The next two days were spent in feverish activity putting those bits of furniture in the best position and trying to ignore the spaces that remained empty. My chief trouble was the fact that I had not been able to buy more than the iron frame and spring mattress for the double bed destined for our own room. There was, alas, no overlay—and no more "cherry-coloured twist." When we had mounted it in its place, those naked springs glared coldly and resentfully in sunlight or lamplight. What to do I did not know, and I seemed to have failed in my task so completely. The rest of the household gods were disposed to the best advantage, but their appearance far from satisfied my artistic sense and I was almost reduced to tears of mortification and dismay.

One of the drollest sides of the affair and one that rather exasperated my mother was the manner in which Joseph Conrad intended to take possession of his first English home. We had been spending the nights at the houses of friends, and the day he was to arrive was to be my first under this roof.

He had written the most minute instructions. I was to be ready dressed for the evening and taking my ease in the drawing-room three days after the arrival of the furniture; the new maid was to be instructed to answer his ring and show him into the room; the meal was to appear; he was to be shown his study, complete with bookshelves and all the necessary paraphernalia, ready for the start next morning on a new masterpiece. It was already the day before he was to arrive and still the iron frame of the nuptial couch gleamed bare and uninviting; the most essential object was conspicuous by its absence. What was I to do?

But imagine my joy that last morning to find a letter waiting for me on the new mat when we arrived there, enclosing a five-pound note. The letter also contained a suggested menu for his first dinner in his own house and ended with the command to "buy myself a pretty négligé for the mornings." Within an hour the overlay was on the bed covering the naked springs and the bed ready for the night.

I think I was more strange and nervous that afternoon than ever before or since. There seemed so much that might not pass muster. The paint on the bookshelves smelled, the stain on the floors was sticky; the curtains all appeared—as they undoubtedly were—horribly cheap and nasty. I knew instinctively that this home was not what he would expect. In vain I tried to persuade myself that I had really laid out the money to the best advantage. Each defect struck me afresh as I sat waiting. I was dismayed and apprehensive.

As it happened it was something quite out of my calculations that called down the trouble when my husband did arrive. At his ring, unable to restrain myself, I dashed to the door to receive him. He was followed by a boy bearing some exquisite fruit and flowers. He received me coldly, and began to reproach me with concentrated bitterness. I had, he said, completely spoiled the whole effect by my childish impetuosity. Scarcely consoled by a subsequent hearty hug and shower of kisses, I preceded him into the room. Alas! there followed some really painful criticisms, sweeping condemnations, indeed, of all or nearly all I had done. I was young, and although we had been married the best part of a year I was too shy and diffident to stand up for myself—as I should have done later. I bowed my head to the storm of invective and thanked God my mother had already departed. My husband seemed to forget that he had at least approved the house a month or so before. As it turned out it was the building itself more than my efforts at furnishing it that exasperated him most. For an hour or so after his arrival, after the meal had been removed almost untouched, I came upon him inserting the blade of his penknife into a crack in the corner of the wall in the room in which he was going to write. When I appeared he left the corner rather guiltily and sank down into his big chair with an exasperated: "Damned jerry-built rabbit hutch."

It was by this time late October and the house seemed to devour heat without ever getting warm and cosy. The damp stood out in discoloured patches on the distempered walls and the woodwork shrunk and cracked. The doors, when they were closed, admitted sufficient draught to fan the heaviest curtains and sweep the manuscripts off the table. The fires smoked or refused absolutely to light on account of the down-draught. It was distinctly a failure.

It was here that John Galsworthy became our first visitor. The most frequent. More than once my husband, while refusing to admit the inadequacy of the amount he had given me with which to feather the nest, had declined to receive other people on the ground that they would soon spy out the nakedness of the land. He had infinite faith in John Galsworthy's good feeling and in the two most intimate friends besides, E. L. Sanderson and Edward Garnett, not to speak of the Hopes.

That dining-room was barely a salle-à-manger, even barer than the one on Ile Grande, or so it seemed, because I suppose it was England, and the dining-room was so terribly unconventionally furnished and lacking even in essentials. The study was extremely bare and uninspiring and, I feel sure, not in the least conducive to the creation of even a trade catalogue. To the end of our time in that villa the gate remained unhung and the bit of ground to the rear as well as the front was a wilderness.

It became my daily pilgrimage to look for something more congenial in every way. The locality was restricted very much, for my partner flatly refused to move far from his old friends, and the Hopes' house had to be within easy walking distance. I had in my mind an old cottage, or small farm-house, standing alone. A farmhouse appeared the most alluring because of the freedom of the ground. Joseph Conrad was intolerant of the restrictions imposed by a fence, and I soon discovered that when ashore his soul hankered for the wide spaces he had known in his childhood in far-off Poland. It became his familiar grouse, "not room in this blamed hole to swing a cat."

I had discovered in one of my rambles, and within the prescribed radius, an old Elizabethan farm-house, which claimed the local fame of once sheltering no less a personage than Queen Elizabeth herself. Gossip had it that she had sought shelter under that old brick-tiled roof the day she had ridden to Pitsea to view the Armada. It was a pretty legend and for aught we knew might well have been true.

My excitement ran high, but for the first few days I contented myself with making every possible enquiry as to its suitability as a habitation for my charge, as I then considered Joseph Conrad to be. The house presented its queer front of one story only, in the middle flanked by a wing of two stories on each side. A narrow hall-way cut it in two, so to speak, the garden door being exactly opposite the front door. Then a letter L passage led to the left, where there was a small kitchen and larder self-contained, and one large room facing a corkscrew staircase. The drawing-room opened into the square hall-way. The other two doors facing belonged to the other wing, which the farmer reserved for a labourer and his wife. Our drawing-room was a big low room with a slit-like window each side of the fireplace, and at the end of the house where the big room was, there was an enormous chimney-stack covered by a gigantic ivy which housed a huge colony of sparrows. These birds were trapped once or twice in the year by the railway porters and found their way up to London in the guise of larks, a great delicacy, it appears. The front of the house was screened from the vulgar gaze of passers-by with a fine row of tall elms. I could hardly contain myself when I discovered that it would be possible for us to rent this dear old place for scarcely more rent than the abominable villa—£28 a year.

As soon as I had my facts hard and fast I set about trying to persuade my husband to come with me to see it, but he had been indulging in an abortive attack of gout and insisted on remaining where he was, enjoying his misery, as he said. However, we were to go to Cardiff for that Christmas, and I determined that on our return he should view my find with my eyes.

CHAPTER FOUR

OUR first married Christmas we were to spend with a delightful family in Cardiff, and I was greatly looking forward to the complete change of surroundings. There was, as always, just that element of chance that became the principal characteristic of all our trips abroad or away from our own home. The date fixed for any excursion, unless undertaken at a moment's notice, was sure to be unlucky. I used to wonder how my erratic husband had ever discharged his duties at sea to schedule time when I discovered that now a fixed date was fatal. To be given a certain day for the delivery of any piece of work seemed to make the accomplishment of that feat impossible. This peculiarity grew infinitely worse as he grew older. Many, many times have I had to keep watch and ward over some promised batch, that in the end had to be sent by rail and special messenger in the desperate hope that it should reach its destination within a reasonable limit of the time it should have been delivered.

I do not for a moment suggest that my husband was the only author who found dates irksome, but it was a habit that I found the most difficult to cope with, in fact on my rare absences from home I never felt at all easy in my mind, if I had left him finishing a piece of work. But if I were to make an assertion that I would finish anything to a prescribed time, he would hold me to that undertaking to the minute.

One accepts the many vagaries when one is dealing with a genius, but I have often wondered what is the dividing line between " a bit peculiar and the claim to being a genius."

We left our "jerry-built villa," just too late to catch our connection for Cardiff, and had perforce to spend the night in town. I had visions of a trying time in that London hotel, because I dreaded an attack of gout, but to my surprise and relief, this strange being declared himself pleased that we had lost our train, and we had quite a jolly evening, visiting our old haunts, and the next morning started for Cardiff in good spirits.

These friends of my husband's to whom we were bound for that festive season had befriended the lonely foreign sailor as long ago as 1885, and the making of that acquaintance was somewhat unusual. He had met a fellow-countryman, who was also a sailor—by the name of Komorowski—and had had undertaken as a small commission to call upon our Mr. Kliszczewski, a prominent citizen in that town, and return to him a small loan that had been made Mr. Komorowski some time before.

We discovered that these Kliszczewskis must have been a family connection of the Korzeniowskis at some time, as their coat of arms was identical with our own. This Pole had come to

Cardiff an exile from Poland soon after the Polish Insurrection of 1831 and had established himself as a watchmaker, having married a Welshwoman. He was delighted to hear his own tongue spoken in his shop and at once welcomed the young Polish sailor—my husband—warmly. A great friendship sprang up between them, and it was this man's son, Josef Spiridion Kliszczewski, with whom we were to spend Christmas.

Our host was a neat, dapper little man who favoured the Polish side of his origin much more than his Welsh, and so also did his three sons. When he met us at the station with all the punctilious politeness of the Poles, I was charmed with him and with my reception by the whole family. My nine months as a wife seemed to have given me no permanent dignity ; I was but twenty-three, and from the moment I met those three boys I became as youthful as the youngest of them. I had a hard matter to preserve my seriousness, even when I caught the decidedly disapproving expression on the face of my lord and master. I could laugh in spite of what might have been a serious accident which happened a few moments before.

I have said that our host met us at the station, and even in the act of greeting him a clumsy fellow-passenger swung his heavy portmanteau accidently under my invalid knee and I had only time to clutch at our friend's overcoat to save myself from falling on the platform. I almost dragged his coat off his back in my effort to preserve my balance. I was in great pain, and neither of the two men with me had seen the cause of my discomfort. I held my peace until the offender had disappeared through the barrier for fear of an unpleasant scene, but that stupid affair rather spoilt an otherwise delightful time for me. My knee had been dislocated some years before and it was constantly giving me pain and trouble.

My fancy even at this lapse of time is distinctly tickled when I recall my get-up on that day so many years ago. Nowadays grandmothers do not dress with such severity and decorum as I had attained at the age of twenty-three. To begin with I wore a sober black gown, long in the skirt and sleeve and high in the neck, a three-quarter dark brown cloak—and, crowning glory, a black bonnet, tied under my chin. Words can give no adequate impression of all this, and it was not until I met these young people that I realized myself—a matron, and knew in a moment how difficult I was going to find it to live up to the dignity of my garb and status.

From that moment my husband began to lament my over-developed sense of humour, but that failing—if it can be considered a failing—has been my salvation. It helped us both, although he would never admit it. That holiday I could think of nothing too frivolous to fit my mood, and no amount of stern disapproval could damp my spirits.

In the evening the boys carried me off to their den at the top of the house and we played cards and I was as youthful as the youngest. It was almost morning when our elders appeared and ordered us off to bed. That Christmas was one of the happiest I remember since my childhood days. I was treated with the good-natured familiarity of a favourite sister, with just that difference accorded to the sister of some other fellow, but without any sentimental nonsense. I became a confidant of each in turn during the week we spent in Cardiff.

There were few visitors to that house, they were essentially a working family, each had their allotted task, even during the holiday. The house was a very substantial one in the Cathedral Road. It was my first introduction to double windows and I got my first thrill the night we arrived when passing along the corridor we glanced down into the depths of the closed business house at the side. Heavy iron gates came up through the floor, shutting in the valuables. But this evening, staring at us out of the darkness behind the bars, we caught the gleam of two baneful eyes fixed in a steady stare.

Later on we discovered that the household cat had been trapped, but for a brief moment it looked as if some intruder were there behind those bars, watching us. Later on the same evening, some enterprising men (probably they were the would-be burglars) rang a peal on the front door. Evidently their idea was that the maids were at home alone, and they were greatly disconcerted when the three sons, their father and his guest appeared in the hall, behind the maid. They mumbled some story and asked if the people either side of that house were at home. The maid had innocently answered their query before we had time to prevent her, and when they turned civilly from the door, we noticed that they must have been wearing rubbers over their boots, for they made no sound departing.

The next morning the police were early with us, asking questions, and two of the sons had to go to identify a man who had been caught during the night. The houses both sides of us had been burgled. My rest had been broken and I had been very frightened when I had been awakened in the early hours by a smothered sneeze. I started up holding my breath and watched the big wardrobe door slowly open, without a sound. I sat on the side of the bed stiff with fright and waited. I had it in my mind to get across the short distance to the door and thence to the room of our host, who I knew had a loaded revolver by the side of his bed. At the end of some moments the door had not fully opened and no burglar had disclosed himself. Greatly daring,

I crept to the massive piece of furniture and closed the door, turning the key as quickly as I could.

I suppose I must have screamed and then have fainted, because the next thing I knew was someone passing a cold sponge over my face and several people standing by my side. The wardrobe door was still closed and I gasped hysterically to see our valiant host armed with his revolver fling the door open and invite my burglar to come forth in grim tones. Nothing happened, no one was there. But I proved that my adventure was not all imagination when a small piece of the lace edging on my night-dress sleeve fluttered to the floor as soon as the wardrobe door key was turned. Of course I do not pretend that there was ever actually a man there, but the smothered sneeze and ghostly opening of the door remained a mystery.

The house was so solidly built, not like our "jerry-built" villa, where anything of the kind could easily have happened. I was teased unmercifully and no one could understand why I had not called my husband to my aid. I explained that I should for a bat, but not for a burglar. I should have rather trusted my power to bluff such an intruder. They all laughed heartily when I related a little episode of a realistic dream which I had had. I told this to Joseph Conrad in the morning when he woke.

"I had such a strange dream last night; I dreamt that there was a very beautiful woman, perfectly nude, coming up the stairs." My husband interrupted me quickly: "Why didn't you wake me up?"

It was during our visit that Christmas that Mr. Arthur Mee called to see Joseph Conrad and some time later published an article on the interview. And for the first time there was a great discussion in that house as to his reluctance to write about the happenings in Poland. But this he declared was impossible, and in fact I fear that his refusal rather caused a breach between the two friends. It was also a very sore point with Thaddeus Bobrowski, my husband's much loved and revered uncle, to the day of his death. In one of the letters that uncle writes as early as June 20th, 1881: "It would be an excellent thing if you wrote for the *Wedrowiec* (the Traveller) at Warsaw. We have very few travellers or even correspondents of that kind. I am sure what you wrote would interest everybody greatly, and after a time they would pay you. It would form a tie with your own country, and it would be an act of piety to your father, who wished to serve and did serve, his country with his pen. Think about this. Put together some recollections of your voyage to Australia and send them in as sketches. The address of the *Wedrowiec* is well known in Warsaw. Six letters a year from different countries will not take up much of your time. It would entertain you and others."

But it was many years before the first book bearing any interest in Poland came to be written. No one could doubt the truth of his shrinking. He would declare that he could not bear to show his wounds to all and sundry, who would feel nothing but idle curiosity as to their scars, without troubling in the least to understand the pain and discomfort they had given.

Then we returned to the place that contained his "torture chamber," as he called his unsympathetic bare room, that faced only a few bare and leafless trees, bordering the main road to Southend. In those days the traffic was little, a few carts and farm wagons, some cyclists, and for the rest a number of noisy children who always seemed to choose the front of our house to yell the loudest.

I grew more and more desperate that first month after our return, and at last I persuaded him to let me begin negotiations with the farmer who was willing to accept us as tenants for Ivy Walls, my ideal farmhouse. It took only a very short time to conclude our preparations and one day when he had made a visit to town, rare for him, he returned to his new home and approved my choice very heartily. The house was certainly less flimsy, quieter and more dignified, only a little longer walk to the village, and from our upstair windows we got wonderful views of the sunsets over the upper reaches of the Thames. There were fresh pathways and even room for a full quarter-deck walk along the path in front of the house, hidden from the vulgar gaze by the row of stately elms that bordered the garden against the road.

With our removal to Ivy Walls, my full responsibilities burst upon me in full force. I was no longer the youthful immature girl I had been at the time of my marriage a year ago. I realized that here was my chance to prove my worth as wife and mother of this author. His dependence upon me touched my maternal instincts, and to the end of his life I remained a willing buffer between him and the outside world.

That first year we spent in Stanford-le-Hope was, I think, one of the most difficult in the whole of our married life. It was some time before it dawned upon me that he must be feeling the isolation from men of his own standard of intellect. The only man who was close at hand was dear Mr. Hope, and he was not always at home. Then the persistent attacks of gout interfering with the only form of recreation I knew appealed to him. Every Sunday he was well enough we would take a picnic lunch and join Mr. Hope on a boating expedition. Fog or rain would not stop us. Often the mist was so low that we could see only a few yards ahead and it was only such landmarks as haystacks on the banks of the narrow creeks and waterways that made it possible for us to tell our whereabouts. But short of being absolutely ill, I soon discovered that those jaunts were not harmful, and all through the early months of the year, most Sundays saw us dressed in mackintosh and gum-boots, nosing our way in and out of the creeks that cut up the Essex marshes; or feeling our way round the powder hulks that lay moored in the upper reaches of the Thames.

As the year advanced the work of constructing the masterpieces advanced but slowly. I was thankful when one of those most intimate friends, John Galsworthy, Edward Garnett or E. L. Sanderson could be induced to pay us a visit, for a long week-end. The effect of their sympathetic and sustaining presence would lubricate the mental machinery, so to speak, and a good advance would be made.

It was about this time that the two artists, Henry James and my husband, first became acquainted, although it was not for some time later that I met him. Joseph Conrad's delight when the copy of the *Spoils of Poynton* arrived, and his keen appreciation of the characteristic and friendly inscription on the fly-leaf touched me very much. There was something almost too gentle and appealing in any expression of gratitude when my husband's real feelings were stirred, as they were for instance by this book and its charming inscription. When I grew to know the author of it I, too, felt his real friendliness as something more than mere polite expression.

The next event that loomed large upon our horizon was the prospect that I was to become a mother. The fact made me realize still further my responsibilities. I had also a very clear notion that my husband was not exactly pleased. I could not refrain from some inward amusement and some awe, when I recalled his assurance given voluntarily to my mother that he did not intend to have any children. It seemed to me that I had played him false as it were—although my common sense showed me that I was not alone to blame. I wondered what would happen afterwards. Could I continue to fill this post of general guardian of my husband's peace and do my duty to my child? I saw quite plainly that my allegiance must be somewhat divided, and with comical flippancy I wondered "which would be God and which Mammon?"

This paragraph of a letter written by my husband to E. L. Sanderson telling of my prospects falls naturally into its place here, and shows his attitude so much better than any words of mine can do.

"There is no other news—unless the information that there is a prospect of some kind of descendant may be looked upon as something new. I am not unduly elated. Johnson (the London doctor) says it may mend Jess's health permanently—if it does not end her. The last he does not say in so many words, but I can see an implication through a wall of words. This attitude does not contribute to my peace of mind—and now, when I think of it, there is nothing very shocking in my not being able to finish a short story in three months. The old practitioner here tho' is very cheerful about it. Well: we shall see—in December, I believe."

Meanwhile, life went on much as usual. Because so much was expected of me I still carried on. I can truthfully say that Joseph Conrad was at once the most exacting lover and husband. I used to call him an "ostrich," for I verily believe he possessed the power not to see anything he did not wish to see. Perhaps some part of his wonderful charm lay in this very characteristic, that and his illuminating habit of presenting interesting similes. One had to stop and think, sometimes very deeply, how these similes bore upon the subjects under discussion. The connection would often be remote, but it was always there.

I came across this letter a few days ago which I will use to illustrate my meaning. It is written from Switzerland in 1895, the year before we were married, and is addressed to Mr. Fisher Unwin, the publisher of the first book, *Almayer's Folly*.

"Thanks very much for the cuttings which have been sent me from your office. Norman has been very kind and I wrote to tell him that. I trust I have done nothing against the etiquette of journalism.

"I have received many cuttings since from the agency. The provincial press is very good to me so far. The *Realm* so-so, but with evident good-will. But the poor old *World* kicks at me (in fifteen lines) like a vicious donkey. It is severe blame (perhaps deserved) but, I think, no criticism in the true sense of the word. I trust you are well. I am living on here in a state of continual exasperation with myself and my work.

"Yesterday snow fell. Jura are all white.

"Yours faithfully,

"J. CONRAD."

This phrase, "like a vicious donkey," is indeed picturesque, and the conclusion shows how very un-English his letters were. I regret exceedingly the whim that made him insist that every scrap of paper that bore his signature on letters addressed to me should have been burnt before we were married.

My hands were indeed full by this time and I jealously guarded each little garment as I finished it, packing it away in my "mystery drawer" as my husband called it. Frequently he would indulge in a fit of gout and I had perforce to be mostly nurse. One time lives in my mind very clearly. As I have said, we had quite a big orchard and the school-children were often very troublesome, getting in to steal the fruit. One day my husband with more than a fortnight's beard untrimmed and his soft black hair falling over his coat-collar, one hand in a sling, was making his painful way round the house with the aid of a stout stick when he came upon these young marauders, some still in the trees and all with their hands full. His well-assumed ferocity and strange appearance put them to instant flight. He threatened to shoot them if he caught them there again. For months afterwards I was greeted with shouts of derision if I went to the village : "Hi, Mrs. Conrad, how's your wild man ?"

Then one Sunday Mr. W. Lutoslawski invited himself for lunch. It had been a week of visitors, of changing round of rooms. We had given over our own room and double bed and had made shift with a small one in order to accommodate Mr. and Mrs. Sidney Pawling. He was at that time a partner in the firm of William Heinemann. They had been staying a night or two with us before making a yachting trip in the *La Reine* which belonged then to our old friend, Mr. Hope. It was one of the hottest August Bank Holidays I ever remember and the relays of visitors had tired me very much indeed. We were still unsettled in the house on the fateful Sunday when this countryman of my husband's elected to pay us a visit. He was our first Polish visitor.

We met the only-one train at the little wayside station of Stanford-le-Hope, and made certain that no other ran from Fenchurch Street until late in the evening. Our guest did not arrive. With a sneaking feeling of satisfaction, for we were very tired, we devoured the lunch I had prepared, and spent the rest of the day in a lazy fashion. About nine o'clock I was nearly asleep on the drawing-room couch ; our only maid had gone for a walk. Blissfully unconscious of impending trouble, I had allowed the kitchen stove to die out. Suddenly I heard the garden gate swing to and the rapid tread of determined footsteps on the garden path. Then a violent and prolonged ring, followed at once by a second. Then came a stream of rapid words in a foreign tongue. Joseph Conrad had himself answered the bell and with a man's beautiful disregard for domestic considerations, he was assuring this delayed visitor that of course his late arrival was of no consequence.

"I'll tell my wife. Dinner ? why, of course, it's sure to be ready now, and a bedroom! Nothing easier. Come in, come in."

The visitor, surely the quickest-moving man I ever beheld, stood before me clicking his heels and bowing profoundly. He explained in his own tongue and broken English, that he had arrived "to the morning train a moment too late. She was already moving out of station, that all-too-punctual train." In vain the officials had assured him that no other would run that Sunday before the nine-fifteen p.m. He remained on the spot so as to be ready if they, the officials, should prove mistaken:

"I stay and sleep, but now hungry, very hungry! Nothing all day. I would eat at once and then to bed."

It was curious that with his limited knowledge of English and in a strange country he had managed to run us to earth. . . .

". . . Well, you see, madame, I ask 'Pan Korzeniowski' (Polish for Mr. Korzeniowski), Dry Wells Farms." He held towards me the heading of my husband's letter and then replaced it in his breast pocket with a gesture of finality, once more voicing his need of "food, hot and plenty," and here he made a wide gesture with his hands: "Plenty, much."

I accepted my fate and repaired to the kitchen and within a few moments had served him a complete little dinner. The moment he had devoured the last mouthful he insisted on being shown to his room and preceded by my husband, who was now decidedly sulky, he trotted quickly up the stairs. I waited a short time without moving, but in a few minutes laughed out loud at the comical expression of my husband's face as he returned:

"By Jove, Jess, he is a queer customer if ever there was one. The first thing he did was to run his hand up and down the bed almost as if he expected to find some hidden cause for discomfort. Then he pulled up the blind and, paying no attention to me, he divested himself of every stitch, Jess—everything, and stood a moment upright on the bed.

"Everyone must have had a good view from the road. He then let himself fall on to the bed, bounced up and down, once or twice, pulled the clothes up round his neck and announced his intention of leaving at six o'clock in the morning. I believe he was asleep before I got out of the room."

"Perhaps he will oversleep himself," I suggested with a stifled yawn. "At any rate, sufficient for the day, etc. . . ."

We silently mounted the stairs, pausing outside the door of our guest's room to listen to the loud regular breathing. The next morning almost before I was properly awake, I beheld the grotesque little person careering rapidly up and down the front path calling loudly for "Pan Korzeniowski." He was distinctly a comical figure. To begin at the beginning, so to speak, he had black side-spring shoes with a big white tag at the back, white cashmere socks, running down over his shoes unheeded, a black alpaca suit, the trousers reaching about the middle of his lean calf, a wide-spreading collar and flowing black tie. A shiny black wide-awake surmounted his shock of untidy black hair and round baby-like face. His cheeks were pallid and drawn.

The effect of the whole was laughable and strangely irritating. By the time I reached the garden, my husband had joined his guest who was loudly clamouring for his coffee. His breakfast demolished, he started determinedly to walk the two miles to the station, gesticulating all the time and far out-distancing his host whose effort to keep up with that flying figure seemed hopeless from the start. I watched them as far as I could see, and then turned back into the house to make a fresh brew of coffee to await the return of my husband. Some time later the railway trap drove up and my poor man descended from it, more dead than alive.

" Good God," he ejaculated, " what a visitation ! " He drank the coffee eagerly, remarking as he handed me back the cup : " What sort of satisfaction he got out of it I can't begin to understand. Eat, sleep . . . ugh, a positive nightmare ! Hallo ! Now what's up ? "

His sudden exclamation made me turn sharply to see a telegraph boy dismount from his bicycle and come forward with a buff-coloured envelope, and the usual query : " Any answer ? "

We read the message together and my husband broke into a grim laugh, repeating what was written in puzzled tones. It was a tersely worded request that we should keep the hurried visit a secret and, if any enquiry was made, disclaim all knowledge of the departed guest. I glanced at Joseph Conrad's puzzled face and dismissed the boy with a shake of the head.

Then I turned away, metaphorically to count the spoons. By mutual consent we refrained from any reference to our strange visitor and no more was heard of him. I fancy though that this unusual secrecy, and in fact the whole incident, left a distaste in my husband's mind, and he found it a little difficult to overlook.

CHAPTER FIVE

OUR next visitor of note was Stephen Crane, the author of *The Red Badge of Courage*. My husband had met him some months before in London, and I felt that I knew him quite well long before I met him that evening in Ivy Walls, in the October or November of 1897. This young man, little more than a boy, was the first American author I had met, and I was delighted to note the extreme good fellowship and complete understanding between the two artists. Both were men of keen imagination and almost uncanny in their powers of observation. Stephen had just completed his book, *The Red Badge of Courage*, which is surely a unique example of his imaginative mind.

Joseph Conrad says of him in his introduction to Mr. Thomas Beer's book that as an author he was the senior of the two, and continues: "I used to remind him of that now and then with affected humility which always provoked his smiles. He had a quiet smile that charmed and frightened one. It made you pause by something revelatory it cast over his whole physiognomy, not like a ray, but like a shadow. I often asked myself what it could be, that quality that checked one's care-free mood, and now I think I have had my answer. It was the smile of a man who knows that his time will not be long on this earth. . . ."

I have used this quotation to show the quality of friendship that my husband was capable of, and in both our hearts Stephen had a little shrine in which he remained till the day of his death at the early age of thirty.

That first evening he had arrived from town with his host just in time for dinner. I was greatly amused by his queer drawl, he told tales of his little dawg, of whom he was inordinately fond. Dogs and horses were a passion with him.

I did not meet this man again until our son was five weeks old. He had expressed himself greatly interested in the prospect before us and had promised to provide the youngster with a little "dawg." Those last months passed all too quickly, even although they dragged at times. Joseph Conrad required very careful handling, and I had my hands full all the time, preparing for the small stranger.

In due time the child was born, and my husband's manner of announcing the arrival is so typical of him that I feel impelled to include it here.

"DEAR MR. CHEESON,

Your unexpected and delightful letter reached me yesterday morning, I would have answered it at once had it not been that the house was in a state of disorganization on account of the arrival of an infant of the male persuasion. However, the fuss is over, thank God. . . ."

I can confidently assert that most of the fuss—not quite all, of course—was made by my good man himself. It was his first experience of any such happening, and in due time he had departed in a jaunty manner in search of the doctor. Arrived at his house he assured him there was no need for any hurry and accepted the offer of a second breakfast with a good appetite. We had to send two messengers before they arrived. A trifle peeved, my unusual man declared himself very displeased with me, 'my behaviour was most unseemly and disturbing.' The house was disorganized indeed.

However, in the end all was well, and it saved a great deal of unprofitable discussion to pass over his impatience, which I knew was due not to indifference but to his nervous temperament. His first words, when he was introduced to his son, amused me, but exasperated my mother very much. "Why: it's just like a human being."

He touched the baby's cheek with his forefinger, and exclaimed in delight when the infant laid firm hold of it and tried to insert it into his mouth.

Everyone who came near that old farmhouse had to view the baby. Asleep or awake his proud father would exhibit him with a curious deprecating air that seemed to say: "That's nothing to what I might be a parent to." Like all fathers he began to make plans at once for his future far ahead, but when the baby was but five weeks old that strange man gave me yet another surprise. We had been asked to pay a visit to the house of Stephen Crane and his wife at Ravensbrook, in Surrey, and to bring the boy, Borys. Another young sister of mine, Dora, was also to accompany us to assist me in the care of the infant.

The day arrived, and, according to plan, we met Joseph Conrad at Charing Cross Station, where he had preceded us. I think I was justly proud of my young son's travelling outfit, and expected his father to express his approval when he saw him. Joseph Conrad approached to within speaking distance and laid down the law in a manner that admitted of no appeal. He had taken our tickets, first class, and intended travelling in the same carriage, but—here he became most emphatic—on no account were we to give any indication that he belonged to our little party. I was rather hurt for I had not then the experience of later years. Soberly we installed ourselves in that railway carriage, and, in due course, he also entered and seated himself in a far corner, ostentatiously concealing himself behind his newspaper and completely ignoring his family. My lips quivered:

then I could not forbear a smile. The baby whimpered and refused to be comforted. I caught a glance of warning directed at me from over the top of the paper. All my efforts to soothe the infant proved unavailing, and the whole carriage re-echoed with his lusty howls. The paper was flung aside and from all sides came murmurs of consternation and sympathy for him—the only man; the stranger in the carriage. No less than four other occupants, all ladies, offered suggestions as to the cause of the yells. Then the whole carriage was convulsed with suppressed merriment when my young sister turned to Joseph Conrad and, forgetting his injunction, demanded that he should reach down the case that contained the baby's bottle from the rack above his head.

That visit was a pleasant one and lives now in my mind. It was here in Stephen Crane's house that the baby first beheld Edward Garnett. The good man peered through his spectacles at the little fellow who, not being aware who was gazing down upon him, greeted him with heartrending yells, which ended in his father ordering his removal from the room in the most peremptory fashion. Edward Garnett, himself a father, hastened to excuse the lamentable manners of my young son. Here it was that we first met Ford Madox Hueffer—or Ford, as he now wishes to be called. It was here, too, that I met Harold Frederic, and Mr. Jack Stokes (a cousin of the late Duke of Norfolk). There was a great deal of amusement caused by the efforts of a Greek, whom Stephen Crane had imported as butler, and who persisted in treating my baby son as a person of importance, setting a big easy chair for him at the dining-table each time close to my side. This man once came to us announcing: "Mr. Conrad, Mr. Stokes he come, he want you, Mr. Crane." I had quite a good time on the whole; apart from some stomach trouble due to my inexperience in feeding the baby, we enjoyed our visit immensely.

On our return to the old farm-house life was uneventful until the boy had reached the age of three months. It must have been on that very day that Joseph Conrad departed to spend the day in town. During the morning I received a telegram that on the next, a Good Friday, I was to expect Mr. Cunninghame Graham for lunch. It was my first introduction to him, although my husband had met him several times before. I can never forget that meeting. With his characteristic goodwill he brought with him a plain gold heart, set with a single turquoise, which he presented to the little fellow on which to cut his teeth. (A grandson of mine has it now.) Borys had only on that day discarded his garb of first infancy and appeared in short clothes. I had made a complete outfit the day his father was in town. I could not help noticing how well Mr. Cunninghame Graham's tall, erect figure fitted in with the old-fashioned farm-house. He needed only a ruffle round his neck to complete the picture and make it all the more probable that Queen Elizabeth had indeed spent the night in that old house, when she rode from Pitsea, after viewing the Spanish Armada. That visit from Cunninghame Graham was followed by many more and the affection between the two artists never wavered or grew cold. My impression is even now so vivid, my recollection so clear, that, as this is a book of memories, it may, perhaps, be the best place to record the evidence of a friendship that lasted to the end, fresh, free and steadfast. Joseph Conrad died on August 3rd, 1924, nearly thirty years after that first visit, and there is more than the irony of fate that allowed the date of the funeral to fall on a day in the gala week (cricket week) in Canterbury. Mr. Cunninghame Graham's account of that sad procession is best given in his own words, words which render his tribute so intimately tender and expressive of their long comradeship. He brings to one's mental vision the pathos of the winding of the solemn procession through the crowded streets of the ancient city, beneath the waving flags and banners; Canterbury was *en fête*. From the study window in Oswalds I watched the *cortège* passing through the park, and my mind followed each turn of the road, each evolution of the wheels, until they must come to rest at the cemetery gates.

There is that wonderful preface to the *Tales of Hearsay*, and its generous praise of the genius of his dead friend: "Genius needs no Old Mortality to clear the lichen from the letters on its tomb. . . . Even if the moss does gather tenderly about the stone, it only adds another grace, as traceries of frost upon a window-pane render the clearest glass more beautiful."

And again: "Read and admire, then return thanks to Allah who gives water to the thirsty and at long intervals sends refreshment for the soul."

At long intervals, indeed! So long that one human life scarcely sees more than one! But to return.

The latter end of 1898 saw many changes, and Borys was about seven months old when Edward Garnett prevailed upon my husband to pay him a long-promised visit. Joseph Conrad had made one or two abortive efforts during these months to return to his sea life, even if he was to be accompanied by our small son and his doting mother. The sea called with an insistent voice, and I should never have been surprised to find myself left alone while he made one or two more voyages before he finally settled down. I am convinced that what proved the greatest influence against this course was his indifferent health and a certain indolence that had descended upon him in consequence. During those early months I held myself always ready for his decision, and I would never have raised a dissenting voice. I was more or less prepared for him to demand freedom, complete and unrestricted. I carefully refrained from the least show of satisfaction when he finally relinquished the idea of going to sea and settled down to his writing-table.

This visit to The Cearne, where Edward Garnett then lived, came as a sort of respite, and I saw unmistakable signs of intense satisfaction on my husband's face when the invitation came. For several weeks I stayed on at the Essex farm-house, enjoying my baby, but greatly disturbed by the huge number of East-end Londonders imported by the farmer to pick the huge fields of peas, workers who were quartered in the big barn only a very short distance from my house. This riff-raff was a menace all the time, and to have one hundred and eighty human beings living in such a confined space, drawing water from the only pump, right at one's back door, was a situation that called for all my tact and not a little endurance. The worst of it was that the peas being gathered they resisted with a great show of ferocity all attempts to shift them from the barn where they slept and ate. Narrow wooden planks divided the men and boys from the women and children, and the fairway or channel down the centre was full of things unspeakable. There was also a fair amount of illness among the children and I was apprehensive, particularly when my young sister developed a sore throat.

My remonstrance with the farmer, a man who appeared to believe only in might, resulted in his coming to my house one night and making, what I thought at the moment, was the most amiable and solicitious of enquiries, until he explained that the reluctance of the barn-dwellers to move from their present quarters was caused by the fact that in a week or so they would be required to pick the hops. He had a brilliant idea to force them to leave, and he proceeded at once to put it into action. His amiability to me in enquiring whether I had sufficient water in the house for the night was the outcome of this brain-wave. He drew me several buckets from the well, then produced a length of heavy iron chain and a padlock from his capacious pocket, and proceeded securely to padlock the pump. I watched him in silence until, his business finished, he turned to walk away. I demanded the key, explaining that I had no intention of remaining in a lath-and-plaster farm-house with one hundred and eighty desperate neighbours who were to be driven from their shelter by need of water and who might easily take it into their heads to set fire to everything. We had only one valiant policeman in the village, and he was two miles away! I told the farmer quite plainly that I proposed to hand over the key at the first request, and that he must make the best of that. All the time I was trembling like a leaf, but I contrived to hide my agitation. The next day I wired to Joseph Conrad asking him to find some accommodation for us in the neighbourhood where he was staying.

In addition to the disgust I felt when the condition of the back prem ises of Ivy Walls became unbearable owing to the uncleanly habits of our pea-picking neighbours in the big barn, the monster maggots that heaved a seething mass in the refuse round the head of the only well revolted me. My nerves were getting completely on edge. I dare not voice the very real reason I felt for instant change, I pictured my husband's distress if—and this was doubtful—I could succeed in making him realize how very trying those last days had been.

The day after he received my telegram he wrote sending me a cheque for £10 for my travelling, and the somewhat curt information that I should remove myself as soon as I heard he had successfully discovered some accommodation.

I made my plans accordingly, arranged to send the two small children, a brother and sister, home, and the evening before I proposed to leave I put my small brother and little son in the perambulator and with the sister of twelve, walked to the village to get my cheque cashed. We left good sister Ethelinda at home.

Our local grocer, Mr. Howard, had some little trouble to give me the whole of my change as the bank was closed, and I was later starting for home than I had intended. It was already dusk when the obliging shopkeeper placed the roll of notes in my hand and bowed me off his premises, laughingly remarking that he thought he should follow and try to rob me.

We had left the last lighted lamp of the village and reached the road between the double line of tall elms that cast a sinister gloom over us, making the late twilight almost dark. Still my mind full of those last few tasks to be done and the children put to bed, I felt no anxiety. I began to urge the kiddies to sing little ditties, more to keep them from getting sleepy than for any other reason. I had placed my bag in the bottom of the perambulator, for safety, and suddenly the small brother, whose speech was not very plain, but whose wits were too sharp to let anything pass him by, suddenly said with a delighted chuckle: "Dess, the drocer man is 'tummin' in the ditch over dere."

I listened in horror, and distinctly heard the stealthy, creeping steps in the dry ditch; we moved on quicker, and cold shudders ran down my back as those shuffling footsteps were now plainly audible both sides of us. For a few yards we ran, but the sounds each side of us grew louder and louder, and I was nearly spent.

A few hundred yards ahead, the lights of our farm-house suddenly shone out; good old Ethelinda had lit the lamps. She was beginning to get a bit anxious. I panted; the children, by this time alarmed, although I had said nothing, started to whimper. I began to think it would be advisable perhaps to fling my bag into the road, money and all. It was only the thought that the men who were following us might not be content with that alone that restrained me.

The three figures now detached themselves from the gloom and evidently intended to cut off our passage to the gate of the farm-house, now almost abreast. I drove the perambulator desperately across the road, there was a sudden hoarse shout and a bicycle rattled into the road, the man jumping hastily off to save himself from a heavy fall. By all that was wonderful I recognized our one and only policeman. He began volubly to explain that he had lost his lamp, could I lend him one? The three sinister figures that had been following faded out of sight before I could give any reason for my distress.

Lend him a lamp! I would have given him my right arm at the moment. I surrendered the children to my sister, who appeared hastily, having heard the commotion, and slid to the ground in a dead faint.

Our departure was delayed a day, but I said nothing on my telegram as to the cause. My husband's greeting the next day almost provoked an outburst of merriment on my part. As in every instance, no matter how unpleasant at the time, my "over-developed sense of humour" overcame me and met with the usual comment, Joseph Conrad's comical disgust at what he pleased to term my unusual timidity provoked me to a burst of laughing when I met him at the station.

"I have done the best I could for you," he began, "but I'm afraid you won't find things very comfortable—for God's sake keep that child quiet; I can't hear myself think, let alone speak"—a remonstrance that was addressed to Ethelinda, my favourite sister, who obediently walked the whole length of the platform in her endeavour to soothe her fractious nephew.

Just then the little ramshackle trap, drawn by an apology for a pony, drew up at the station, and we were wedged into it. The journey passed in complete silence. I forbore to make any remark because I distrusted my powers of speaking in a natural voice. Clearly it would be impossible to attempt to give a correct impression of the life we had led in the Essex farm-house. I tried once, only to be met with the incredulous remark:

"Oh, stuff and nonsense! This is England. You are exaggerating, my dear."

We arrived in due course at the old Mill-house on the Limpsfield Chart. Here, Joseph Conrad descended somewhat stiffly from his seat in the dicky, where he had been balancing the trunk. He helped the men carry it into the house. (" Out of all proportion, let me tell you, for the needs of a fortnight's stay.") I held my peace.

A curt command to the driver to wait followed, and we were hustled into the front room, and, with a hurried command to make the best of it, we were left with only an exasperated " Good night. I shall be late for dinner as it is. I shall see you no doubt to-morrow."

I think I felt more " womanish " then than I have ever done before or since. I determined silently that if he came the next day I would be out, no matter what time it might be. I felt truly vicious, and only the expression of comical concern on my sister's face and the renewed lamentations of the baby recalled me to myself and my usual philosophy. I mumbled to myself: " Well, anyhow the farm-house was impossible and, even if we are not exactly comfortable, this is something fresh anyway."

My short-lived resentment was soon a thing of the past. Joseph Conrad was not the sort of creature with whom it was either profitable or possible to remain long at variance. Moreover, I had come to realize that he was at best unusual, and could not be expected to concern himself about silly trifles.

All this time my young sister, with abnormal tact, had offered no opinion of anything or anybody. We stayed the first week alone at the old Mill-house before my husband decided to join us. While we were there we made the acquaintance of Mr. E. V. Lucas and his wife and daughter, a pretty little baby some few months either younger or older than my boy, anyway, very close in age. There came also to the house of Edward and Constance Garnett, Ford Madox Hueffer, Elsie, his wife, and Christina, their eldest daughter, a child of nearly two.

Thus commenced the close acquaintance between Ford Madox Hueffer and Joseph Conrad. F. M. H., on page 15 of his book, *A Personal Remembrance*, gives the following fantastic picture of that first meeting. I cannot recognize my husband by this description, but I include it under protest.

" Conrad came round the corner of the house carrying a small child (F. M. H.'s memory plays him false, my husband was alone when he called upon the Hueffers—my baby was too young to trust alone with his father) that did not impede his slightly stiff gait and the semi-circular motion of his head as he took in the odd residence, the lettuces protected by wire-netting from the rabbits, or the immense view that lay before the cottage. He was conducted by Mr. Edward Garnett. In those days the writer had been overcome by one of those fits of agricultural enthusiasm that have overwhelmed him every few years, so that such descriptive writers as have attended to him have given you his picture in a startling alternation as a Piccadilly dude in top-hat, morning coat and spats (note the omission of the further necessary garment is his own), and as an extremely dirty agricultural labourer. Mr. Garnett lived an acre or so up the hill ; Mr. Conrad and his family were staying on Limpsfield Chart. . . ."

Certainly F. M. H. made a contrast that was startling in the extreme. In dress—whether as the dude or labourer—the two artists were miles apart. My husband, I claim, had the appearance of a man whose garments are whole and in good condition all through. But personal appearance is so very individual, and in many instances if manners "make the dog," clothes do almost as much for the man. These purely external factors troubled me a great deal more than they did my husband. His characteristic habit of not seeing, or admitting anything he did not wish to see or acknowledge was at first rather a trial to me. But after a time I could afford to disregard this peculiarity, and I am bound to agree that this attitude once understood was a save of much time in useless argument; it was often a good deal trying in practice.

I would recommend many husbands to adopt this attitude, providing they began at the start. If by some unlucky chance Joseph Conrad were to burn a hole in a sheet or tablecloth with his cigarette his only reply to any reproach was the inevitable : "I will give you the money to buy more, but I don't wish to hear anything more about it."

I have said that when we first returned to England I could not help being aware that my husband was finding his writing life rather isolated. It is not enough for a man of genius to be warm and comfortable, to have a devoted wife to cook for him and attend to his creature comforts. He needed a mental stimulus, and in the early days F. M. H. provided that. I cannot admit though that his statement as to being literary god-father was exactly true. My letter, written in December, 1924, to *The Times Literary Supplement*, was a protest against that statement and also of the many fictitious and fantastic claims made by the man who collaborated in the fabrication of the following books only : *The Inheritors* (which is practically all F. M. H.), *Romance*, and a short book, *The Nature of a Crime*. Why the false claim to so much of the work my husband left behind him, what provoked F. M. H. to make such unfounded statements I am at a loss to understand. And surely from pure motives of gain, his pretensions should have been made while Joseph Conrad still lived. Perhaps this aspect of the matter has not yet struck the mind of F. M. H. As it is he appears to spend his time producing one bit of

"RAVENSBROOK," THE HOME OF STEPHEN CRANE

STEPHEN CRANE AT WORK IN BREDE PLACE IN 1900

" fiction " after another, claiming such absurdities as the following :

" Conrad was Conrad because he was his books. It was not that he made literature, he was literature of the Elizabethan Adventurer. . . . Think of setting out in an old wickerwork chaise drawn by what appeared to be a mule to persuade a Hythe grocer to give you three years' credit. . . . Think of setting out from Stanford-le-Hope, a safe harbour where at least there was contact with ships, estuaries, tideways, islands, into an unknown hinterland of savage and unknown populations, of bare downs, out of sight of the refuge of the sea to persuade an unknown wielder of the pen, the finest stylist in England, to surrender his liberty to a sailing partnership—to surrender too his ' glamorous subject,' for all the world as if you had adventured into the hinterlands behind Palembang to ask someone only just known to give up to you for your joint working the secret of one of those mysterious creeks where gold is found. An adventure like that of Victory itself. . . . And then to insult the owner of the creek with groans, sighs, O God's contortions. . . . Well all we who supported Conrad to his final victory, were the subordinate characters of his books, putting up with his extortionate demands for credit, for patience or for subjects. . . . The Steins, the Whalleys, the Captain MacWhirrs . . . and now the Marlowes."

It would have been unfair to have given only half this long quotation which is taken, word for word, from pages 25 and 26 of a *Personal Remembrance.* Exactly what it means, I confess utter ignorance, it is beyond my comprehension, but it is typical of all the books that have come from the pen of the *great stylist.* Why, as I have said, suffer in silence from the greedy and unscrupulous foreigner, during his lifetime, only to revile him when he is beyond the power of defending himself ?

By the time we returned to Ivy Walls the autumn had advanced and already the trees were, for the most part, bare and leafless. Our landlord's wife had taken offence at some trivial happening due in fact to a mistake on my part. I had called upon her at the moment when she was going for a drive, and of course departed at once. I had my sister and the perambulator containing my small son with me when the lady overtook us on the road. She said something as she passed, and I thought she was offering me a lift home. A merry laugh from my sister who had heard the remark exactly, and which she at once repeated, as soon as she could control her mirth, showed me the *faux pas* I had made. The lady had said : " You will come and see me another day ? " And I had said : " Oh, no, thank you."

By such trifles are big things governed and with no chance of an explanation we received notice to " Quit," and accordingly we removed ourselves at speed. Then it was that F. M. H. suggested that we should rent the old farm-house in Kent, Pent Farm, together with a good part of his furniture. Amongst this were some really fine specimens. There was a writing desk that had once belonged to Christina Rossetti, a big table designed by William Morris, and a picture cupboard belonging, or having belonged, to Ford Madox Brown. There were also hanging above the couch in the front room a death mask of Dante G. Rossetti and one of Oliver Cromwell, gruesome relics that held for me a good deal of awe, especially in the dusk or firelight. There was a great dignity in these pieces of furniture, and when in the course of time these heirlooms were removed, our efforts to replace them according to our means, fell very far short. I believe my husband rather missed these things. By that time we were the real tenants, having taken the place over from F. M. H.

Walter Crane had once been a tenant of the dear old place and had written the following couplet above the front door: "Want we not for board or tent, while overhead we keep the Pent."

Christina Hueffer and our small boy Borys often filled me with anxiety when they both started on a voyage of discovery round that old house. There was a small four-foot well right in the "fairway," as Joseph Conrad would say, and more than once I came round the side of the house and found the two children kneeling on the wooden rim, with the lid open looking into the water. This was when the Hueffer family were staying at the Pent with us during the collaborations. Sometimes the two would elect to start work as we, Mrs. Hueffer and I, were retiring for the night. For hours after I had gone to bed the voices would reach me through the floor. Sometimes the tones would appear to mingle in pleasant accord, their ideas flowing easily, amused laughs and chuckles. At others sounds of wordy strife and disagreement penetrated to my ears, and raised voices came distinctly into my room. Then F. M. H., who was a very tall man, would relieve his feelings by thumping the oaken beam that crossed the ceiling below and my small son would stir in his sleep and mutter sleepily: "Mama, dear, moo-cows down there."

The small house seemed at times full to overflowing and there were days when the two artists with their vagaries, temperaments and heated discussions made it seem rather a warm place. Still, to give F. M. H. his due, he was the least peppery of the two, being a native of a less excitable nation and his drawling voice made a sharp contrast with the quick, un-English utterances of the fellow collaborator.

One day stands out very vividly in my mind, a day that presaged an attack of gout. The two men had been working late the night before and both the children were a trifle peevish. It must have been the first time they had been in the house when this illness was threatening and both F. M. H. and his wife were jumpy and apprehensive. Joseph Conrad had scarcely touched his lunch, and I was heartily glad when the uncomfortable meal was over. I was feeling the strain very much of trying to be a buffer between my guests and my invalid.

Joseph Conrad wasted no time in civility that afternoon, but indulged in a show of ferocity, the real accompaniment of a coming attack, not often displayed before anyone but myself.

He stalked through the dining-room with the terse request that I should at once prepare him a dose of gout medicine. He then announced to all and sundry his intention of retiring to the next room and trying to rest. He wished to be alone there, too, and in a tone tantamount to a command he added : " And keep those two children quiet, and out of this, where they can't disturb me."

Totally disregarding his guests, who looked, as they must have felt, uncomfortable, he closed one door after the other with considerable violence behind him.

This first experience of their host as anything but the acme of politeness and courtesy was received in silence, except for the rather sarcastic suggestion from F. M. H. that we, my sister and I, should take Christina with my boy with us for a walk.

He then walked slowly to the window-seat and seated himself, a gloomy silhouette, his drooping bulldog pipe at an even more depressed angle than usual. His wife flung herself on the couch the other side of the room. When we returned nearly two hours later they had not changed their position. F. M. H. still sat on the window-seat, a book in his hand and many more on the floor at his feet, together with both the lady's shoes.

Just then Joseph Conrad appeared refreshed after his nap, and quite ready to make himself agreeable, both his irritation and the threatened gout forgotten. It was often a matter of much conjecture and discussion, friendly, of course, as to cause and effect. But I still maintain that in nine cases out of ten the irritation produced the gout.

He greeted F. M. H. with jocular friendliness and the wife with a show of ceremonious politeness that might have been taken as an apology for his lack of good manners a little while ago. He stopped short at the sight of the miscellaneous collection on the floor, and turned to me with a pained expression and rebuked me rather severely for not leaving the room tidy for my guests before going for my walk. "I am very surprised and displeased," he finished up, as he held open the door with a return of his rather grand manner, inviting the couple with a courtly gesture to precede him into the other room. I gasped, and turned away to hide a smile. Once again my sense of humour threatened to overcome me. I marvelled at his want of understanding, but by that time I had ceased to be upset at trifles that certainly had their humourous side. This attitude on the part of F. M. H. was typical of both him and his wife for the whole of that close acquaintance. Sometimes I boiled inwardly and my sense of justice was outraged, still I prided myself upon my complete self-control, and did not lose my temper.

CHAPTER SIX

THROUGH all the maze of conflicting and fantastic statements made by F. M. H. contained in the books he has written about my husband *since his death* I have found nothing about myself, in fact, although he refers on several pages to the existence of Joseph Conrad's son—I conclude that this infant must be like Topsy "just growed." One thing only I know he did say and that was in the early days when someone asked him about my origin, and this was "that I was the daughter of a Folkestone boatman." I have never been able to discover from what source such a fictitious notion could have come, and my only answer to the report when I heard it was a trifle flippant. I merely remarked that there was a saying: "Happy is the child who knows its own father, if its mother were good-looking—and mine was." I am wondering if I owe the forbearance of F. M. H. to the fact that I am still in the land of the living, for he did not begin to belittle Joseph Conrad until after his death.

There was one instance that might have rankled in my mind if it were not for that sense of humour, so much deplored by my husband. It happened that we had rooms in Winchelsea for the furtherance of the work of collaboration, and on that particular day the two families were invited to take tea with Mr. Henry James at his house in Rye. One roomy fly had been commissioned to transport us *en masse*. F. M. H. had been working with my husband during the morning and had asked him to beg me not to change my dress for the afternoon as his wife had no gala garments for the visit. But when the fly drew up at the door, having already collected the Hueffers, both were arrayed in their best and were resplendent. For a second Joseph Conrad hesitated and turned questioningly to me. But true to my principle, and with, I hope, becoming dignity, I merely clambered into my seat in the fly and we drove off.

That tea-party was quite amusing. Dear Henry James himself presiding and for some reason, or more likely from inadvertence, passed the first cup to Mrs. Hueffer. This provoked the lady to remark unpleasantly to me on the homeward drive: "Did he give me my tea first because he thinks I'm older than you?"

I controlled an inclination to laugh and then gravely replied: "I don't know, but anyhow, you can hardly expect me to make a scene and insist on having mine first on that account, can you?"

By mutual consent this small episode was not referred to, but I knew my man well enough to know that it had not passed unnoticed. It was one of those little happenings that made for such a solid basis in all our relations. My trumpeter is dead, so I must needs applaud myself. I remember many years afterwards when Joseph Conrad was feeling more than usually irritable and my well-meant ministrations were unwelcome. He turned to me fiercely and ordered me out of his room at once. My mild reply took him by surprise. I merely said : " Very well, but you know if you should need me after I *have* gone, you will have to ask me to come back." Perceval Gibbon was staying with us at the time and I overheard this little incident being repeated to him. Joseph Conrad seemed impressed, but Gibbon, who understood me very well, put on a serious face and answered : " Well, my dear chap, I expect you will have to ask her to come when you want her." He told me Joseph Conrad glared at him a moment and then burst into one of his rare sardonic laughs and flung his cigarette in the fire.

On the whole I managed rather well on these visits to Winchelsea. I discovered that my complacency was the very best weapon of defence, and I contrived to hold my own quite well. On one occasion we were staying in a cottage opposite the Hueffers, and here the domestic arrangements provided me with ample source of fun. The good landlady had dispensed with her male partner legally while living in South Africa, and soon after coming to reside in Winchelsea had engaged him as cook-handy-man—this apparently unknown to her mother, who was partly supporting her. One day I was convulsed to hear the youngest kiddie enquiring of his mother : " Granny is coming to-day, is father father or cook ? "

Altogether the intimate years of our connection with F. M. H. and his family could hardly be considered dull, the intercourse being so considerable a help and stimulus to Joseph Conrad. I was careful that my feelings in the matter should not intrude themselves unduly and I was too grateful for what help and pleasure the connection gave my husband to make a fuss.

When Borys was two and a half, Christina six months older and their new baby about four months old we tempted Providence indeed. A connection of my husband's family, called by us affectionately Aunt Marguerite (Madame Poradowski), came on a visit to us in Pent Farm. She was, I think, the most beautiful woman I had ever seen. When she arrived Joseph Conrad amused her greatly by telling her that if she required any assistance in dressing she had only to summon me. The dear woman laid her hand affectionately on my shoulder and shook her head at my husband. " I wonder, my dear Conrad, have you any conception of the many duties this little wife of yours is fulfilling now ? We understand each other, but I could not add the smallest trifle to her tasks. I can manage, I am not used to being waited on."

I enjoyed that visit immensely, and grew to know and value the friendship of the truly noble Frenchwoman who had married Alexander Poradowski. She told me many characteristics of her husband and I understood even better after she had done so the great temperamental similarity between her late husband and her beloved Conrad. This similarity must have been national. Both were typical Poles.

The outcome of her visit was the suggestion that we should take a holiday in Knocke later in the year. She gave us a very alluring picture of this Belgian seaside resort, and I was eager to go. My ardour was, however, greatly damped when my husband returned from a short visit he had been paying to F. M. H., and told me that they intended to accompany us. I was tempted to cry off, I sensed difficulties that were going to spoil my holiday completely. It was only the plea that it would be possible for the two to do heaps of work together that induced me to go.

As it turned out their party, husband and wife, a Belgian lady-help and their two children left a month before we did. We joined them in Bruges. F. M. H. met us in Ostend, and I can see his tall figure now, bearing my small son asleep in his arms as carefully as he would his own. He gives a most fantastic account of this in one of his books, pretending that my husband was completely helpless when travelling, incapable even of getting through the Custom House without his aid. (*Personal Remembrance*, page 225.)

This holiday to which I had looked forward was a complete fiasco and we very nearly left the small boy behind. The child managed, with his usual facility to get anything going, to catch enteric fever, which was very prevalent that year on that coast. Nearly every kiddie in the hotel went down with it, but none, I think, became so ill as our small boy Borys. At this crisis I have nothing but praise for F. M. H. He earned my gratitude and appreciation by the manner he showed his practical sympathy. He was always at hand to shift my small invalid, fetch the doctor or help with the nursing. It was a nightmarish time, that terrible August we spent in Knocke. Naturally no work was done, and all our nerves were completely frayed long before the child was well enough to be taken home.

As part of the party had preceded us there, so they made the home journey first. I heaved a sigh of relief, for a week or ten days we could at least rest, and I think my husband had had enough of the double household for a time, at least abroad. The rest of the *Rescue* was written after our return at the Pent. This book I managed to keep clear from collaboration.

One of our first visitors after our return was Sidney Dark, who spent a day with us; the poor fellow was suffering greatly from a terrible headache. Then came W. H. Hudson, who appeared one day out of the blue at the back door opening into the big farmhouse kitchen. I was busy getting the lunch for the two artists, F. M. H. and my husband, and my instinct led me immediately to recognize the tall man at once. It is not often that the image you have in your mind of any stranger is so completely correct, and you feel certain who it is at first sight.

I think Sir William Rothenstein's portrait of W. H. Hudson is one of his best, although when he came to draw Joseph Conrad I insisted upon some indication of shoulders. Poor Hudson's head appears to be floating in a mist. Sir William, Will as we always called him, quite readily acceded to my request, and even included a flowing tie—that was not familiar.

I think I can claim to be one of the friends with whom W. H. Hudson was the most completely at ease, and I know that I was one of the very few to whom he brought his wife. Even his oldest friend, R. B. Cunninghame Graham, was not aware that he was even married. Hudson's reply to the question : " How long have you been married, Hudson ? " " Ever since I can remember," was characteristic.

On the whole our stay at the Pent was productive of a large portion of the writing, it saw a good deal of joy and some sorrow. We were now much nearer Stephen Crane's home and they frequently drove from Brede Place, a house that had been lent them together with the services of an old retainer of the owners. We had spent a very enjoyable fortnight in their home when the boy was just learning to walk. In fact the first time he succeeded in sustaining a vertical position for more than a few seconds was on the slope at Brede Place close to Stephen's study window. An excited exclamation from the interior of the study brought both Stephen and Joseph Conrad out in time to see the baby totter a few steps down the steep slope. He had begun to walk, a great stride towards growing up.

Brede Place when the Cranes had it was only partly furnished, just a few bedrooms and the drawing-room and dining-room. The study only just habitable as regards necessities. Cora Crane was of a somewhat monumental figure and affected a statuesque style of dress. The house, even the unfurnished part of it, was occupied. Harold Frederic, the author of *Illuminations* (which is one of his books I can readily call to mind at the present), was there a great deal, not long before he died. There was also a lady whom we all knew as Mrs. Frederic and three young children, two girls and a boy, who lived the simple life tucked somewhere out of sight under the roof, and who only appeared for a short time in the evening in the drawing-room. All day long these three intelligent little folks ran about barefooted, but every evening saw them clothed in some coarse bronze plush frocks, terribly ornate, their socks mended with weird cobbled darns in some colour that swore violently with that of those pitiful little garments. How I longed to spend a few days on their sketchy wardrobes.

Stephen, after riding one of his two horses along the edge of a narrow terrace past the drawing-room windows, would come into the drawing-room with an old violin and accompany himself singing some ditty in a thin but tuneful voice. Robert Barr was also a guest and had shown an excess of nervous apprehension when he once slept in the same room I used afterwards that opened into the picture-gallery, because of the ghost.

Brede Place was supposed to be haunted, and it was impossible to persuade local servants to spend the night there. The only two who would sleep there were the old butler, who fortified himself with liberal potions, and an excellent cook—who did likewise. She had often to be bribed to function in the evening with a bottle of brandy. The chances of dinner—at eight—were often very small, especially when there were many people expected. The cook would appear and announce in the most truculent tone that she was even at that moment departing. Cora Crane, at her wits' end for the moment, would wring her hands and appeal to Stephen. He in turn would give her one glance and solemnly ring the bell. Like clockwork the old butler appeared and handed a bottle of brandy to the thirsty woman, who retired with no further comment to her kitchen, and an hour or so later a perfect dinner would be served, complete in every detail. One night the old butler, who had primed himself a trifle early, knocked over the lamp and set the table alight.

While we were still living at the Pent John Galsworthy became again one of our most frequent visitors. He would appear walking over the fields from the station with his black Cocker Spaniel Chriss in close attendance. In contrast with the F. M. H. he was always the most easy guest to have in the house. Chriss, in his doggie way, was as finished a gentleman. I remember one Sunday when my preparations for lunch were complete and there remained some half-hour or so before our guest could reach us, I persuaded my husband to accompany me across the fields to meet him. The small boy Borys came with us.

Two fields off we made out a familiar figure coming steadily towards us, the dog gambolling at his heels. As they came closer the countenance of a total stranger was disclosed. We gasped and looked at each other in bewilderment. The smile faded from the puzzled face of the man before us, but a moment afterwards Borys rushed into his arms. "I know it's Mr. Jack, only he's had his moustache mowed off." It was characteristic of this kiddie that he often used the farm terms he heard during those days when he lived the life of a little savage. I could never have believed such a change could have been possible. Another time the boy rebuked me when I spoke of the old sheep dog as a she. "Mama, dear, that's not a she dog, that's a ram dog."

There was always such an inherent propriety about John Galsworthy that I dare to tell the following little anecdote without fear of being misunderstood. It was during one of these week-end visits, while the guest was still a bachelor, that John Galsworthy developed one of his rare headaches and retired to lay down after lunch. He was leaving us by an evening train. I had a new and desperately pretty housemaid, and all that Sunday afternoon she had been upstairs. When she appeared at last I asked where she had been. With an exasperating show of self-consciousness she hung her head and twisting her apron in her fingers in seeming embarrassment, she murmured without raising her eyes: "Mr. Galsworthy asked me to stop and help him pack his bag."

The Pent contained perhaps the happiest days of our married life. I tried once to regain possession of it after it had been renovated, but for some reason my husband was disinclined to return to live once more under the old red-brick roof.

Two brothers, whom we call affectionately Big Claus and Little Claus (two men by the name of Dawson), spent many week-ends with us. It amused the small boy very much to see the difference in the size of the two men. Stephen Crane was also a frequent visitor while we lived in that farmhouse. There was a curious telepathy between this young man and myself. I remember once, when we had not heard anything for some months of him and did not know he was desperately ill, I had a most vivid dream one night which I told my husband in the morning. I had had a vision of dear Stephen lying on a stretcher being placed in an ambulance with two nurses in attendance and Cora Crane, and of the ambulance being driven to the coast as quickly as possible. The dream was curious because we had not spoken of the Cranes or seen anyone connected with them for some months. When the post arrived an hour later a letter told us the exact substance of my dream and begged us to go that morning to the "Lord Warden" in Dover, where the poor fellow lay awaiting a calm sea to cross and try to reach the Black Forest in search of health. For poor Cora it was a pitiful business, she had not the means to pay for meals in the "Lord Warden." The nurses were fed outside, but I know that the wife often went without.

The small boat we shared with Stephen had been in Rye for months. That arrangement was not very satisfactory as far as we were concerned, and Cora Crane's illogical request made to my husband rather took his breath away. We had bought the boat, *La Reine,* from Mr. Hope on the understanding that Stephen and my husband were to be joint owners, and half the time we kept it in Folkestone and the other half of the time Stephen had her in Rye. But he had never paid his half-share, and his wife's proposition was that she should allow their local wood merchant to take her over in payment for their wood account.

A few days after that this queer telegram arrived for their man of business, who was not aware that they had taken the favourite dog with them to Germany: "God took Stephen at 11.5, make some arrangement for me to get the dog home."

I always thought that it was a terrible pity the poor corpse should have to lie in a London mortuary waiting for a passage to America for so long. There was a glass let in the lid of the coffin, and people were allowed to take a last look at poor Stephen, and leave their card at the mortuary.

It was to the Pent that H. G. Wells came, bringing G. B. Shaw, George Gissing and many other men, and not a few young ladies. I always remember a lunch that H. G. Wells partook of and one that exasperated my husband very much. He arrived with a terrible headache and would eat nothing but a slice of dry bread, washed down by a glass of quinine and water, while G. B. Shaw made a tea off Van Houten's cocoa and a dry biscuit. It looked such a small meal for such a big man to exist upon.

H. G. Wells often amused me extremely in those early days. We spent many very happy days in his home, Spade House in Sandgate. He had apparently a passion for breaking crockery, which vexed his wife's tidy mind, and she used to keep some cheap vases, etc., for those occasions. His handkerchief drawer was also a model of tidiness. All along the edge of the drawer neat little slips of paper appeared bearing the following descriptive legends: "Handkerchiefs to lend, handkerchiefs for everyday use, evening handkerchiefs"—I think the only omission were black-bordered ones. I once met there a dear little old lady, his mother. The quaint little figure dressed in her stiff, black silk dress, and black apron, a lace cap with black ribbon inserted along the front and with long lace strings hanging each side of her face. This vision was complete, sitting on a chair with her black cashmere side-spring boots mounted on a low stool by the fire. In deadly seriousness she would try to instil the idea of shopkeeping into the heads of her small grandsons standing at her knee.

Other good friends who came to the Pent were Mr. and Mrs. Hugh Clifford. His first wife came with him many times to the old Pent. They would appear cycling, stay perhaps a day and depart, leaving both of us the better for their visit. Then came to us the tragic news that Mrs. Clifford had been killed as the result of a driving accident abroad.

Mr. Hugh Clifford (now Sir Hugh Clifford) was quite

inconsolable. He brought with him on each subsequent visit a very beautiful miniature of his wife which he would always place upon the mantelshelf in his bedroom. Then one day I saw he had left it on the drawing-room shelf when he retired to bed. A few days after that visit we saw the announcement of his second marriage in the paper, and we became friends of the second wife. Lady Clifford was extremely kind to me, and I remember many pleasant visits she paid to us, the last during the first year of the war.

They arrived, breaking their journey on their way from one country house to another, and Sir Hugh had the whim of leaving his wife to be entertained by Joseph Conrad, while he took me for a run in his car on the marsh. I was at a loss to understand the meaning glances directed at us from the different cottagers we passed who knew me very well by sight. Then it dawned upon me that our friend's luggage was still on the carrier. It was said that I had eloped.

He has told me of this rather amusing incident when he was Governor of the Gold Coast. The natives were greatly awed and impressed by the first aeroplanes that flew over their heads, and demanded to know " How will they get their food up there to them ? "

Before I met Sir Hugh I remember my husband went one day to lunch with him in London, and there he met Sir Maurice Cameron, and some twenty years afterwards we met him with Lady Cameron by chance in Corsica.

This quotation from Sir Hugh's memoir article touched me deeply, and I can see no better place than this to record this extract :

" Yet, all the while, I have a saddening feeling that I am missing much that is accessible to other readers of this book (*Almayer's Folly*) ; that the expert knowledge of the men and women of a little-known race, with which the circumstances of my life have chanced to endow me, and to which, be it said, Conrad was the last ever to pretend, mars for me the enjoyment that, lacking that knowledge, would have been mine. None the less, I like to recall that it was through a review of this and others of Conrad's early books, which was far more outspoken than anything I have promised to write and through a signed review by Conrad in the Academy of my *Studies in Brown Humanity*, that in 1899 he and I first foregathered. His lament was that, while I possessed unusual knowledge, I made of it an indifferent use ; mine that though his style was a Miracle, his knowledge was defective ; yet it was upon this unpromising foundation that a friendship was built up which endured without a falter for a quarter of a century, and ended only on that sad day in August, 1924, when I stood mourning at my old friend's graveside in the quiet Kentish cemetery where he lies sleeping."

This mature criticism would have greatly pleased my husband could he have read it, even although he, to the end, regarded his first two books with a touch of impatience. He used often to say: "If I kept the manuscript by me for ever there would always be something I could alter or improve." I can remember only one story that was completed even before I saw it, typed within the space of a week and posted to the publisher, and—I had almost said—for the moment forgotten. *The Secret Sharer.* I remember bitterly reproaching my husband for not having ever spoken of this episode to me before he wrote the story. He gave a hoot of delight, and then as soon as he recovered from his unusual outburst of mirth, gave me a great hug and explained: "My dear, it is pure fiction. I don't know where the idea came from, but I've taken you in beautifully. Hurrah."

Other visitors who graced the Pent in those early days were John Galsworthy's favourite sister, Mrs. Sauter, and her husband, and their young son, Mr. Robert McClure, who arrived one night very late and left very early in the morning. F. M. H. and his family were with us at the time and it was then I had the fright of my life when I came upon Christina Hueffer with her long fair hair and china-blue eyes, sitting on the rim of the well with our own boy Borys. The two children would have made a charming picture if I had dared to wait long enough to enjoy the effect, but with my heart in my mouth, I grabbed one kiddie with each hand and hauled them to a place of safety.

There had been a somewhat prolonged spell of work, and the two artists were feeling the strain not a little. I was rejoiced when their dog Cromwell disappeared, and there was a frantic call from their cottage in Aldington, where F. M. H. was living at the time, for the animal to be placed immediately under rigid control. It was, I reflected, an ill-wind, etc.

As was always the case, Joseph Conrad took refuge upstairs and retired to bed to nurse the first symptoms of a threatening attack of gout. I decided that he required a complete rest and was very glad to have the house to ourselves. I found my property (my pet name for my husband) inclined to be distinctly difficult and requiring much attention. It was, unfortunately, Sunday, and he had nothing interesting to read. It happened that my choice the day before at the local bookstall had not been at all successful. No one to speak to and nothing at hand worth reading, a calamity indeed. We had no near neighbours whose store of books I could raid, and I was at my wits' end. Then suddenly as a last resource, I remembered a pile of old *Edinburgh Reviews* in a dusty cupboard. I knocked the dust off these, and creeping up to his bedside while he slept, I put a goodly pile within reach and, lighting the lamp, retreated out of sight.

A subdued chuckle came to me from the room I had left after half an hour, and my dainty tea was greeted with every exclamation of satisfaction. The next thing was a request for something decent for his evening meal. This anxiety to know what next he would have to eat used sometimes to shock strangers. It sounded greedy, but it was at once so characteristic that I had ceased to notice it.

I once had a cutting sent me which must have been inspired by some malicious mind. It was supposed to be a man at breakfast in the saloon of an Atlantic liner. The steward had just finished attending to him when the passenger asks : " What time is lunch ? " and the steward says : " You can have it practically now, sir." Then in brackets (" We don't know whether this is correct, but we will ask Mr. Joseph Conrad "). I was careful to put this paper on the fire at once.

This evening my husband lamented loudly at the prospect of cold meat, the usual weekly Sunday supper meal in most houses. He became extremely petulant and turned his face away, banging the pillow with his bandaged hand. Then turned brightly to me and demanded a small dish of cauliflower-cheese. " You said you had some cauliflower in the garden." Nothing loath and relieved with a suggestion at once practical and possible, I acquiesced and at once departed in search of the required vegetable.

I must explain here that our kitchen garden was a broad strip of ground in the orchard which bordered the road, but it was quite a distance from the house. The late twilight was not light enough for my purpose, so having lit the candle in the stable-lantern and armed with a sharp knife and my walking-stick, I set out. I looked back at the house when I got into the gloom of the thick trees and felt a bit comforted by the lights. That farm-house was very lonely, quite half a mile from the nearest human habitation and at home there was only my husband lying upstairs and a maid with the small boy downstairs.

A few more steps and I reached the garden gate and turned the key in the rusty lock. I stepped carefully over the rough ground, having a regard for my lame knee, and came at last to the row of young cauliflower I had noticed a few days before. I raised my lantern and the flickering light fell upon the face of the most repulsive tramp I had ever seen. He showed his few yellow fangs in an angry snarl and rose slowly to his feet. I reflected rapidly that my womanish impulse to scream would not be very likely to be helpful. Who would hear me ? I gasped, but managed to say in a voice I scarcely recognized as my own, pointing to the pile of cauliflowers at the man's feet : " If you have got all you want, take yourself off." I trembled violently, I was out of reach of any help, I had one or two rings on, and the intruder was most terrifying to look upon.

"Show us a light," he growled, and proceeded to stow his ill-gotten gains into the capacious pockets of his ragged coat. I waited while he passed me, stooping his head to extinguish my lantern as he moved towards the gate by which I had entered. Without haste, he went through and closed it behind him loudly, turned the key, and shambled up the slope on to the road above the orchard.

I knew instinctively that he had locked me in and taken the key before I heard his voice jeering at me as he disappeared round the hedge. I stood still trying to pull myself together, the moon suddenly swam clear of the cloud and showed me that there were still one or two of the young vegetables uncut. I secured two and thought rather ruefully of how I was to get out of the orchard. The man must have entered from the road, through a gap in the hedge, but from where I stood I had a shallow river to cross and two deep banks to negotiate and no matches to re-light my lantern. Just then from the road I heard again the same hoarse chuckle and a small object fell with a metallic rattle on a stone at my feet. I stooped and picked up the key and made my way back the way I had come. I was not a little proud of the fact that I locked the gate behind me. I said no word of my unpleasant adventure when I took my little dish upstairs. Not even when I was reproached for the "unconscionable time I had taken over such a trifle." However, he enjoyed it and was as usual loud in praise of my culinary effort.

It was soon after that evening that I awoke one night to hear voices outside my bedroom door. I found our faithful village maid seated on the top step of the stairs in her nightdress weeping bitterly and protesting that someone was knocking on her bed-room window with a wooden prop. Joseph Conrad stood a few steps lower down the flight that led to the spare room. He had been using this room on account of his recent indisposition. He was insisting that she was mistaken, and not too gently he commanded her to get back to bed and forget all her nonsense.

I was touched by the very real distress of the maid and invited her into my room, and she lay on the side of my bed trembling and sobbing till she fell off to sleep.

About half an hour later I heard the spare room window opened violently and my husband shouted: "Damn, there is someone about."

Clad only in his pyjamas and with bare feet he dashed down the stairs and out of the house. In my nightdress, with my hair flying behind me and also barefooted, I followed him. At the open front door I hesitated, wondering which way he had gone. It was a brilliant moonlight night and I could not help wondering what we must be looking like flying round and round that old house, one behind the other. In a few moments I caught a sound of a familiar voice muttering the most appalling threats. Old Hunt, the gardener, an old veteran of the Indian Mutiny. We passed round the house once more, then, with all my strength, I forced my husband into the little hall, panting out: "Go back to bed, dear, it's only Hunt, he has been drinking again."

The next morning we saw the old fellow seated on a fallen tree stump outside the orchard gate with a scythe (with a broken handle) leaning against his knee and his eyes fixed on the house. I concluded that the weapon he had with him the night before was that identical scythe, formidable enough, especially with the will to use it. Without a word Joseph Conrad strode up to the man and, gripping him by the shoulders, shook him violently, then as suddenly released his hold, and the old fellow rolled on the ground at his feet. My husband stood over him with clenched fists and shouted fiercely: "Get out of this, you pig, pig, pig."

Not many days afterwards the old man was found lying in the orchard very ill, and was removed to the infirmary, where he died.

By this time Borys was getting to the small boy stage and inclined to make a row like other children of his size. The story, *Falk*, was finished, and the effort of writing this had taken its usual toll, and for the last three days poor Joseph Conrad was held fast in the grip of one of the most severe attacks of gout that he had indulged in since our honeymoon. Any untoward incident seemed to produce a painful attack as an immediate result. I used to be exasperated sometimes when a plan was made and its fulfilment depended entirely on whether or not the "bogey" gout would stop away or not. In fact, once my husband had invited an almost stranger to come for a long week-end, and almost on his arrival took a sudden dislike to him. Before the first meal was over I was commanded to take charge. "Keep that man out of my sight, or I might do him an injury." This expression I grew to value exactly as it was meant, but it took some time.

The particular occasion I have alluded to above, the attack, although seemingly conjured up at will, became in a very short time, as I have said, very realistic. I forget what particular vexation was directly responsible. It remained a matter of argument between us as to which was the cause and which the effect, but as the sufferer said himself, since it was there it hardly mattered—and he preferred to consider the gout the cause and the irritation the effect.

My command on this day had been to keep the place perfectly

quiet, and the boy out of the house altogether—thank God it was summer-time. Accordingly I had taken the child as far away as possible from the sick room and was playing engines with him at the entrance to the big yard. This yard lay below the road and was the principal entrance to the garden. It was possible to make a wider detour and to get right round it in the fields and keep within sight from the windows.

There was a tinkle of a bicycle bell, and looking round I beheld a stoutish stranger ride into the yard, dismount and lean his cycle up against the wall, while he came purposefully towards me. I did not fancy the man at all, and was not disposed to be particularly gracious when, without the least preamble, he began : " I 'ave gom to make zee acquaintance of Mr. Conrad."

I answered rather shortly that this was impossible as my husband was very ill in bed, and not allowed to see anyone. The stranger stuttered with excitement, and declared in guttural tones : " I gom again, I vill gom many times." He glared at me in a truly vengeful manner, and as I turned my back upon him, his hand flew to his hip pocket in a significant gesture. I felt a moment of some satisfaction as I thought to myself : " Ah, my friend, a touch of rheumatism."

Without further parley he turned his machine abruptly, mounted and rode out of the yard.

When I re-entered the house I told my husband of this visitor and of his determination to make his acquaintance. " He was a foreigner," I concluded, " and a bad-tempered one at that. I wasn't particularly civil to him either." We dismissed the matter from our minds without any further thought for the time being. My invalid had enjoyed a good sleep and was anxious for his tea. After I had administered the medicine and re-bandaged the suffering limb I retired to the kitchen to set the domestic machinery in motion before I put the small boy to bed and settled down to my needlework.

The next morning there was little or no improvement in my invalid's condition, and I felt anxious and depressed, although I had seen him as bad before. I busied myself with my usual morning tasks, and took the boy out into the garden as I had done the day before. My youthful groom came to me with the remark that the visitor of yesterday seemed to be keeping his word as to coming many times in the hope of making Mr. Conrad's acquaintance. " He was hereabouts late last night and he has been prowling round the fields since quite early this morning," he announced in an important tone, " there he is over there, wonder what he wants to see Mr. Conrad for and who he is ? " This youth was intrigued by the stranger's determination.

I dismissed the matter shortly, remarking that there was very little prospect of Mr. Conrad seeing him very soon as he could not put his foot to the ground. I tried not to think of that watching figure, for the house was lonely. I almost wished that he would give me some cause to order him off, but there was a right-of-way through the fields, and I decided I should only make myself ridiculous if I mentioned the matter to our old landlord, the farmer.

The days passed, lengthened into weeks and still my invalid kept his room. My household staff at that time consisted of one daily young girl and my old maid, and the youth I have mentioned. Every morning this young man would report having seen this mysterious figure sitting in the fields watching the house or taking his restless way round and round, but he made no further attempt to speak to any of us.

Then the day came when I had cause to be thankful that the gouty attack had been more than ordinarily persistent and my husband still a prisoner. A messenger left a note for me at the back door and made off before I could ask from whom it might be. I turned it over and over in my fingers, curiously reluctant to break the seal. My dismay is easily understood. The note bore the signature of a friendly farmer who lived about two miles away, and he proceeded to tell me that this man, a German by the name of Meen, had been lodging in his house for the last three weeks, and only that morning he had discovered that his lodger was in the possession of loaded fire-arms. Further, in the course of a somewhat heated conversation, the fellow had declared his fell intention of shooting Mr. Conrad at sight. He had a copy of the book containing *Falk*, and had decided that the character Hermann was meant for himself, and thus this dangerous lunatic had conceived his expressed enmity against a perfectly innocent person.

I crumpled the note in my fingers. It was easy now to understand his persistent watching of our house, and his sinister movement I had mistaken for a twinge of rheumatism. I was frankly nonplussed. What could I do to protect my husband from the madman ? Then I noticed a postscript. The farmer went on to say that when he found he had a loaded revolver in his possession he had ordered him out of the place, refusing to house him any longer. This was some three hours ago, and now he was distressed for he had no idea where the man had gone. He assured me that the fellow meant mischief and warned me to take care.

Suddenly the full horror of the whole thing came home to me with such force as to rob me of all my strength and power of thought. What could I do to prevent this man from forcing his way in, for instinct told me that he would not be long before he used that weapon he had carried about with such concentration of purpose for nearly a month.

I knew I must depend entirely upon myself and I began to take stock of my resources. I could not make a confidant of either the girls or the youth, I distrusted their courage profoundly. I could only hope that fate would send some visitor to the house to whom I could relate my worry. Meanwhile I decided to keep everything to myself. If I had occasion to leave the back of the house I locked the massive oak door of the kitchen, and if I had to leave the front I locked that door. I could give no explanation of my action to the girls, and I sensed some surprise in their glances.

I could only give the excuse that I did not want the small boy to go out that morning, and knowing the bucolic mind pretty thoroughly, I threw out a suggestion that there was to be a fair passing through the village, and that there might be some rather light-fingered folk among them. Further than that I encouraged them to do double work that day, promising them the price of a visit to the fair when it was open in two days' time. My ruse succeeded, and only my anxious heart was troubled and apprehensive. From the window we actually saw the elephants pass along the road, they were bound for a town four miles distant, but that I did not think necessary to explain at the moment.

I never let the child out of my sight, and I kept away from my invalid as much as possible, fearing my face might betray me. The climax came when the child had gone to bed, and I sat listening for the sound of the trap being driven into the yard. The youth had been sent for some medicine for my husband and to buy certain books or magazines. What a day! At other times there would have been life on the farm, but a distant market had taken every available man on the place. Even the postman gave us a miss that day.

It was after nine when the sound of wheels fell on my ears and I opened the door to let the groom in. I noticed at once that he was deadly pale and very subdued. He unloaded his parcels on the kitchen table in silence, then he said solemnly, turning his pale face towards me:

"You know the German fellow, mum?" I nodded. "Well, he's killed a convalescent soldier who was walking on Folkestone Leas this morning, because he laughed out loud as he passed him. He turned round, our German did, and shot him dead."

True enough as we read in the paper the next morning. The man was indeed a German, and he had in his possession a copy of *Falk*, with the passage he had decided referred to him, marked in red ink. The last we heard of the affair was that the lunatic was to be detained during His Majesty's pleasure. He had been living in the care of an elder sister for years in the West of England.

It was several days before I could bring myself to tell my

husband what a narrow escape he had had. Here again comes comedy close on the heels of tragedy. I came upon the small boy hammering two flat slabs of wood together with his toy hammer. The nails he had used protruded right through the masterpiece he had fabricated. A wooden sole to keep his father's gouty foot dry when he went with his son into the garden. I had to provide long tapes with which it could be attached. That sole was treasured by Joseph Conrad long after the boy had gone to school, and it provided a never-ending source of fearful pleasure to the child. There was such a queer expression on the kiddie's face at the mere mention of an attack of gout, half-sympathy and half-intense gratification because his sole would come into use.

CHAPTER SEVEN

THERE must be many women who, like myself, have found themselves in the double position of mother as well as wife. I mean mother to the man they have married, and have found, too, how very exacting that overgrown baby can become. This is not said unkindly or in any way bewailing my fate. I can think of no greater happiness than the recognition of some wifely service. But—and this is a big but—that service must be rendered in a certain way, without any suspicion of self-satisfaction, and the wife must be content with reflected glory if married to a famous man. It may often happen that the shadow—or reflection—looms bigger than the object, for a brief time. But I think a wife or a mother needs to be on the spot when needed and capable of effacing herself—when the first, second or third act is complete without her.

My husband's wonderfully fertile imagination had its moments when it would have been wise to have let it lay fallow. It could be productive of no good result to sit and fume because the inspiration necessary for the work in hand had for the time eluded the artist. It was very unfortunate that he had no pet hobby to fall back upon, now that those precious little sailing jaunts were a thing of the past. He was not fond of any kind of outdoor sport, disliked walking and had no patience with cricket or football, and took no interest in racing.

Sometimes he would take it into his head to try to teach the small boy to splice a rope or make knots. He had the greatest contempt for a "granny knot," he was in fact very clever with his fingers at knotting ropes. It was very remarkable that even after those years before the mast and walking barefooted in Africa the palms of his hands and soles of his feet were velvety in their softness. When I came upon the father and son in the garden or the boy's den, making knots, I would creep away out of sight. But his small stock of patience was soon exhausted and it always ended in a burst of exasperation out of all proportion to the matter in hand.

One morning something like this had happened early in the day, and when passing an open window I heard the small boy reproving the house-boy for something he did or did not do.

"I shall tell my farver."

"Who cares for your faver?"

Borys, in his A.B. fatigue dress of white duck, answered quickly: "Let me tell you, my farver's a very furious man." This was said with such earnestness that the yokel moved off with some show of concern.

I was desperately sorry when a state of mind held up his serious work, such as is shown by the following extract from a letter he had written to E. L. Sanderson (Headmaster of Elstree School): . . . "All goes well here . . . and for that I am indeed thankful. I work. I reproach myself with my incapacity to work more. Yet the work itself is only like throwing words into a bottomless hole. It seems easy but it is very fatiguing.

And so I've taken to writing for the press. More words . . . another hole. All the degradation of daily journalism has been spared to me so far, there is a new weekly coming. Its name: *The Outlook*: its price threepence sterling: its attitude, Literary, its policy—Imperialism, tempered by expediency, its mission,—to make money for a Jew. Its Editor Percy Herd (never heard of him) one of its contributors, Joseph Conrad—under the heading: 'Views and Reviews.'

The first number comes out on Saturday next. There will be in it something of mine about a Frenchman who is dead and therefore harmless. I've just sent off a second contribution. It is a chatter about Kipling provoked by a silly criticism. It's called 'Concerning certain criticism.' I'll send you the number in which it appears, probably No. 2."

This is one of the letters he was fond of writing in those early days and the mood, which he would call jocose, brought tears to my eyes very nearly. Why I have never been able to understand. The following will show his power of exaggeration even in matters that should be merely a statement of fact. It is addressed to his friend J. B. Pinker, perhaps I should have said the man who later became his very real friend.

. . . "The American publisher need not be ashamed, tho' the fact is that all my prose has been published in the States. Publishers are not supposed to be able to read. I can write a little, but God forbid that I should break upon the blessed ignorance of a stranger far from his native land.

My method of writing is so unbusinesslike that I don't think you could have any use for such an unsatisfactory person. I generally sell a work before it is begun, get paid when it is half done and don't do the other half till the spirit moves me. I must add that I have no control over the spirit, neither has the man who has paid the money.

The above may sound fanciful to you but it is the sober truth. I live in hopes of reformation, and whenever that takes place you, and you alone, shall have the workings of a new Conrad. Meantime I must be content to pander to my absurd weaknesses and hobble along the line of least resistance. . . ."

About this time one of those weaknesses having been finished we took ourselves off to London into some rooms in Gordon Road, near Church Street, Kensington. This was to be in the light of a change for me, and for my husband a unique opportunity to get a great part of *The Mirror of the Sea* written. F. M. H. and his family had a house close at hand, 13 Airlie Gardens, which house belonged to his brother, Oliver Hueffer.

It sounds somewhat absurd, in the light of my previous experiences, that once again we were to share household expenses, at least in the matter of meals with the Hueffers. What a weird adventure it was, it is as clear in my mind to-day as if it had happened yesterday. I never felt at home and welcome there. But this curious fact is worth recording. F. M. H. has made the most fantastic claims with regard to my husband's various plots, yet *The Mirror of the Sea* owes a great deal to his ready and patient assistance—not perhaps to the actual writing, but that book would never have come into being if Joseph Conrad had had no intelligent person with whom to talk over these intimate reminiscences. The book is absolutely built upon personal experiences.

F. M. H. was then of the greatest help and encouragement and for that I am grateful. The situation was a bit complicated because John Galsworthy, my husband's old and trusty friend, had a studio-flat very near and Joseph Conrad alone had the privilege of writing at a table in that studio while his old friend worked at a stand-up desk a few yards away. I found John Galsworthy's attitude of toleration, his distant politeness in all matters connected with F. M. H. at once understandable. An attitude I do not believe any other man of my acquaintance capable of sustaining a week. And yet there it was. Never for one second was John Galsworthy hoodwinked by the other's style or pose. He denied him none of the glory and distinction that he claimed, but personally he never recognized it. I used to be amused sometimes, it had its comic side, but I had the sense not to discuss the fact with my husband, who was ready at all times, in those early days, to take up the cudgels in defence of his collaborator.

It was while we were staying in Gordon Road that I once more met W. H. Hudson. I believe it was my one and only journey by tube and I had my small son Borys with me. The great naturalist had in his hand the manuscript of his book *Green Mansions* and we began to talk about it. So absorbed were we that we had three times completed the circle before the boy drew my attention to a gaudy advertisement that he had seen three times. I enjoyed that talk greatly and when at last we parted I promised to call in the course of the next two or three days and renew the acquaintance of Mrs. Hudson, whom I had met once before.

They lived in a big block of flats in Bayswater and the afternoon I called was damp and cold. I had some trouble to find the place and then still further to find which flat in the block the Hudsons were at that time occupying. Mrs. Hudson had a fad of moving from flat to flat as each in turn might become vacant. The property was hers and poor Hudson was a portable part of the contents of those different flats.

I think I shall remember the picture of that home, which was hardly a home, to the end of my days. I climbed the stairs to the top of the building and then was shown into a big room where chaos reigned supreme. The principal piece of furniture was a plush-covered seat, or rather several seats, joined together such as one sees in the vestibule of an hotel. The green plush back surrounded a big palm. Pictures rested against this with their cords dangling on the uncarpeted floor, which was covered in piles of books and ornaments, chairs one inverted on the other and a miscellaneous collection of rugs and other small objects covered the couch against the windows. There was literally no place to sit. Then W. H. Hudson appeared with a few sticks of wood in his hand and his overcoat flung cape-wise over his shoulders. He swept the things off a portion of the couch and prepared to light a fire in the cold empty grate. But I assured him I was not in the least cold and he settled himself on the cleared space by my side and resumed his discussion just where we had left off in the Tube some days before.

Mrs. Hudson did not appear until I was on the point of leaving and then as she knelt one knee on the plush erection she kept up a string of complaints as to her husband's shortcomings as a helper in putting things in order. I was consumed by pity for the poor author, and I could not help thinking that a training such as I had been privileged to have would perhaps have been beneficial. I reported the terrible discomfort to my husband on my return and slyly asked him how long he would endure such conditions. His only answer was a hug.

I was considerably proud of my friendship with Hudson. It was a standing joke that one needed to be a bird to interest him as a rule. I only saw him once after my visit to his home and that was when I was in the Nursing Home in 1918. It was a somewhat embarrassing moment for a call, 7 a.m. I was more than a little unpopular in the Home by reason of my early visitors, although with the one exception they were all medical friends who came to see me so early. Dr. Scot Skirving was one who used to call in on his way to Mill Hill Hospital. (He was an Australian surgeon.) We met him and his wife during the war. Another was an old friend, Major Kenneth Campbell, who always looked in on me as he passed to and from his home and Salisbury Plain, where he was quartered.

The morning Hudson appeared was specially awkward as my room was in an uproar and all the staff was occupied with some extraordinary case or cases and I was considerably startled when

BORYS AND HIS MOTHER IN 1899

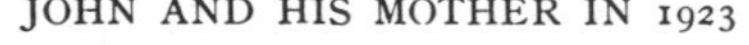

JOHN AND HIS MOTHER IN 1923

JOSEPH CONRAD, JESSIE, BORYS AND JOHN IN 1908
Someries, Luton, Bedfordshire.

my dear little Scotch nurse appeared and said: "There's a very tall civilian downstairs, who insists upon seeing you at once. He won't give his name and it's very early for visitors." She got no further with her objections for the visitor quietly entered the room in her wake. Of course I knew him at once, and hastened to assure my attendant that he was an old friend.

His manner of greeting me gave no indication of the number of years since I had last seen him, and I was at a loss to know how he had discovered me in that Nursing Home. His first words were a rather fretful complaint that Joseph Conrad should not have answered a letter he had written him some years ago. I made many excuses and managed to sooth my caller with the assurance that no slight had been intended and that I was sure his letter would be answered as soon as I reminded my husband of it.

My breakfast tray appeared at that moment and the dear fellow was induced to partake of some refreshment to the extent of coffee and fruit.

Joseph Conrad was intensely pleased when he heard of the visit and the two old friends lunched together the next day, and the misunderstanding was cleared away.

But to return to those earlier days when F. M. H. lent his valuable help in finishing *The Mirror of the Sea.* I managed, unfortunately, to slip both knee-caps at once one morning, when I was walking in Church Street. This disaster kept me at home in the rooms, and eventually I returned to the Pent before my husband. Those were days of excruciating pain and perhaps that is why my memory was not too retentive of other happenings. I was too full of myself, my pain and misfortune.

Next November we went again to London and an operation was decided upon. That Nursing Home was a nightmare and I have only horror of the first time I had faced a surgeon's knife.

It was typical of Joseph Conrad with his inherent extravagance of everything that the night before I left the flat in Addison Road to go into the Nursing Home, we had some thirty guests for a kind of impromptu supper. I remember Mr. and Mrs. E. V. Lucas, A. J. Dawson—who returned in the small hours of the morning after an absence of some few hours, to tell us he had sold "his soul to the Standard"—Henry Tonks, Augustus John, among many others.

Then after a few hours spent in the vain effort to rest, I departed for the Nursing Home with my husband and small son. It was practically my first parting with the boy and I had hard matter to keep a straight face. But the child with a wisdom beyond his years stayed only a few moments after they had seen me in bed, before he assumed control of the business with a mature "Come along, Dadda," and marched his parent out of the house.

That week after the painful effects of an examination of the injured limb while the surgeon debated the need of an operation was, I really believe, the longest I had ever spent. I was in too much pain to care what might happen to me. And the morning of my first adventure with the knife as in every subsequent adventure, my over-developed sense of humour stood me in good stead. I remember telling Mr. Bruce Clarke when he appeared dressed for the fray of something I had been reading in "*The Times* Memoriam"—"In Memory of dear father: His end was Peace, with God all things are possible." My levity relaxed the tension more than anything else could have done and both doctors burst into a laugh.

Meanwhile poor Joseph Conrad paced to and fro on the pavement outside in the chilly mist of a November morning. Three hours was a lifetime of horror to the super-sensitive man. And I was really much more sorry for him than for myself. Anxiety, after all, is the worst kind of pain. As in every case, he suffered greatly and his apprehensive mind could never justly appreciate what was to happen.

I have a hazy notion that the Nursing Home was at the end of a cul-de-sac, at any rate, Joseph Conrad's restless walk up and down seemed restricted by the end of the road. He told me when it was all over and he was allowed to see me, that he must have acted subconsciously part of the time he waited, and when he found himself he was standing in front of an old dray-horse with his arms literally round the animal's neck. The carter stood by all the time apparently divided in his mind as to whether the swell was hopelessly mad or merely intoxicated. He shook his head ominously, but accepted the half-crown which was offered him with injunctions to give the old horse an extra feed of corn. He pocketed the money with a wink and grumbled discontentedly. "He's broken-winded, that's what he is, an' he can't eat 'ay. I'll 'av ter get rid of 'im, too 'spensive." He took up the reins and clambered into the cart, touching his cap and muttering: "Extra feed indeed, I'll watch it."

Then followed weeks of pain and discomfort with little that could tempt a smile. But before long my room was the play-room for any hapless kiddie whose misfortune and ill-luck had sent them there for an operation. I like to think that the time of waiting was made more pleasant for the poor mites because of my love and devotion to children. Here there was some loved dolly who wanted a new frock, shoes or bonnet, or a mechanical toy that yielded to persuasion in the matter of a little oil or small adjustment I had learnt by experience to perform. The adult patients rather regarded me as a kind of William Whiteley or G.P.O. in one. My stock of periodicals, stamps, even cigarettes

—these I kept for visitors—were in constant request. I had many little notes of thanks and requests while I was there. Then as each patient left and had to pass my room, a few words of farewell our good wishes were spoken through the door.

Among my most valued visitors was Mrs. Galsworthy, mother of the late John Galsworthy. The dear old lady would climb the long flights of stairs bringing her gifts of jellies, fruit and flowers. I saw a good deal also of her son and his wife while I was there. My small boy came every day either with his aunt, his father or or old maid.

At the end of the fifth week my surgeon decided that I should have a better chance of recovery away from the home, and accordingly preparations were made for me to be transported back to the flat in Addison Road. That morning Bruce Clarke appeared and tried to give me a first lesson in using crutches. I made a sorry show of learning to keep my balance, I fear.

I spent in all three hours sitting bolt upright in the hard chair waiting for the carriage, which was more than an hour late.

When I got back to the flat the next two or three days were almost a blank, and except for the pain of my wound, which was still open, I took very little interest in anything. It was arranged that as soon as I was able we should start for Capri. Why such a hilly place should have been even suggested is even now a matter for wonder. The surgical nurse I was to take with me had the misfortune to run foul of Joseph Conrad long before we were ready to leave. I tentatively suggested that we should give up the idea and stay in England, but once my husband had an idea in his mind it was difficult to get him to give it up. Moreover, there would have been considerable loss attached to the abandonment of the plan. We had perforce to travel in the most expensive and luxurious fashion, if at all. Carrying-chairs were ordered all along our route, and rooms obtained in the different hotels on the way. Accordingly we left to schedule on the appointed day. Our seats had been booked from Victoria, and if we had missed our train all our connections would have been broken.

The fates seemed against us that morning from the first, almost I was in despair. Joseph Conrad had a favourite pair of eyeglasses, and these that morning could not be found anywhere. I was convinced that had I been able to have joined in the search I should have found them, but I could not move. Then I tried to persuade him that the pair he wanted were cracked and the rims rusty. All to no purpose. We left at the last moment, and he lamented all the way to the station, turning towards me a most reproachful face. In the general distress I had forgotten part of my own dentures, but of that I dared not speak.

My failure to produce those glasses appeared to have cast a

gloom over our first day's journey and it certainly impaired my serenity. I was not then as wise as I became later, and it never dawned upon me that he was unconsciously taking refuge in the first tangible cause for complaint he could find to hide his real nervousness. Looking back I can see what a tremendous undertaking that journey was for him. Apart from the fact that my transport was so difficult there was the knowledge that the wound was still open, his faith in the nurse nil and the doctor who was to take charge of me in Capri very many miles away and a stranger as well. He was a man of wide reputation, but that was small comfort.

Embarking at Dover was very nearly a tragedy, and I shudder now at the recollection. Alas ! I am not and never was a fairy. Joseph Conrad used to tease me by saying that " he knew when he got married that he had quality, but he had been specially favoured because in a few years he had quantity as well." I used to retaliate by calling him a " stupid British subject, and a lean and slippered pantaloon."

The men who handled my carrying-chair in Dover were rash or inexperienced, for by some mischance one of them got his hand stuck firmly between the chair and the rail of the gangway. No doubt it pinched horribly and my fortitude was severely tried while I sat poised aloft, in a frail chair without arms even, on the top of the rail, watching the swirling waters between the ship and the quay, and listening to the howls of dismay from the onlookers, who expected every moment to see me tipped into the water.

Perhaps the man was, after all, a bit of a hero, for when he got his hand free he assisted in finishing my transport right into my cabin. He pocketed a very liberal tip, but discretion was apparently the better part of valour, he was not to the fore when it came to unloading me in Calais.

My husband had chosen an hotel far from the railway station, in a sudden desire for economy. In vain I had pointed out that under the circumstances as I was so helpless and had to be carried in and out he might have saved at least two cab-fares, and thus have equalled expenses. As it was, so it would be, and I was commanded to let well alone and leave the arrangements entirely to him.

My one desire when we did at last arrive was to get to bed at once, but here again I was forced to draw upon my reserve of strength and humour. When I proposed bed, and a light supper in my room, he came to me and with grim determination declared : " I will not sit down to a meal alone with that nurse. Please to understand that."

Poor fellow, in addition to his anxiety over the journey, he had taken a violent dislike to my attendant. If such a contretemps had happened in later years I should simply have suggested that he should have sent our meal to our room and have himself dined alone. But in those days I was much less assured and I meekly made a painful journey to the dining-room on my crutches. The next day we boarded the *train de luxe* and began the next stage of our journey to Naples. We had got severely told off by the Italian officials when my husband insisted that I could quite easily get to the dining-car on crutches. I was the veriest duffer in using them anyhow, and to get along over the shifting platform between the coaches would have needed an expert. I got that far but here some four or five officials, loudly complaining, seized me and transported me bodily back to my berth. It took some palm-crossing to pacify them, they were loud in their protests, but in the end their nationality overcame them, and they accepted the apology, verbal and material.

I enjoyed this part of the journey, especially after I knew that no strenuous efforts were to be made on my part, for I had not been without some considerable apprehension during my attempted passage along that moving train. I faced the corridor from my lower berth and the country through which we passed had all the allure of something fresh and unknown. The boy and his father found plenty to interest them and the tension of anxiety seemed to be relieved for Joseph Conrad, at any rate for the moment. The small boy's excited claim to have " discovered the Alps " amused us both not a little.

We had engaged the two double sleeping berths with a dressing-room between, the boy and his father occupied one and my nurse and I the other. From the moment of starting that good woman went out of her way to annoy and irritate Joseph Conrad. It taxed all my tact and ingenuity to keep even a semblance of peace, to prevent him from showing the most violent antipathy, and her from the equally disconcerting burst of tears. If, for instance, both might want to use the dressing-room at the same time. She had the most exaggerated idea of her claims as a mere woman, and a truly exalted notion of her privileges as the nurse in charge. Yet all the time she proclaimed her abhorrence for the opposite sex. I was soon to discover this to be a mere pose, and I fancy my husband, with his well-known gift of intuition, resented this from the very beginning. I have known only one other person who knowingly set herself to irritate him, but that was many years afterwards, when I was more experienced and able to act as a buffer between them.

At the time of our journey I was very helpless and distressed for the same reason, but such is human nature the following little incident caused me intense amusement.

I have said that I shared a compartment with my nurse, she

having the upper and I the lower berth. The first night we were passing through the Alps and the small boy had been allowed to remain up until we were clear of them. For the same reason I had kept the door of the compartment open. My nurse issued from the dressing-room prepared for retiring and from my point of vantage I watched the good woman mount the ladder. I retain a mental picture to this day. I had been half-dozing when this apparition issued from the dressing-room, crossed the compartment and placed one stockinged foot on the ladder. A subdued titter came from the group in the corridor, and as I gazed I almost laughed outright. The effect was droll in the extreme. That lean form, clad in a tight red underskirt surmounted with a short fur coat exposing the upper half of a lace-trimmed under-garment. Some of her long hair still on her head and the rest in her hand with a small hand-bag. She mounted the steps slowly, more for effect, I thought, than caution, and remained poised a moment on the top step exhibiting a long black-stockinged leg, then hoisted herself ungracefully over the edge and subsided.

There was little variety in the rest of the journey except that, for a mere matter of form, the train was drawn up once or twice and some unnecessary brass-work cleaning done. I had forgotten to mention that there was supposed to be a railway strike on at the time.

We had to change trains in Rome, and I was nearly torn in two by the well-meant efforts of the porters and the misunderstanding of my efficient nurse. I was left hanging by my arms to the carriage door, or rather to the ledge above the open door, while the chair was taken away. It was extremely difficult to make myself heard above the clamour, and I knew no Italian. However, just as I had almost exhausted my strength to hold on any longer a passenger intervened and I was released from a very unhappy position just in time.

CHAPTER EIGHT

WHEN we reached Naples we were made extremely comfortable and our stay for the week or ten days we were waiting for a favourable wind for our passage across to Capri was restful and happy, although I was a close prisoner.

Then came the day when we were to cross over. Again I travelled like a bale, sitting on an ordinary wooden chair lent us by the hotel proprietor, a black ribbon sling to support my foot, at the end of a long splint. My limb had not been "unpacked" since I left London, and already it felt sticky and very irritated. However, the good doctor had been warned to expect us and I was looking forward to being made more comfortable.

Our little party, with the exception of my nurse, thoroughly enjoyed the trip. She was most exasperating, she loudly lamented having left London all the time. She must be sent back at once, she must have something she could eat, a glass of sherry or some Bovril. Then when my long-suffering husband managed to procure either for her, she turned away her head. "How could he expect her to eat or drink or even think of food." But even that passage came to an end and at last in the flood of brilliant moonlight, we saw the island of Capri lying in the calm sea, with its twinkling lights all over it.

My landing was accomplished in a truly marvellous manner. A number of Italian seamen appeared and amid loud, unintelligible chatter, I was hoisted over the side of the vessel and passed by willing hands down the gangway into the small boat lying alongside. I simply shut my eyes and let myself go. Still in the wooden chair, I was landed on the "Granda Marina," without a pause as it seemed to me. Poor Joseph Conrad was loud in praise of the feat performed by the seamen—after it was all over. "It took a sailor to do things properly." The dear man appeared to have forgotten his agitation during the process.

Once ashore, I stood supported by my crutches, while all the women—or so it seemed at the time—passed their hands up and down my fur coat, exchanging opinions all the time. I was a bit disconcerted at all this attention by complete strangers, but I was soon to know it was only a little pardonable curiosity on their part. I got very friendly with all the inhabitants before I had been long on the island.

We had rented a villa from an old peasant, one of whose sons was a priest. This charming young man, Père Raffael, was on the quay to meet us with his Superior the Canonico di Farra, and the two were very kind and cordial in their greetings. My nurse and these two preceded us in the first little carriage and we followed up the steep road to the piazza, from where I was transported in another chair borne by two scented natives. Ugh! garlic, it was my first introduction to it in quite such strength. I had, perforce, to clasp each of my bearers round the neck to keep my balance on the slippery seat of the chair. I was still tickled at the recollection of the two priests and the nurse, and the personal laundry that she had wrapped insecurely in some newspaper just before we left the hotel in Naples. The Canonico had been nursing this package on his knee, and the last I saw of the preceding carriage was the wave of his plump white hand hovering over the erratic under-garments, with which the rather strong breeze was taking liberties. It was so incongruous, somehow, two priests and the vagaries of the waving and fluttering lady's embroidered underwear.

That little episode and my inability to persuade the good Canonico that I could stand without support, made a truly amusing interlude in our somewhat unusual arrival. My bearers having reached the top of the long flight of stone steps, and thankfully deposited me just inside the principal room of the villa, my new acquaintance, the senior priest, conceived it to be incumbent on him to clasp me round the waist from behind and to resist all my attempts to release myself. The more I protested the tighter he hugged. I really think it was the expression of Joseph Conrad's face more than anything else that induced him to relax his hold, and my husband drew me none too gently from the good man's grasp.

The next morning, while we waited for the first visit from Dr. Cherio, my nurse, who had been sitting by my side, suddenly collapsed in a dead faint. We were puzzled, for she had made no recent complaint and we were rather given to disregard her frequent lamentations anyhow. She came round very soon, but she was evidently ill and I induced her to retire to bed without delay.

This was the beginning of three weeks' sharp illness and there was no possibility of getting another trained nurse for her. I did what I could and followed Dr. Cherio's directions to the best of my ability—and this on my crutches. Meanwhile I dared not think what might be taking place under my bandages, but at the end of the three weeks I could bear it no longer and the doctor spoke rather to the point, saying that if my nurse was still unable to attend to her charge he would be forced to procure help from elsewhere.

I should say Capri was one of the most difficult places for anyone to move who had anything wrong with their lower limbs. There was only about half a mile on the whole island level and possible for me to try to move. On most days when my husband could spare the time from his work, he would have me transported in a chair to our " quarter-deck," and with the aid of my crutches I made my painful way up and down until I had so far recovered the use of my limb to move a little more freely.

That time in Capri has some very grateful memories, and as with all our jaunts abroad, I enjoyed the country and the good few friends we met there. Norman Douglas, the author of *Siren Land*, was one of our first visitors. He and his two young sons had a very fine villa on the island. He remains to me a unique personality, a man of great charm of manner and conversation. His chief attraction for Joseph Conrad lay in his wonderful erudition. His presence was such a distinct flavour to any company. His success with my sex was certain and assured. He came to our house on one occasion with Frank Harris and Austin Harrisson.

I mention this visit here because it was one occasion on which Joseph Conrad went completely off the deep end, as the boys would say, without any warning, and sparks flew for some moments. These three men arrived early one Sunday afternoon, and coffee was brought at once. I stayed in the room some half-hour or so and Frank Harris, to everyone's surprise, rose and without a word to either of us, coolly rang the bell for more coffee. The impertinence nearly took my breath away, and the air was tense for a few moments. Then some remark made by that extraordinary man, who must have forgotten he was in an English drawing-room, brought Norman Douglas to his feet with a bound. But consummate gentleman as he was always, in his dealings with a woman, he merely offered me his arm and led me to the door. I don't even remember that my husband had heard the remark. I never referred to the incident even when asked to give my opinion of the guest.

But to return to Capri. It was here we met a countryman of my husband's, one of the most charming men I have ever met, Count Szembek, who lived in part of the Canonico's villa not very far from the Villa di Maria, where we stayed.

The good old couple where we had rooms started life with the traditional bedstead and wardrobe. When we were there their family numbered some eight or nine children, of whom Father S—— was, I believe, the eldest. The second daughter was our maid and the family dwindled in age down to a boy of eight or nine.

The younger children still slept on straw in one of the lower rooms, the priest was housed in two rooms immediately beneath our windows, on the next terrace. I do not pretend to be shocked, and certainly not surprised when I heard that his conduct being distinctly improper, the young man had been banished for a term of punishment to the seminary on the mainland. I could not help comparing the Italian father's philosophical acceptance of his son's shortcomings, with the attitude of an English father. One would almost think that Papa di Maria was indulgent to that particular failing, that of raising a number of the youthful population of the island! He had simply held up his hands in a familiar gesture, and made a sign to avoid the evil eye. I half-regretted my chance enquiry for the young man whom I had missed from his usual haunts.

As soon as I was able to get to the piazza, some little distance from the narrow lanes between the high stone walls which surrounded the villa, we made many trips to different parts of the island. One trip by sea I remember best for the fact that one of Norman Douglas' small boys, when he saw the boat tilt as I put my foot on the side, without waiting to see if my weight would cause it to capsize, scrambled over the side on to the quay and was away up the steep street before we knew where we were.

In all of our sea trips we were three, my husband, the small boy and myself. Nothing would induce my nurse to venture in a small boat, and nothing, I am convinced, would have induced my husband to include his " P.A." (pet abomination) in those little jaunts. At the most, when he strained a point and tried to be polite, he would procure an English plum cake from a certain stores or now and then a bottle of sherry.

Mr. and Mrs. John Galsworthy were staying at the principal hotel and afterwards they went to Amalfi, and while they were there we three hired a boat and four oarsmen and made the passage along the coast from Capri to Amalfi. That was a very pleasant passage and we had thought to return the same way. But as usual, " man proposes etc." While we were lunching with the Galsworthys a wind sprang up and they decided that to return by boat was impracticable.

Nothing loth, although I always hated not to accomplish anything I had set out to do, I bowed to the superior wisdom of my husband, and as it happened the boat's crew were unable to make Capri until the small hours of the next morning.

I remember that night so well. Our friends had no difficulty in lending night clothes to Joseph Conrad and to me, but the small boy was another matter. At last he consented to retire in one of our host's shirts. The boy was absurdly sensitive of ridicule and I dared not smile at the strange little figure. He had been to sleep and woke in his improvised small bed to see a door we had taken for an entrance to a cupboard open slowly before his eyes in the dim light from the passage. He had been disturbed by the sound of voices heard half unconsciously, but the opening door drove him in terror from the room.

We were sitting in the big salon when the flying object rushed into the room, upsetting a table and glasses en route. The long tails of the shirt flapped behind him and it was some time before we could get a coherent story from the terrified child.

The long drive back the next day to where we made the short sea passage to Capri, took nearly the whole day, but the little interlude had been very pleasant and I smiled when I recalled the picture of Mrs. Galsworthy and our young son playing ball on the terrace with oranges they gathered from the trees.

We met a strange assortment of human mysteries on that island, for Capri, then unlike Corsica, seems to be a refuge, or perhaps I should say a retiring place for those who desire to live in the subdued light of obscurity. Socially one had to step warily, few people were just what they appeared. But one can always sift one's acquaintances in the calm consideration of absence, later on.

One person we met there, introduced to us by my nurse, filled me with apprehension within the first week of the meeting. She was more than a little queer. She lived alone in a tiny villa in Ana-Capri with her small son, a boy of seven or eight years. I never heard her exact story but I believe she was the widow of a Colonel, and her other children were not with her in Italy. The first visit to her home I was induced to make for the purpose of trying to get her to let her son and mine become sufficiently friendly to be companions. She received my request with as much ceremony as if she had been of Royal blood and I felt rather disconcerted. My strained manner pleased her mightily and she condescended to unbend to the extent of explaining. She declared solumnly that her boy belonged rightly to the Holy Ghost, and that she had to return him to that deity—when he was dead. I started and looked round for my husband. I was glad to get out of that house and away from the neighbourhood. We heard afterwards that she was used to sleeping on the flat roof of her villa and that she had been frequently heard praying to be shown the best way to sacrifice her son.

I had shuddered to see her kiss my child, but that must have been pure intuition, for at the time I did not know that she was actually unbalanced. Later on she scared the good natives out of their senses by appearing at the top of the steps from Ana-Capri leading down to Capri proper in her white nightdress with her hair flowing about her and a lighted candle in her hand. Those steps rose almost perpendicularly and the apparition of that figure coming down them in white, must have been truly awe-inspiring. On that occasion she was shepherded into the hotel and left in the care of a nun till the arrival of a doctor. In a struggle she bit the lobe of the nun's ear off with those cruel even, dazzling teeth. I remembered my horror when she kissed my boy.

The most intimate friends we made in Capri were Norman Douglas and his sons, and of course Count Szembek. Douglas was a host in himself. I recall a remark made by his youngest boy who used to make his holiday home with us later on. It was so typical of his father and the tone in which it was said absolutely identical. I had reproved him for sitting with his toes turned in. "Oh Mum, don't you know that most thoroughbred dogs and all Chippendale chairs turn their toes in?" He always called me Mum.

We enjoyed our last fortnight or three weeks in Capri, after my first walk without crutches. Here again the choice of that first walk was fantastic. We went to Pompeii, and I refused to have a sedan-chair because the small boy was not quite well and I was afraid to get far away from him. As it turned out he must have got some direct throat infection, for when we reached Naples, where we were staying the night, he developed a temperature and indulged in a bout of Naples fever.

I don't think we went to Naples more than three or four times from the island. Joseph Conrad made one memorable journey when he went to the dentist. Fancy my dismay when I met him on his return, still with the offending tooth in his head, and nearly crazy with the pain of it.

That night he elected to share my very narrow couch. We had two very small beds, side by side, but that night he wanted mothering and thought my shoulder the best resting place for his poor head. He kept filling his mouth with cold water from a glass that I had perforce to take from his hand each time and he held the liquid in his mouth with his cheeks bulging out. If he swallowed it in the end all well and good, but more than once he dropped off to sleep and the water ran unheeded from the corner of his mouth. The result was that I was rapidly getting wet through. But like a good wife I endured and he got snatches of sleep through the night. When he roused himself in the morning he rose hastily in great disgust, declaring that my bed was damp.

This is only one instance of his complete detachment from the mundane happenings of this world. The amusing part of it was his absolute determination not to allow any argument if the matter were referred to later on; he would still give his version of the incident, no matter how unreasonable it sounded.

Those last weeks in Capri were the easiest for both of us. My nurse had been dispatched overland on the return journey, and we all heaved a sigh of comical relief. I say comical because it was droll in the extreme the power that one person had to spoil and mar every little pleasure my husband took so much trouble to arrange. The little extract from one of his letters shows that the manner of our return journey was not mere chance as I had thought it to be.

. . . " The Stage Society wishes to perform ' To-morrow ' next June. Colvin wrote me. Several men (whose names I can't recall just now) and amongst them G. B. S. have professed themselves very much struck. But alterations are demanded and I don't know whether I can return in time. I've written to London to hurry up enough pounds to take us home—but I don't know. I own I would like to secure that chance of the stage, I still cherish the hope of getting away by the 12th inst.

We go by sea to Marseilles, where I want to have a day with M. d'Humières who is translating my poor ' Nigger.' I fancy two days at sea will do me good. We would go by one of the small boats of the Adria Co. or Florio Co. I shall look forward to the view from the bridge. And in Marseilles I did begin to live thirty-one years ago: it's the place where the ' puppy opened his eyes.' Marguerite Poradowski is also there—who really seems to love us."

How well I remember leaving Capri. At that time our post was being brought to Naples by a warship, on account of the railway strike. The " pounds " to pay for our return journey were delayed and had not arrived the day before we were due to leave for Naples on the first stage of our journey. It was then we knew Norman Douglas for the friend he professed to be. Without hesitation he offered the loan of £100, and accepted with some reluctance an I.O.U. for the amount. The morning we left our money arrived by the first post and Joseph Conrad immediately sent our good friend his money back—but gave no instructions to the messenger to wait for either a receipt or the return of the I.O.U.

All our peasant friends were on the quay to see us depart, and urged us to come again. Baskets of wild flowers, lemons and oranges gathered from their trees were pressed upon us. An instance of my husband's hasty manner is expressed in the fact that the small boats in which our peasant friends were returning from the steamer after bidding us farewell, had not reached the shore before he had cast the whole contents of the baskets overboard. The oranges and lemons bobbed saucily up and down in the wake of the steamer and there was some lamentation on board at the waste. I felt not a little regretful, it seemed so ungracious. He, of course, thought of nothing but the inconvenience of carting the " stuff " through the streets of Naples. " Impossible, out of the question, my dear."

We spent two nights in Naples and my strange man was rather annoyed than otherwise when Norman Douglas arrived there soon after we did, bearing the I.O.U. His irritation was, of course, only due to his disgust with himself for not being more businesslike. However, with his usual charm and tact our visitor managed to interest Joseph Conrad and we spent a very happy evening all together. The next day we boarded the tramp steamer in Naples Bay.

I was a bit disconcerted when the little boat came alongside her, and I looked up at the broad good-natured face of the captain who leaned over the rail. I found I had to climb up a rope ladder from the small boat, dancing on the waves below. However, I would trust my arms if not my nether limbs, and commending myself to luck, I managed to climb that ladder and with the help of the hand outstretched to help me, clambered over the side. Then I looked down into the boat and watched my small son and his father after him as they, too, came aboard.

I have nothing but pleasant memories of that passage, in as far as the food and friendliness of the officers went. We were the only cabin passengers and as such were highly privileged. I spent many hours on the bridge and shuddered to see the huge rats that raced familiarly among our less fortunate steerage passengers. These poor folk were provisioning themselves and from the vantage post on the bridge there was little that happened beneath that I did not see.

I shall always remember the wonderful bread we had on board that ship and the cooking was very good in every way. I had managed to preserve a large bunch of pink carnations the proprietor of the hotel in Naples had given me, by packing them in a cardboard box. Joseph Conrad had eyed that box with interest several times on the passage from the hotel to the ship, but I held my peace and the flowers were proudly displayed on the cabin table by the dear old captain to whom I had presented them.

We were amused at his quaint way of answering our question as to his family, which he was never tired of talking of afterwards. I had asked if he had any children as he showed such a great interest in my small boy. " I was married, five year, and come no children, then come five." I wondered exactly what he meant by that mass production.

We had been nearly two days out from Naples when I noticed a certain preoccupation and concern in my husband's manner and several times I came upon him emptying his pockets, when he fancied himself unobserved. At last I demanded to know if anything were wrong. With his usual extravagant gesture and flinging away his freshly-lighted cigarette, he rose and paced the length of the cabin before he said, abruptly:

" I left my damn' wallet on the table in that café the other day. Every blamed cent. Well, it's no use crying over spilt milk, we shall have to wait in Marseilles till I get some more sent us, that's all. Don't pull that face. It's gone, I tell you, and whining over it won't help any."

I pondered deeply, and that night after he had gone to sleep I crept into his cabin and surreptitiously I removed his clothes to mine. As I had hardly dared to hope, safe and sound in the wash-leather pocket I had sewn inside his waistcoat lay the wallet and two letters I had given him to post, unstamped and addressed to my relatives in England.

My mind was soon made up. I replaced the letters and the money and early next morning I went to him, reproaching him bitterly for not posting my letters, which I declared were most important. I scarcely deigned to remark on the fact that the wallet was safe after all. My little ruse succeeded so well that I felt almost ashamed of my duplicity. He promised to telegraph our news as soon as we got ashore. I left it at that. The letters were of no great consequence, but they had been useful in diverting his attention from my raid upon his pocket.

It will be remembered that he had said in the letter I have included a short while ago, that he had written for the pounds to enable him to get to London for the alteration or correction of his little play 'To-Morrow.' In the face of this assertion his eccentricity will be appreciated by my readers. The night before we were due in Marseilles he came to my cabin and announced: "We shall have to wait when we land, after all, for some more money. I have used what there was in that wallet to tip the crew, just out of gratitude that it was found, you know."

He marched jauntily out, whistling his familiar three bars of "Carmen," and I burst out laughing, half in vexed exasperation. My little bit of "play acting" had been quite wasted.

On the whole, I reflected afterwards, we had indeed saved the tipping but that was all. We spent the two or three days while we were waiting with Madame Poradowski, and I saw a little of the city in which "my puppy" had opened his eyes. No other event of any consequence occurred during the rest of our journey, except the news when we reached Folkestone that the pet sister Ethelinda was married.

Once again we settled down at the Pent, and life went on much as before. It was while we were living there that yet another of my husband's early acquaintances crossed his path once more.

Sir Roger Casement, a fanatical Irish protestant, came to see us, remaining some two days our guest. He was a very handsome man with a thick dark beard and piercing, restless eyes. His personality impressed me greatly. It was about the time when he was interested in bringing to light certain atrocities which were taking place in the Belgian Congo. Who could foresee his own terrible fate during the war as he stood in our drawing-room passionately denouncing the cruelties he had seen.

But life goes on, some pass out and others seem always ready to fill the vacant place. Only a few retain to the end tender memories and real regrets for the departed. I am finding it very much easier to record the happenings of our life together at the distance of ten years. I am anxious to reach the end, but I shall miss these pages terribly when this end is accomplished.

It was after our return from our Italian holiday that the small boy embarked seriously on the steep path of learning. He did not find it easy to learn to read. Joseph Conrad, who would make no allowance for the different conditions between his own early youth and that of his son, was bitterly resentful. " Disgusting! I could read in two languages at his age. Am I a father to a fool? "

I waited awhile to let my husband cool down a bit and then I betook myself to the " lion's den." I felt that some kind of understanding was necessary after his last outbreak. I found him decidedly more reasonable and for once ready to listen to my argument. I pointed out that first of all, the conditions of his early days had helped greatly, because as a child he had been entirely with grown-ups and educated people at that. Whereas the boy, at his father's expressed wish, had been allowed to run wild on the farm. Moreover, while my husband had been thrown entirely upon books for companionship, his son was much more in tune with the realities of life. I warmed to my subject and further declared that the boy was anything but a fool, and ended by urging him to be a bit more patient with my small son.

There was nothing wrong with his intelligence. Before he was a year old we had come upon him mimicking the cat making its toilet. I had candidly admitted that I had not before noticed that the cat moved its face and kept the paw still, while washing its head, until I saw the baby doing the same thing.

Not long after this we had the temerity to endeavour to combine two functions, that of tutor and secretary, and to that end we secured the services of a good earnest man, who shone at neither and taxed my good-humour to the full. He began to teach himself typewriting, and his waste-paper basket would be full each morning with the last words of this cheerful essay: " And she died a holy and edifying death " ; this line was repeated over and over again. I began to wonder if he were referring to some passage in his past history, or simply getting ready for some other's untimely end. He was a simple soul, a good Catholic, who would make a wide detour when crossing the home meadow on his way from church. I was puzzled by this for several Sundays until one lunch-time I asked him why. He explained that he was rather nervous of a "colt"—in reality a very aged and harmless hunter who had been turned out in the field to end its days. He must have been a stranger to the country and country ways. He was terribly anxious to know if I thought a fox could climb into his bedroom window, and he had a holy terror of wasps.

The climax came when he was trying to take down some letters from dictation. I was quite sorry for the man, he appeared with his pad and pencil, each of which he dropped in turn, and wandered round the room distractedly. "Where would you like me to sit, Mr. Conrad?" We had in the room an old chair with a piece of tapestry on the high back, depicting two owls on a tree stump. Joseph Conrad, irritated beyond endurance by the poor man's inefficiency, turned upon him and, with concentrated fury, rapped out without turning his head: "Oh, take the owl-chair."

He looked owlish, I decided, although I had not found an appropriate name for his cast of countenance before. I left the room hastily.

During the months that followed, while the secretary-tutor earnestly endeavoured to perfect himself in typewriting, I did the first copy of the big batch of work that got itself written. It was soon plain that there were other walks of life that were more suited to our tutor, and we were both greatly relieved when that fact dawned upon him and he retired from the scene.

Joseph Conrad had remembered his promise to be a bit patient with the boy's difficulty in mastering the art of reading, and I had encouraged the efforts by every means in my power. At last, Borys could read quite well. His delighted father thereupon had a pedal-car made for him and what was more, would patiently help the boy to climb the steep hill behind the house with the clumsy machine and watch from there his rather dangerous descent again. It meant one of his devoted parents mounting guard on the bend of the road down hill, to warn him of anything coming. But in those days, thirty years ago, very little traffic came along, and what there was, usually a slow wagon or traction engine, made enough noise to give notice of its approach.

A pedal-motor in those days, even although it was a clumsy turnout, was a great interest to the boys of the surrounding villages and this afforded many an excuse for the proud owner to exhibit his treasure. It had a tragic result, for some of the children who intruded into the garden must have been infectious from scarlet fever, although I had no notion of any such thing at the time. But of this a little later on.

My reward for some months of real hard work was to be a week or so in town, to show off my "glad rags," as my husband said, and incidentally to see a few people. We secured rooms in a first-class boarding-house in Bayswater and there we installed ourselves in due course.

But fate was unkind indeed. Joseph Conrad and his small son went to see the Rothensteins (I don't remember where I was that day), but when the hansom drew up at the boarding-house and the child was lifted out, I saw at once that he was ill. For two days I kept close watch beside his bed, fearing I knew not what, till one day the doctor came in and declared it to be scarlet fever. I had a letter from the old maid at home telling of an outbreak in a village, and it was easy to trace the infection to the boys who had been so interested in the pedal-motor.

As long as I live I shall remember the nightmare of the next day in the boarding-house. If either my husband or I appeared outside our room, our fellow-boarders scampered away out of our reach like a lot of rabbits. At last we managed to put the boy into a fever home in Kennington and were able to secure rooms close by.

It was a curious coincidence that took us to that part of the world in which I first saw the light of day. And, further, I was born in Shepherd's Place, and my first sweetheart was named Shepherd, he was a newspaper editor, so it seemed as if I were predestined for the world of letters.

We had a very nice nurse for the boy who did night duty, and I was allowed to nurse him myself during the day. Nowadays these rules would be considered rather lax, especially as I was never asked if I had had the disease myself.

All this time I was terribly lame, and every morning and afternoon I had to be taken in a cab to the Nursing Home. I had tried to arrange to get my midday meal in the Home, but unsuccessfully. Those six weeks were full of anxiety, pain and discomfort. My husband, as was usual under any stress, developed a bad attack of gout that lasted most of the time, on and off, while we were in those rooms in Kennington.

I am sure if he had seen the child while he was ill, I should have had two fever patients on my hands. As it was I was often forced to spend the night on a couch or a couple of chairs. Gout is the most unreasonable complaint, or perhaps I should say makes the victim most unreasonable. I would be asked the first thing when I arrived from the Home for news. But almost before I could answer, my attention was claimed by my senior patient and it was pointed out that he required his share of my ministrations. There would be a pile of letters to answer, dressings for the painful foot or ankle, or some dainty dish to be cooked.

But even under these strained conditions I found some cause

for mirth, and I am sure only my sense of humour kept me going. The landlady had a son who combined more functions than I have ever discovered one capable of. The young man was very attentive and useful to my husband and worked well under his mother's eye and direction. By degrees I discovered that some love affair that his parent had disapproved of, had induced the young man to join the army. He had been slightly wounded in some scrimmage abroad. The wound, although very slight, had been the cause of an immediate reconciliation with his mother and an exit from the army with all possible speed. She managed by dint of frequent references to the savings she was reputed to have to keep him by her side, and by this time he had lost any inclination to get married. I knew that he frequently met the young woman, grim of face and taciturn by habit; she was a cook somewhere in the neighbourhood, but although his mother must have known of those frequent meetings, she never made the slightest allusion to them. But she insisted upon his accounting for nearly every moment he spent outside, which led the fellow to romance persistently.

Once, when he had been telling me at length of his wound, I asked him where it had been. "In the heel, madam," came the answer promptly, and I burst into a laugh. "You must have been running away," I gasped as soon as I had recovered breath. I don't think he ever quite forgave my levity. I suppose a wound anywhere—even in the heel—in those days held some sort of distinction.

That place was irritating in the extreme. One was requested to board oneself, and the consequence was that with strict regard to economy and the fact that there was no question of entertaining visitors, or at any rate for meals, I ran the "ship's" provisions as low as possible. But after a time F. M. H. became assiduous once more in his attentions to Joseph Conrad. I was glad to know that he had someone to talk to, but the unfortunate part of it was that I never knew whether he was coming for lunch or not. If I provided for him he never turned up, and if I ran the stores close, there he would be when I arrived home from the Nursing Home. I never dared come into the room where they might be talking, before I had had a bath and changed my clothes, and this formality left me no time or energy to make the shortage good in time for the meal. It usually ended in my becoming a vegetarian from force of circumstances.

There was also the landlady's propensity to dispose of any surplus of stores if I ventured on any extravagance. I once purchased a brace of pheasants which I cooked for the evening meal. Only one had been eaten, so that I felt no qualms when I heard the drawling voice through the half-opened door, when I returned as usual the next day. I had the shock of my life when the young man followed me to know what was for lunch. "Why the other pheasant of course." I answered shortly, as I reached my bedroom door. Without the least hesitation the man said: "Oh, mother says she knew it wouldn't keep, so she has given it to the charwoman."

After that there had to be a hurried raid on the nearest cooked-meat shop, and the great stylist was kept waiting nearly an hour for his lunch, until the young man returned with the supplies. But I was past attempting to defend myself from the stream of reproaches that greeted me when I entered the dining-room. Joseph Conrad was decidedly sulky and his guest more supercilious than ever. I felt the salt tears very near, but I managed to keep a calm face.

When I did explain the delay that evening, my husband protested against my suggestion that F. M. H. should at least let me know when to expect him. "Certainly not. Why all this dam' formality, you never used to want a day's notice for a big dinner, let alone a simple lunch. It's plain enough in all conscience. I for one am heartily sick of it, and shall be glad to get back home. And, besides, think of the hours of boredom I have to spend alone while you are out." Clearly there was nothing to be gained by expostulation, and I retired as hastily as possible, biting my tongue to keep back my tears.

But even these awful days came to an end at last, and I returned home two days before my invalids to get the house ready for their reception. Then when they arrived with the nice nurse in attendance my troubles were not over. In her zeal the dear woman had used too much lysol in the bath she gave the boy before starting, and had set up carbolic poisoning. The child kept fidgeting and worrying in spite of having everything clean, and I was at a loss to understand why. He had his own little bedroom, and mother-like I made a call on the boy about four, just as it was getting light, and what was my consternation to see his face swollen out of all recognition. His lips were like cushions and his fingers stiff, his heart thumping like a sledge hammer. Fortunately a week's rest put the boy right enough to be out in the garden and he began to pick up. The doctor told us that he had a very sensitive skin, and very little lysol had been necessary to cause the trouble.

For the remaining months of the summer we made a very good arrangement with the schoolmistress in the nearest village school, a very clever woman who undertook to continue the boy's lessons after the school hours. We intended to go to the South of France after Christmas, and for that reason we did not want to get a resident governess in a hurry. The idea was to get someone to fill the post of secretary as well.

About this time I discovered that I was to become once more a mother. I believe my husband was more pleased this time than he had been when the first one was coming. He declared that he had more faith in me this time, because he knew what to expect, and as I have said before, he played ostrich—there would be plenty of time to worry when we got back from our trip.

It was while we lived at the Pent that I had, perhaps, the strangest experience of my husband's fertile imagination, and it gave me no little cause for reflection. We had a youth, a very decent boy, who had been some four years with us and who as the phrase has it " slept in." His various functions included the care of the mare, and one evening towards the end of November he had bedded her down and leaving the light in the stable had come to the kitchen to get the hot water to mix her mash. I spoke to him then, and some half-hour or so afterwards I looked over to the stable hearing the mare whinny and I noticed the lantern still burning across the yard. Together with the old maid we made a tour of the sheds and stackyards, but there was no sign of Walter. By eight o'clock still no sign, and the light still burning. I became alarmed and penetrated the sanctuary, my husband's study. For the space of a few seconds he gazed sadly at me when I explained why I had invaded his privacy, then with a deep sigh he rose from his chair and put his hand on my shoulder. Together we walked into the kitchen and he put minute questions to the serving maid, as to when Walter had last been seen, how he looked, what he said? Then, throwing up his hands, he turned and without another word went across the yard, fed the mare and closed the stable door, bringing the lantern back with him.

He came slowly into the kitchen and motioned me to follow him into his room. His next words startled me out of myself, he began walking to and fro the room and then stopped abruptly before me and said:

" That fellow's committed suicide, my dear. I heard of a case just like it on board once." He laid his hand none too gently on my arm to silence my indignant protest. " You don't know these young men; his whistling and being, or appearing, happy is nothing to go by." At last I spoke: " But if there is anything in what you say, we must do something. I have been all over the yards."

" Don't go near there," he burst out, " it'll be no sight for you. I must go and send someone for his father." He turned to the door and called for the maid to bring him a pair of boots. Without any further parley I hastily caught up a large shawl and insisted on going with him to the village.

I did not stop to suggest that we should get the trap, and yet the walk was a very painful one for both of us. Arrived at the village, it was nine o'clock, and he had to wake one of the farm-hands to ride to the next village with the grim news. I am sure every head was out of the window listening to the story, and quite half of the male population crept downstairs half-dressed, a few half-intending to journey to Lyminge to give the tale due importance. But our cyclist was ready a little too soon and departed with a liberal tip and full of ponderous importance. His last words were: "I'd better bring a policeman as well."

Slowly we prepared to retrace our steps. My mind was very uneasy, yet I utterly discredited the idea of suicide, but the notion was firmly fixed in my husband's mind. Dear man! going back he helped me along, and even began to talk lightly of all sorts of things under the impression he was diverting my thoughts from the tragic reason for our unusual excursion. Half-way back the sound of a familiar whistle came to our ears, and looking ahead we made out in the bright moonlight the figure of the "suicide' striding unhurriedly along the top of the high bank bordering the road. At the same moment the tinkle of a bicycle bell betokened the fact that the messenger had also seen the youth and had returned with all possible speed to his home. We heard in the distance a loud guffaw, that ended in strangled effort to restrain it. The men must have suddenly realised that we were still within earshot.

Joseph Conrad, beyond a short "dam" which might be due to relief or impatience as to his ready explanation of suicide as the cause of the youth's disappearance, said nothing more till we reached the house. Then as he took his arm from mine and continued his way to the front of the house, I entered from the back, he spoke over his shoulder: "Tell that fellow I'll see him in the morning."

The explantion was a simple one, and it was well that my husband had had time to cool down before he heard it. I was relieved to hear him laughing heartily when he was told it. Simply this. Three huntsmen had ridden into the yard the afternoon before to look for some hounds that were missing, and had offered the young fellow a liberal tip if he helped to find them.

CHAPTER NINE

IT must have been early in February 1906 that we started, after Borys had sufficiently recovered for us to make the journey to the South, according to our plans. The journey was fairly uneventful, and we seemed at last to have broken our ill-luck, at least for a time. We installed ourselves in the Hotel Riche et Continental, Montpelier (Place de la Comédie), and there settled down to enjoy the sunshine. It was a charming old French town, and our rooms faced the principal place. Joseph Conrad who was another creature when the sun shone on him, seemed in better fettle than he had been for sometime. He began to work while I typed as usual, and between whiles sewed industriously, fashioning the little garments in readiness for the expected small stranger. Most of this work was done in the Public Gardens, while Borys and his father sailed toy boats or constructed bridges and wharfs on the little stream. We discovered a charming French woman who readily undertook the boy's French lessons. Mademoiselle Seé was lively and very amusing. Her pet name was "Madame Barb-à-Bleu"; she boasted of a fictitious husband whenever her business took her out of her native town. We had a great regard for this dear lady, and many were the hours she spent with us, either on our various jaunts or sitting with me while I worked.

There was no bathroom in our hotel, and by this time I was disinclined to take my bath in one of the Bath Houses, and preferred to make shift in my own room. I ought to explain that the trams ran past the hotel on two sides, the building being on a corner. I was busy with my ablutions one day, locked in my privacy and the bath before the fireplace. A tram passed and dislodged a big metal shield from the top of the tall clock on the mantelpiece. It had evidently been placed insecurely, for it fell and struck the back of my right hand a sickening blow. My plight was rather awful, I was desperately lame, and with my right hand out of action—and in a nude condition—I had to keep a strong hold on myself to keep from fainting. I managed somehow to clothe myself sufficiently and summoned assistance. Joseph Conrad was very angry at the carelessness of someone. It was a fortnight or so before I could use my hand in a normal manner.

I had been driving most days a pair of spirited horses before the accident, but it was out of the question after that for the rest of our stay.

Judging from the following extract from a letter written to John Galsworthy, about this time my husband was not very satisfied with his work on the whole.

. . . "As to myself, my dear Jack, I have always that feeling of loafing at my work, as if powerless in an exhaustion of thought and will. Not enough. Not enough. And yet, perhaps, those days without a line, nay, without a word, the hard, atrocious, agonizing days are simply part of my *method* of work, a decreed necessity of my production. Perhaps! But if it is so, then nothing can repay me for such a sombre fate,—not even Pinker's satisfaction with the stuff I send him, 14,000 words was all I could achieve. It's simply disaster and there's nothing in them, it seems to me, the merest hack novelist could not have written in two evenings and a half. I doubt not only my talent (I was never so sure of that) but my character. Is it indolence—which in my case would be nothing short of baseness,—or what? No man has a right to go on as I am doing without producing manifest masterpieces. It seems I have no excuse under heaven or on earth. Enough.

We shall be starting off for home in a week of so, and then I shall run up at once and see you. I must see you both and get braced up in the contact of your friendship and affection. And I must read the play—must."

Most of my small son's trousseau got itself finished before we returned to the Pent, to take up our life there again. Borys had now mastered the art of reading, and was my constant and attentive companion. Those days would live in my mind, bright spots in any darkness, if only for the comfort and joy of the boy's loyal affection. No matter what the future holds for any of us, there is the past, with its tenderness and affection, the memories we can recall at will, at any time day or night. And in most cases the past can compensate for present ills.

I suppose the expected event had a good deal to do with my husband's excess of restlessness. He could settle to nothing for long enough to achieve any measure of work that would even begin to satisfy him. About this time F. M. H., who had been busy over his own domestic affairs, which were not exactly to his liking, suggested that we should occupy his house in Winchelsea for a week or so, just to see if we inclined to change our abode for some place in that village. For a few moments I was somewhat alarmed at the mere idea. Joseph Conrad could see only the friendliest motive for the suggestion. I would have given a good deal to have shared his belief. However, there was a definite need for a change of scene for my husband, and I felt sure that the experiment would also convince him of the advisability—let us say—of keeping our distance. F. M. H. had been rewarded by the Railway Company with a first-class pass to and from Winchelsea—season ticket—for his book *The Heart of the Country*. According to his suggestion we met him in Ashford where we were to change trains for Winchelsea. I am sure my readers will appreciate the fact that by this time I was acutely conscious of my appearance,

MISS ELLEN GLASGOW AND JOSEPH CONRAD IN THE GARDEN AT CAPEL HOUSE IN 1910

THEODORE ROOSEVELT AND WARRINGTON DAWSON, BIG-GAME SHOOTING, 1907–8

WARRINGTON DAWSON IN 1909

and the day was terrifically hot. I was anxious only to install myself in the carriage out of sight as quickly as possible.

With the one idea in my head, as I have said, of stowing myself out of sight and as rapidly as I could, I approached the nearest first-class carriage. F. M. H. appeared as if by magic and placed himself across the doorway, barring my entrance, and said in his usual drawling fashion : " Oh, but what class are you travelling ? " I gasped, then the words tumbled out of my mouth : " I came thus far in a cattle-truck, but I am going first from here." F. M. H. fell back without a word, and I scrambled into my seat and said nothing. My disgust was complete.

I think every conceivable thing happened that fortnight to make me regret coming to Winchelsea. The two long week-ends that F. M. H. had stipulated he should come down were the longest I have ever known, and a fit punishment for any sins I might have ever committed, or even contemplated.

In the first place he countermanded the trap I had ordered at Winchelsea and our luggage did not arrive in time for the evening meal. The Hueffer family plate was locked up and the key lost. Fortunately a porter, who sensed a possible tip, brought the trunks up late on that Saturday evening.

The next day I was cooking the lunch when he appeared with a Panama hat he had washed, and to my amazement opened the oven door and placed that hat on a sheet of paper above my joint. It was a real Panama, but his washing had been strictly confined to the outside only, there was too much grease inside the lining for my liking—even had I not had our meat beneath, and I would have liked above everything to have put it on the fire. I removed it to a chair as close to the fire as possible, and resolutely closed the oven, voicing my displeasure in as few words as possible.

My next surprise was a request put forward by my husband that I should, on a Sunday morning, out of the blue, so to speak, provide a new black ribbon and put it on the hat. But even this fantastic request was possible as it happened that I had some few yards of black ribbon I had been giving the maid to tie her collar with. I dutifully sewed it on the hat.

The next morning before F. M. H. started to go to the station, which he did after nearly making me break the rule I had set for a guest under the same roof as myself—although it was somewhat difficult to fix who was host and who was the guest under the circumstances. He had entered the dining-room for his breakfast after Joseph Conrad had left the room. The first thing that caught his eye was a small cut in the tablecloth. " Look at that, Elsie will be furious." I paused in the act of pouring out his coffee and said indifferently : " I don't suppose she will ever see it." F. M. H. jumped to his feet with surprising energy, and almost forgot to drawl: "Not see it, what do you mean? It's the first thing she will see. I must say that when I lent the house I expected ordinary care. . . ." I rose quickly to my feet and hastily turned another corner of the cloth towards him, saying slowly and distinctly: "I said she most probably would not see it. You see my name is on the corner. I brought my own linen, and I shall take it home with me. Are you satisfied?"

He uttered a short vexed laugh and stalked out of the house, or rather had started to do so when I recalled him with the remark: "Oh, by the way, be kind enough to look at the date of the laundry book you gave me last night. You will see the last entry is three weeks before I came into the house, and that week's laundry is entered in the name of Hyde. Moreover, I put away the first day I came into the place everything of yours in the shape of linen *without using it* and we have been using our own."

I could cheerfully have devoured my husband who entered the room at that moment and caught something of the last remark. "Pay the laundry bill, of course, my dear fellow." F. M. H. gave me a supercilious glance and a condescending "Good morning." But I took care to forget to settle the account which was distinctly not mine.

The next week-end put the "lid" on it even for my dear ostrich, who had his eyes opened with a vengeance. With characteristic disregard for me, F. M. H. announced on the Sunday morning that he had several friends coming to tea that afternoon. He had declared this in his usual lofty manner, and as was his wont, my husband mentioned the fact off-handedly to me just after lunch. I was disconcerted and very disinclined for any extra effort, but I was also pretty certain that this charming host-guest sought to put me at a disadvantage. I had noted a particularly lordly air about him and had been for a moment at a loss to account for it. Joseph Conrad came to me when I had retired to the kitchen to prepare the sandwiches, etc., and kissed me, remarking that one of the guests was to be Henry James. "Are you sure you can manage, you won't be too tired?" I shook my head. I meant to go through with it, in spite of the heat in the little kitchen and my very ineffective help in the shape of the young maid. I protested that I should do very well if he could fasten the kitchen-door back so that I got a little air. The kitchen was immediately facing the front door, but it was clean and tidy. F. M. H. stalked out of the big living-room, and remarking that "he could not have his guests regaled by a sight of his kitchen," he cut the cord and let the door close. Quick as lightning I whipped off my overall and prepared to take my painful way upstairs, merely saying, "Very well, then, you must get your tea yourself. I cannot stand the heat." He threw me a furious glance but did not attempt to shift the chair the young maid had placed to prevent the door from closing. That tea eventually satisfied even Joseph Conrad, who was wont to be terribly fastidious and critical over that particular meal. As it happened more than once I would provide only a very elementary meal, of plain bread and butter, if lunch had been late. This would exasperate my lord and master beyond endurance, and every time he came within earshot he would mutter under his breath, " A damn rotten tea, let me tell you, my dear, a damn rotten tea."

I presided on this Sunday with as serene a countenance as possible, but it is no untruth that I hardly felt able to do so. Dear Henry James came to me afterwards voluble in his tender concern for my trouble under the circumstances, and very apologetic for his own presence. I was very fond of this dear man, who was so essentially a gentleman in every sense of the word. I could read his work, too, with very real pleasure, in spite of his wordy and often terribly involved style. The following little incident that took place near his home in Rye is typical of this habit of his. Some three or four little girls caught his attention, and in his most ingratiating manner he stopped to talk to them. He began by presenting each with some pence and then proceeded to harangue them far above their understanding. The kiddies at last flung the coins on the ground and burst into loud sobbing before they ran away.

I believe the dear man was terribly distressed by this. But to return to my statement that my husband was at last forced to take his head out of the sand with regard to F. M. H. The morning after the tea-party, was incidentally the last day of our rather uncomfortable visit, as well as the last we ever paid to the house in Winchelsea. The host-guest had only left the house an hour or so when the young maid appeared at the kitchen door with a miscellaneous collection of masculine garments crumpled out of all recognition in her arms, and asked what was she to do with them. Some she had found on the bed occupied by F. M. H. and some beneath. They turned out to be my husband's robes of ceremony. Frock-coat and striped grey trousers. I was puzzled for it was my pride to keep my husband's wardrobe in proper condition for instant wear. I had carefully pressed and ironed the crease myself and had also laid them flat in the drawer when we had taken temporary possession of that house. I made my difficult way upstairs, and such was my disgust I could not forbear calling Joseph Conrad and drawing his attention to the wanton treatment of his dress suit and other garments. It was quite plain to see what had happened. F. M. H. had not found the curtains thick enough in the room he had occupied to keep out the early morning light, and had hung one of the blankets over the window. Then not finding himself warm enough in bed, had removed the suits from the drawer to pile on the bed. It was an effective eye-opener to the owner. For once he could not blame me for this calm appropriation and misuse of his wardrobe, because there had been too little clothes on a guest's bed. F. M. H. was in his own place and any responsibility for the dearth of covering was his own, not mine.

F. M. H. had an uncanny way of picking out people from the point of interest, and having found anyone to his mind was extremely tenacious of them. There was also some, one might almost say, promise held out to the other, either of material gain or some intellectual reward, which cemented the acquaintance between them. Certainly very few lasted very long, but there was some kind of fascination about the man. A fascination that I could never understand. All the blemishes were to me much too apparent, as if I had worn magnifying-glasses. But the next person introduced to Joseph Conrad by this extraordinary man, usurped a place completely in my husband's regard and esteem. It must be remembered that any influence on the mind and work of my husband had depended very largely on personal contact. After our visit to Winchelsea, and, I think, due a little to the fundamental change wrought by the hand of time on the mind and temperament of both artists, the intellectual influence began to irritate instead of to stimulate. My husband, being much the elder, grew tired of the younger's insufferable air of superiority.

The first time that Arthur Marwood came under our roof was barely a month before my second boy was born. F. M. H. acted then in direct opposition to Joseph Conrad's expressed wishes, not to bring any strangers for the time. But I must pride myself in detecting any unusual force of intellect, and here was a man who certainly was mentally far above many of his fellows. The fact that his health was very bad through all the years of the long friendship between Arthur Marwood and my husband, would have been more than enough to spoil Joseph Conrad's interest in any other case. He had a morbid horror of ill-health in others, in spite of his intense sympathy. I have tried through all these pages to prove by the use of my husband's written word the point I am trying to make. The short extract from the only letter he wrote to Arthur Marwood that has been preserved will, I think, show this. It is dated April 1915.

"MY DEAR MARWOOD,

I am much relieved by your letter as far as 'Victory' is concerned, but I am distressed by what you say of that extreme feeling of lassitude from which you suffer. Of course, this is a season of queer sensations, and it may not mean much,—a matter of a day or two. Perhaps you will drop me a line. For various reasons I can't fix a day yet for my visit this week, and I want to know how you are.

You, my dear fellow, are the real Wise man of the Age. I am so convinced of the truth of what you say that I'd have cabled to U.S. the correction you suggest, if it hadn't been too late. By the same post I received to-day a clipping of the *Boston Transcript*—review of Victory! The only thing I can do now is to delete the lines pointed out by you in the English edition. I can't tell you how grateful I am for your friendship, which speaks aloud to me out of the lines of your letter so indulgent and so careful of my good fame and fortune. . . ."

I have used this extract, as I have said in the preceding paragraph, to show that this friend had a great and beneficial effect upon my husband's whole conception of his work, and that the intimacy between the two men, so widely different in temperament and views, was a stimulus, generally. Also his great erudition made him a prop and mainstay, at a time when badly needed. In spite of Arthur Marwood's indifferent health he was never behind the times with matters of state or diplomacy He would have been, but for his health, a great tactician. His reason was always so calm and considered, his understanding so clear, that his companionship could not but help such an artist as Joseph Conrad. Moreover, my husband would always accept his criticism, if not exactly without argument, at least with a reasoned and considered one. I can trace Arthur Marwood's influence in most of the books written during the period of his close friendship. Curiously enough my husband took more out-of-door exercise and interest in material things in Arthur Marwood's company during those years, than he had done since he had left the sea.

It must have been only a very few days after our first meeting with Arthur Marwood that we were due to betake ourselves to London for the birth of the second boy. This baby was to have a much more auspicious birth than his brother. He first saw the light in the house of the Galsworthys. With his innate courtesy and kindness John Galsworthy had offered the loan of the house and his domestics. These were nondescript, three married women whose husbands had proved unsatisfactory as partners, and whose subsequent departure abroad had been made possible by our philanthropic host. They were not at all satisfactory from the servant point of view. Inefficient and grudging in their work. I made the mistake of taking to town with me, importing so to speak a desperately pretty girl who made matters very much worse. Tradesmen developed a passion for leaving their vans outside the house while they foregathered in the kitchen. Two petted my good-looking maid, she sat on the knees of one, and the other nursed her feet, while the elderly "ladies" of the kitchen looked on. It was, I found, when I came to investigate, the occasion for much liquid refreshment, of which the three women had their full share. There was only one thing to do, to send the girl back into the country, till such time as I returned home.

As usual the sublime and ridiculous attended my transport to town. A car was hired to transport me in the greatest ease and comfort from the Pent to the house in Addison Road. My nurse was to "join the ship" the end of the following week. Joseph Conrad was calmer than I had known him for sometime, and the study in the garden belonging to our host held golden possibilities for work. "I shall start work at once, you must amuse yourself," he declared to me. We had arrived on Thursday, and too soon it was evident that the calm was but the precursor of a storm. Sunday saw my husband helpless in bed with a sharp attack of gout. He was ill and desperately irritable and unreasonable. A favourite bedside book had been left behind at the Pent. Like a spoilt child no other would do, he must have that book and at once.

In vain I tried to give the maid a minute description of its appearance, size, shape, colour and title. Joseph Conrad could not remember exactly where he had left it. It was one of my fairly good days, and as usual any discomfort or inclination for laziness left me immediately occasion arose, and I was called upon to act. I readily fell in with the suggestion that I should take the next train to Westenhanger, the nearest station to the Pent, and fetch his treasure myself. Neither of us appeared to remember that Sunday trains were not so frequent as those on week-days, also at that time there was no one near the Pent with a telephone. From all accounts when I got back, which I did some four or five hours later than he had expected, those in Addison Road had had a bad time of it. It did seem somewhat incongruous as my good Doctor Tebb pointed out: "You came up to town in every comfort and when I come three days later to see you, I find you have taken yourself off by train, and on a Sunday too. You will go straight to bed, or I won't be answerable for the consequences. Yes, and stay there till I come in to-morrow." The good man departed in more haste and much greater displeasure than I had ever seen him show. But I was glad to go to bed. It had been a hot tiring journey, but not I was glad to say unsuccessful. I did not tell of the long search I had, or the improbable place where I had discovered the book. The very last one in the world I had expected. Face downwards on the bathroom floor, under a forgotten towel. Of course poor Joseph Conrad was full of compunction, at least at first, but in the end he finished up by declaring : " Of course, Tebb doesn't know you, my dear. You're not one of these frail, hysterical women, who go to pieces at the mere idea of a little exertion. Bless you ! "

Then, only two days before the baby arrived, one of the derelict serving women chose to turn up her toes with a bad headache, and we had guests due for lunch that day. This was not one of my good days, but I rose to the occasion and retired to the kitchen to cook the meal; as usual my dear man was touchingly grateful and enjoyed my efforts. Then followed some rather trying days till the young man arrived, and when his father was introduced to him he declared positively : " That fellow is an Italian." His concern was so comic, I burst out laughing at once. Borys was as amusing; his first words were. " Well, I must give him half the dog and half the cat," a profound sigh, and then : " And I'll let him sleep in Mum's bed." This last remark was another protest to something that had been said to him a couple of years before. He had been told that he was too big to sleep in his mother's bed. " I'm perfectly furious, Mum ; why my father does it now."

The next few weeks were full of apprehension. John Galsworthy had left all his trophies, silver cups and the like, just where they usually stood. I had tried hard to get my husband to allow them to be placed in a cupboard in safety. " No, certainly not, he might wonder what had become of them if he happened to come into the house while we are here." But my anxiety was very real and I never had a moment's peace. My husband was used to a remote country place, without electric light, and there were no precious trophies in the old Pent. Then he would frequently go to bed at night and leave the lights blazing through the house, and all the windows wide open. The house backed on Holland Park, and there was literally nothing to prevent a thief entering at his leisure and removing the treasures at will—then indeed poor John Galsworthy might have been forgiven for wondering what we had done with his prizes. Many were the nights we were knocked up by a zealous policeman because the windows stood wide open and the lights were full on. My nurse began to complain that my husband was a little too regular in this habit, and on more than one occasion there were a few heated passages between them. She even went so far as to declare that nothing would have induced her to take the case if she had met him before she came into the house. One day a message was brought to me that a young woman had called for an interview regarding the berth as parlourmaid. I was startled as I had not even thought of engaging a servant in that capacity. I made my way somewhat hastily into the hall, and there I found the girl busily examining the Yale lock on the front door. Nothing daunted by my quiet approach she stated her business as if what I had seen was the usual manner to wait for a desired interview. She showed no undue haste to be gone either, and I, who was in that house alone but for a young maid and the intruder, began to feel decidedly uncomfortable and anxious. She departed at last so abruptly that I had no time to do more than gasp as she closed the door after her. Her movements were so suspicious that I decided to remain in the hall until someone returned. It was not an hour afterwards that a policeman arrived with the news that my wily visitor had been given into custody on a bus; he had been told that she had been seen coming out of John Galsworthy's house about an hour before. He advised that the lock should be changed at once, as the woman had been proved to be one of a gang, and by what I had told him was evidently taking an impression of the lock when I came upon her.

I was intensely grateful for the loan of that house, but I must admit a great satisfaction that nothing untoward had happened while we occupied it. I had been desperately anxious several times, first for fear my husband might brand some treasure with a burn or that something might be stolen owing to his careless habits. It was curious that after all the real attempt to rob that house should be made when the Galsworthys themselves were actually there, very soon after we had left. The little episode speaks so well for the calmness and generosity of our friend.

One night he had been disturbed by unmistakable sounds downstairs, and entering the drawing-room found a bona-fide burglar busy making a neat stowage of his valuables into a big sack. John Galsworthy chatted pleasantly to that bad man, and ended by taking him into the dining-room and giving him a good meal, a little more sound advice and opening the door wide for him to go out. I have often wondered if his clemency was productive of the fulfilment of the promises the miscreant made. The next morning our friend had iron bars fitted to the window through which the would-be thief had entered.

Our return to the Pent was heralded if not exactly with a roll of drums, at least a considerable stir. Many people came from quite a distance to see the baby. Among them was a dear old cottager, a descendant of some old Huguenot family, a Mrs. Hoddinott. This old dame had long been a protégée of mine, she wished to cross the baby's hand with a silver coin, according to a gipsy custom. The dear old lady would talk for hours in a high falsetto voice liberally dotted with H's, and a strange mixture of dignity and deference.

The groom we had at the time looked long and fixedly at the baby face, and declared his immediate intention of erecting fences everywhere without delay. One would have thought the baby was to begin to walk at once. The child had the great distinction of having his perambulator pushed by no less a person than Sir Sidney Colvin. The dear man even swallowed some very moist cake the kiddie offered him, by way of a great favour. The two of them, Sir Sidney and his wife, were very dear to us both. John, this second boy, was just four months old when we started once more for the South of France, and this journey was accomplished with ease. A baby travels like a bale, very little trouble as long as it is kept warm and comfortable. But ill-luck came upon us once more before we had been two months out of England.

CHAPTER TEN

I HAVE said all through these recollections that I needed to be a philosopher and the need for this attitude grew more and more necessary as time went on. The journey was by no means either an anxious or difficult one, and except for an incident that happened when we were within the last few miles, I would have said it had been most enjoyable.

We had had the carriage to ourselves, six of us, including the young nursemaid and my cousin who was to combine secretary-governess, and I had been busy putting my young son into a fresh rig to leave the train. I had but just completed my task and the little maid had made a neat bundle of the discarded kit ready to put into a case. Unfortunately the bundle lay on the floor of the carriage right in the fairway, and my husband stumbled against it as he re-entered the railway carriage. Quick as thought he stooped and before any of us could imagine his intention, he had hurled the things through the open window out on to the line. I was confounded. There, lying on the foot-way at an ever increasing distance, reposed months of hard work. A complete set of infant's clothes. At last I laughed, the expression of my husband's face was so comical. " Now what's wrong ? " I bit my lip, then I said calmly : " Well, I am sure the man who finds that bundle will be looking for the baby's corpse." " What do you mean ? " He turned on me as if he had an idea that I had taken leave of my senses. " Oh, nothing much, but didn't you know that you have thrown away half your young son's wardrobe ? " A shrug of his shoulders, and a promise of the money with which to buy more, was all the satisfaction I got.

The first two months were very enjoyable. Fine weather, no gout and a great interest everywhere. Then came a stroke of bad luck. Borys developed measles in that French hotel. By great good luck the baby escaped, and for that boon we were indeed thankful, but it was a nightmare all the same. I fed my baby and nursed the other boy, and my poor Joseph Conrad worried through the next six weeks somehow. The dear man was under the impression that the child had slept through the night because he, himself, had done so, had even slept too soundly in his chair to hear him. And directly the measles left the boy, he and his baby brother indulged in whooping-cough. The good French doctor declined to agree that it was that distressing complaint. However, I proved to be right. But previous to this tragic development we had had a fortnight's respite of comparatively fine weather—as to health. That is as far as the children were concerned.

Joseph Conrad, true to tradition, had indulged in a fit of gout and irritability, and one day I left him after I had dressed his poor gouty hands and given him his medicine, to rest for an hour or so. Imagine my concern when we got back in about two hours to see the chamber-man coming out of his room with his arms full of smouldering bedclothes. Of course he had dropped off to sleep with a lighted cigarette in his mouth, and he had fidgeted the bandages on his wrists until he had exposed the cotton wool. The rest is simple. It looked very alarming, because the narrow airless corridor allowed the smoke to hang there thick and heavy. I own I did growl at him when I found he was safe and sound, and for once I could see nothing to laugh at in that incident.

As the children developed their distressing cough the good doctor was loud in his advice to take them away for change of air, and accordingly we removed ourselves to Switzerland. By this time the governess and the young maid had returned to England, and our old maid Nellie Lyons had made the journey across France alone, and was to help me with the children.

At each development this time it really seemed that I could endure no more, yet as soon as I saw that poor Joseph Conrad showed signs of a collapse, I became once again efficient and calm. It was then when he escorted the governess and the maid to Calais on their road back, and was to bring the old maid back, that I found myself alone with the two children in Montpelier. Everyone was kindness itself, and we had our meals served upstairs in our rooms. It was a curious situation, because I could not carry my baby across the room, on account of my lameness. I hit on the plan of having his perambulator brought up whenever we went to the rooms, and amused Borys very much by using that conveyance as a kind of " lighter," allowing the small boy to drive it up to the side of the bed or couch as the case might be. I had not realized how difficult I was going to find it to handle the kiddie alone. I had to get one of the waiters to carry him to the lift on the two occasions we went for a drive.

There was a lady and her grandson staying in the place, her son was paralysed and the grandmother had been staying with the son and his wife, and the boy. Our acquaintance began by a meeting one morning in the gardens. She had her son in an invalid chair, and I offered the poor fellow my magazine. A few days afterwards I met the grandmother alone, and heard with consternation that both the child and his father were laid up with measles. By the time my husband was escorting the governess and maid to the boat, the boy was recovered, and when I went for my drive I offered the old lady a seat in the trap for herself and the child. Never have I had such an uncomfortable drive. The boy would have been quite good and tractable if only he had been left alone. He was sufficiently in awe of me to sit still, but his doting grandparent found that state of affairs so unusual that she must needs say: "Wouldn't you like to stand up, darling?" Darling stood up, on my toes, climbing over the seat, woke the baby and ended by pinching his hand in the break. I record this little episode because this very small boy but a short time ago was in trouble for shooting his mother in Draguiguan. The defence was that the mother had begged him to shoot her, as she was dying of an incurable complaint. It goes but to show how small the world is after all, and I am blessed with an unusually retentive memory, as this incident proves.

The two days and nights I spent alone with the boys were rather anxious ones, and I was relieved to see my husband on his return. The first few days were, perhaps, the freest from worry. He had a spell of hard work, and our crowning ill-luck had not then overtaken us. But the lull was short-lived, and when the baby was seven months old, it was not any longer possible to ignore the fact that both the children were indulging in whooping-cough.

The good doctor, as I have said, advised us to get away into Switzerland. The night before we left was one of the worst I have ever spent. Joseph Conrad was still handicapped by having his right hand in bandages, the gout had twisted his wrist and left it very weak and painful, my baby was fretty, as all sick children are, and the small boy was limp and easily moved to tears. The old maid absolutely fuddled. I was glad when my husband left me to finish the packing and retired to another room to read. But I was busy all night. It was no light undertaking to be responsible for everything and everybody. I subsisted that night on biscuits and a glass of champagne.

In the morning we started up to time intending to spend the night in Lyons. When we arrived at the station there and began our quest for a resting place, our luck was dead against us. Every hotel we got to and were just thinking we had at last secured rooms one of the two children would cough, and we were politely told that they were sorry but there was no room available. We were almost in despair when the cough hung fire just long enough for us to get into the place at last.

The two rooms we secured were divided by a long narrow corridor. As soon as I had fed the poor baby, and seen that he was fairly easy, I left him with the old maid, and walked down the corridor to the other room my husband intended to share with Borys. The boy looked very tired and I had a good deal of difficulty in coaxing him to eat a little before he, too, dropped into a fitful sleep.

My husband I had persuaded to go down to a lonely dinner while I laid out what he might require for the night. He returned before very long, with a book he had managed to buy somewhere near the hotel and a waiter followed with a light repast on a tray for the maid and myself.

I was on the point of leaving the room when he, my husband, asked for something out of the trunk, and as I turned to get it I noticed subconsciously that he was placing the wallet containing all our money beneath his pillow. At the same moment the door opened without any preliminary knock, and a man appeared showing another guest into the room. It was a second or so before he retired with a muttered apology, this in answer to Joseph Conrad's exasperated "Well I'm damned." I retired from the room with a quiet good night, followed by the waiter with the tray.

That was an awful night. Neither the maid nor I undressed, the baby gasped and coughed, and nothing we could do would ease him. It was nearly seven when my husband came hastily into the room with such an air of excitement that for a moment I feared that something was wrong with the other child. I turned to him with a scared face.

"Oh, you needn't look so frightened, the boy's had a very fair night, but I'm just sending for the manager. We've been robbed. You remember that man coming into the room last night when I was putting that wallet under my pillow? Well he must have been a dam' light-fingered thief when he returned, for I never felt him take the thing away. I—here where are you off to? I tell you I've looked everywhere, I'm not a blamed fool. It makes me angry when you think you can find things when I tell you . . ."

He followed me protesting irritably down the corridor. "Look at your hair, you're positively a guy, and you won't find it, I tell you." He closed the door after us when we reached the room, and gripped me by the arm, none too gently. "I tell you it isn't there. And if it is I will fling it out of the window. I won't be treated like an imbecile."

In a few moments he changed his mind and flung the pillows into a heap on the floor. I stood still while he raged, then I laid my hand gently on his arm. "Look, dear, last night you put the wallet under the bolster, and"—I plunged my hand underneath —"here it is."

He gave a short vexed laugh, and then hugged me like a big bear, gave me a quick kiss and ended up with a favourite quotation from Louis Beck's *South Sea Island Stories*, "Long Charlie's good little wife."

All was peace once more, but he insisted that we should get along to Geneva as quickly as possible. "Out of this infernal place, where one gets robbed in the night."

I forbore to correct him, and left the room. In a couple of

hours we were in the train, and his exasperation was renewed when he found he had left his book in the hotel.

The movement of the train seemed to soothe my small son, who lay in my arms, and after a time I too closed my eyes. I had, perforce, to put my left leg up on the seat so that there was no danger of the child slipping off my lap, and I had been two nights without sleep. Borys amused himself by counting the telegraph posts, while Joseph Conrad had settled himself in a corner and was soon sleeping soundly.

There was a good deal of agitation when we reached the hotel at Geneva but there was no objection raised to our taking possession of the rooms we had engaged. Very soon we had to fetch a doctor, who shook his head ominously when he saw the tiny sufferer. He declared there was very little he could do, but he left me some kind of fluid in which to soak some cotton cloths to hang at the head of the bed above my baby's pillow. The good man had forgotten to warn me that everywhere a drop of the stuff fell a big hole would appear. I would have forgiven him probably if his remedy had been effective, but the child grew worse and worse.

The next day we took possession of our rooms in the Pension la Roserie Champel. It was in this very pension that my husband had twice before been staying to recover from his bad attack of illness when he came back from the Congo, and again the month or so before we were married. Because of the children's complaint, we had to be content with a suite of rooms at the top of the house. I was virtually a prisoner because of the long flight of stairs, I had to stay either up or down.

It was here poor Joseph Conrad tried to find some small corner in which he could concentrate, but for weeks our anxiety was too great for him to give any heed to his work. Both children were very gravely ill. John was nothing but skin and bone, and the elder, a few days after we reached the pension, augmented his bliss and our own by indulging in rheumatic fever. This, in addition to the cough that left him little peace, seemed the climax.

This extract from a letter written by my husband to John Galsworthy gives a good impression of the situation in his own picturesque language.

. . . " To-day the baby smiled very distinctly the first time in the last thirty days or so, and with a pathetically skinny paw reached for my nose nippers. I mention these favourable symptoms lest you should think this letter unduly pessimistic.

From the sound next door (we have three rooms) I know that the pain has roused Borys from his feverish doze. I won't go to him. It's no use. Presently I shall give him his salicylate, take his temperature and then go and elaborate a little more of the conversation of Mr. Verloe with his wife. It is very important that the conversation of Mr. Verloe and his wife should be elaborated—made more effective—more *true* to the situation and the character of these people.

By Jove! I've got to hold myself with both hands not to burst into a laugh which would scare wife, baby and the other invalid—let alone the lady whose room is on the other side of the corridor. To-day completes the round dozen years since I finished *Almayer's Folly*." . . .

After six weeks of nightmarish worry and anxiety, fate again smiled upon our little family, and I was able to keep the children all day in the garden. The baby recovered more quickly than did Borys. He for a long time seemed to be wearing the clothes of some other bigger and plumper person. His stockings hung round his lean shanks in a pitiful fashion. I had to take a reef in most of his under-garments. Still, that time passed and the boy and his father at once resumed their nautical pastimes. There was a stone-rimmed flat basin with a fountain in the grounds, and the two amused themselves by making docks, and constructing bridges across from side to side. Joseph Conrad would be perfectly patient at this kind of game for hours on end. Edward Garnett himself alluded to this in his introduction to the volume of my husband's letters he has published.

. . . "When Conrad wished to surrender himself to anybody he did it single-heartedly in an irresistible fashion. I remember on the occasion of a visit he and Jessie Conrad paid to the Cearne in 1898, coming suddenly on him and my son David, aged six, sailing on the grass plot, in a big basket, rigged up with a broom-stick, a table-cloth and a clothes-line. The illusion of a real boat was strangely complete with Conrad shifting the sheet in the breeze, going on fresh tacks and giving sharp orders to the boy in nautical language. This gay buoyancy of spirit, while more in evidence in early years, contrasted curiously with the antithetic mental atmosphere of Conrad's sardonic brooding and disenchantment with life."

It came at last to the day we were to leave Champel to drive to Geneva, and my husband's elaborate plans included a careful arrangement with Borys as to the difference of the central European time. They had carefully fixed the difference by their two watches, one was an hour less than the other. But . . . and it was a big but, Joseph Conrad refused to allow the boy to remind him of this compact. He disposed of the argument by declaring one watch to be slow, and his own, showing the hour according to the one in the hotel, to be the correct time. We were hauled away without being allowed to finish the dinner we had but just begun. All I could get in the way of any concession was, " If there's time I will get some sandwiches cut for you to eat in the train." But in spite of the fact that we had over an hour to wait before the train drew out of the station—he disappeared in the distance to a book-stall—not a buffet, and my sandwiches were forgotten.

Then he once again mislaid the wallet and forbore to mention it for the first half-hour or so. Then in answer to my rather anxious query as to the whereabouts of the tickets, he admitted that he had no notion where the wallet might be. Once again my subconscious mind stood me in good stead. " Wallet, well, my dear boy, you gave that to the attendant when he asked for the passports." He almost jumped out of the carriage in his indignant excitement. " Well, you do take me for an all fired ass," . . . he choked with rage, but the official appeared at that moment and handed him the wallet without a word.

One could have no doubt but that Joseph Conrad's seeming carelessness in regard to the care of his wallet was due to his constant preoccupation with matters beyond the ken of such an ordinary mortal as his wife, but I maintain that one commonplace parent is very necessary, to make existence in an ordinary world possible.

The night wore on and beyond an irritable " damn " or two, no word had passed his lips. He sat in the corner of the carriage, a small electric torch fixed in the corner of the window-frame to enable him to read, but for the last two hours he had slept soundly.

I was beginning to feel somewhat faint and my vision of the beloved face rather blurred in consequence. He looked thinner than usual, I fancied, but the two children were now quite recovered, and I glanced with great satisfaction at both sleeping faces. John was just a year old and a bright merry little soul. He was greatly entertained by a negro whose broad black face and woolly head had been thrust into the carriage window at each stop. I had thought it an unusual physiognomy, but the baby crowed and gurgled delightedly. Even when the coloured man held out a big black paw for him to grasp, he seemed quite at home.

It was on the whole an uneventful run from Geneva to Paris, but I was hardly in a condition to enjoy the drive across Paris in the early morning. I was still the baby's sole means of sustenance, and it was by that time some fourteen hours since I had had even a drink of water. Our jehu seemed to drive at a furious rate and I was so giddy that I had to hold on to the sides of the trap. More than once he was on the sidewalk and once the end of the shaft cut a long scratch across the crupper of one of the gendarme's horses.

I was glad when we reached the station, and I don't remember anything that came as such a welcome sound as the voice of the Cook's agent when he said: " Take your time, Mrs. Conrad, don't hurry. I'll have some coffee sent to your carriage at once."

The dear old Pent looked very homely when we arrived there some four or five hours later. Borys was delighted and rushed out at once to see Escamillo, his good dog, whom he had not seen for nearly a year. The brothers were good friends, and Borys was very disgusted by my well-meant attempts to assure him that the baby would not be likely to covet his favourite toy motor-car, because it would most likely be out of action before he would be old enough to understand how to play with it. " I don't want John to be a thousand years old before he is big enough to play with me," he muttered and stalked off in high dudgeon.

We stayed only a few months longer at the Pent, and some of our abortive efforts to find something at once a trifle more modern as to comfort but out of a town, were laughable. On one occasion when the baby was just eighteen months old, we went to look at a place in Aldington. We had hired a rather tall trap and the horse was not a " goer," anyway. John was seated on my knee, and was greatly concerned when the driver " took the butt-end of the whip, as he said to wake the horse up a bit." The expression of the little fellow's face was so mature in its concern. He leaned forward and said gravely: " Man don't 'mac the go-go."

Our quest this time was unsuccessful, and we returned to the Pent once again. Then Joseph Conrad betook himself to Bedfordshire where he had seen a farmhouse advertised. It was his one and only house-hunting jaunt, and I for one was determined it should be the last. I did not see the place until I arrived with the children, and the furniture. That was an adventure that nearly robbed me of all my philosophy. The leaving of the old Pent had been a wrench, and our departure greatly delayed by the obstinacy of the men who were conducting the move. The old house lay under the hill, much lower than the road, and was approached by two deep slopes, one much steeper than the other. When the vans were packed, these men made determined efforts to force the horses to draw the heavy load out of the yard by the steepest slope, because they should save two miles by going through Westenhanger than by Sandling Junction. They yoked on three cart-horses belonging to the farm, and broke most of the farmer's harness chains, to no purpose. It was distressing to see the van take charge time after time, and drag the animals backwards with their mouths bleeding.

I don't think I was ever so pleased to see my friend the farmer that I was that afternoon. He soon put the matter right and sent the van the long way round. Then when I came to examine the cheque my husband had left me, with which to settle up the last charges and pay my travelling expenses, I found he had not endorsed it. However, here again my farmer friend came to my assistance, but the matter delayed me several hours, and my baby was very young.

Joseph Conrad had gone to stay with John Galsworthy, and there I too repaired for the two nights the furniture was to be on the road. His wife was away on a visit, or he would not have been able to put up the whole of the Conrad family.

After a few necessary purchases of carpets, etc., I left the second day with the two children and the old maid. On my way from Luton station I called at the principal grocer's and obtained provisions, and armed with these necessities I arrived at the Someries about three in the afternoon.

My husband had assured me that there was a fine drove of cows on the farm. My consternation can well be imagined when we arrived to find the vans already half unpacked, things strewn everywhere, pigs in the kitchen, the well in the process of being cleaned out—which meant there was no water available—and the fine drove of cows, every one a bullock. There was not a cow on the place. My provisions included a half bottle of champagne, and some tinned milk. Some instinct must have warned me, I think, that the cows might not be cows. I had intended weaning the child as soon as we were settled, but I had after all to make a very unsatisfactory arrangement by which the old gardener brought the milk each day with him from Luton, two and a half miles away. The old sinner watered it religiously every day.

I don't think I was prejudiced against the house unduly, but the fact remains that I was not very happy there. It was barely six o'clock the night I had arrived when my husband drove into the yard, all excitement and anxiety to start work at once. He first of all made what he declared was the most reasonable demand—his dinner, it was nearly seven o'clock. Time any decent man was fed.

And, I smile now at the recollection—his dinner he had, and a hot one at that. "Not as well served as usual, my dear. You must see to it. Put your foot down at once."

It was easier to say nothing, and he could not see that he was desperately unreasonable. By twelve the next morning he was able to take possession of a room in which he began to write at once.

That house was another "jerry-built rabbit hutch," only much larger than our first. Noisy and with only a muddy yard by which one could drive anywhere near an entrance. The big kitchen garden ran past the whole length of a row of cottages. These good people, less scrupulous even than most, had but to step out of their kitchen window to find a fine field of loot, vegetables and fruit. They certainly made good use of their opportunities. I, who can usually get on friendly terms with the cottage class at once, felt hopelessly at sea. You could hardly call them exactly country people. I did in the end establish a common ground, but it was some few months before I managed to do so.

It was while we lived at the Someries that John had the privilege of being driven in his perambulator by our dear old friend Sir Sidney Colvin. He stayed with us many week-ends, but we never were able to persuade his wife to come with him. It was in this house that the first number of the *English Review* came into being. That was a time of great excitement and no little weariness and discomfort for me. There were six bedrooms, but these were not enough to put up all the various people that F. M. H. deemed to be necessary for the editing of that first number.

I have wondered many times since where he would have found anyone else so accommodating, and I had almost said foolish, as to allow him to take such complete possession of his home, as Joseph Conrad did on that occasion. Lights blazed from every room downstairs—no expense was spared. To have some four or five strangers quartered on one without more notice than an hour or so was not exactly comfortable. Only the baby and the maids slept that night. Orders, directions, or suggestions were shouted from room to room. It was an uproar all night, and the next day the house was in a chaos. My monthly stock of provisions were soon devoured, and the great trouble was that we had to use lamps and candles. However, that nightmare came to an end at last—and there was that great amount of distinction according to my husband in the first number being edited under our roof.

F. M. H. had come to the fore once more, much to my dismay, and he reverted to his old habit of treating our home as if it were one of his own. He did now and again condescend to wire the time of his arrival, carefully timing the telegram to be delivered at the back door while he was even then entering by the front, and lunch half over, more often than not.

I remember once my husband had hired a dog-cart to drive to the station to meet him, and Borys, who was continuing his riding, had been allowed to ride his pony behind the trap. F. M. H. was in a teasing facetious mood, and Joseph Conrad nearly flew all to pieces. Borys was only a novice at the time, and had been told to ride close to the side of the trap. F. M. H. could think of nothing better to do than to continually make motions of seizing the pony's bridle, or pretending to hit him on the nose. I suppose he thought to worry the boy into a tumble or reduce him to tears. The child was dutiful and obedient as a rule, but his temper was not equal to the occasion. Exasperated at last he touched the pony with the whip, and disregarding his father's order " keep by the side of the trap," he cantered back home and came hurriedly to me. " I don't want to ride the pony any more. Please tell Dadda so." I came upon him some time afterwards sobbing his heart out.

It was Hueffer who brought Conal O'Riordan to the house; this was one of his unexpected visits, but I could forgive him that time because of the very precious friendship I instantly made with his companion. A friendship that lasts to this day. None the less sincere because we so seldom meet. I had a very happy meeting between Conal and my old friend Josef Kliszczewski more than once, and I hope to see Conal soon again, and have a long talk over so much that happened to us both since last we met.

The Someries also saw the first meeting with Stephen Reynolds, whose book *The Holy Mountain* is firmly established in the world of letters. That is to name only one. Another friendship that was begun in this house was one that was perhaps the closest and for both Joseph Conrad and for me, the most intimate. Perceval Gibbon was a most arresting personality. Everyone who came into contact with him felt the man's mental attraction at once. People of any walk of life, of any school of thought, or any nationality. That virile creature with his wealth of blue black hair, and gentle sensitive mouth was able to impress himself upon everyone. Gentle Lady Colvin felt his charm instantly. He was a stimulus all the time he remained in the room.

A power to reckon with, and a steadfast friend on whom to rely. If he were but alive to-day, I should feel that my hold on everything that makes life worth living were more, much more tenacious and lasting.

He was a master of short story writing, his imagination was stored with real life episodes which his able pen could reveal in the most arresting language. His affection for my husband was deep and sincere, and I knew he had sufficient feeling for me to be indeed a real pal. This extract from one of his letters written during the war shows the depth of understanding and affection between that artist and my husband.

UFFICIO STAMPO,
COMMANDO SUPREMO,
ITALIA.
Feb. 27th, 1917.

MY DEAR OLD CHAP,

If you could imagine—if I could only convey to you—what a pleasure it was to get a letter from you, you'd write again. I never get any letters from anybody, nowadays, and have ceased to look for them! I am living in a cell, that never widens, which goes with me everywhere, and your letter is almost the only glimpse outside of it I have had for months. And if I had to choose who I would hear from, whose handsome scrawl of a superscription I would wish to see when I go in to H.Q. and stroll down to the Censor's I would assuredly have said "Conrad's!"

You are wonderfully right, dear old fellow; so far as I am concerned at all events—no words and no silences can affect the friendship and affection which I have for you and yours. That is one thing which is assuredly *au dessus de la mêlée* and of any mêlée. Borys is an ass! he has nothing to be grateful to me for. I have something to be grateful to him for, though, and that is that jolly, boyish sort of respect which he gives me, which always stimulates and refreshes me. I have the very biggest kind of liking and belief in that kid. And by God, hasn't this business made a man of him! You ought to see him by a muddy roadside with his wagons and his sergeant, and his calm competence and appetite, and his infantile bad language, and his little half-conscious swagger when he invites his uncle to come and have a drink. I took him to dinner at the war correspondents' mess, and the fellows after first being impressed by his ancestry, took to him unanimously. Which is a dam' sight more than they ever did to me, because, not to put too fine a point on it, they were a set of . . . mantelpiece ornaments.

I heard of you in the North Sea, commanding either a battleship or a beef boat; I never learned which. I was sick with plain yellow jealousy. To think of YOU—that man Conrad—leaving word to call you if the weather changed, then going below to your berth, taking the bottle from the drawer under your bunk (the locked one) and the glass from the rack and giving yourself a drink before turning in, while I—well . . . was bumming around battlefields ashore like a blarsted boarding-house runner—let us change a painful oath-fraught topic forthwith.

Had a telegram of congratulation from my kind master, Donald, on my eye-witness story of the Gorizia fight. It was an ear-witness story, rather, for they brought it off in the dark, and by the pig of St. Anthony, they tore my renowned Bedford-cord riding breeches with something bigger than a bullet, and smaller than a twelve-inch shell. There should be some real fighting soon, though. If Donald leaves me here long enough I ought finally to land a pretty good news-story.

Sorry to hear wine is scarce in England ; it's other things which are scarce here. I have not tasted butter since I last left Switzerland, but wine in some quantity I have not lacked. Had also a pleasant letter from old Jess, to whom please give my love. I'm awfully sorry she isn't fit. When in God's name shall we all three be together again ?

Forgive the typewriter—I have nearly forgotten how to use a pen. Dear love to you all. Don't quite forget me.

Always Yours,

PERCEVAL GIBBON.

This letter had to be included here, although it was written much later than the events in this narrative took place.

We spent in all only some fourteen months in the Someries. It was not our home county. John was barely three when we left Bedfordshire, and came back to Kent to look for some congenial home. Borys had been a weekly boarder at a small school in Luton some six months or so when we decided to leave. That move was accomplished with the usual " cart before the horse " effect. Joseph Conrad had been a little gouty, sufficiently so to make me grateful to a dear friend, Dr. Mackintosh, who came with Perceval Gibbon and his wife to fetch him to stay with them while I conducted the move.

I was directed by my lord and master to hold myself in readiness to abandon everything, leave the furniture on the road to take care of itself, should the attack of gout become in any sense severe. His manner of leaving the Someries was a fitting contrast to his arrival. First of all he had declined to allow any of the carpets to be taken off the floors or the pictures off the walls, before he should have departed with our guests. In vain I pointed out that the removal men were already at the back of the house with the vans. They had, in fact, removed the biggest furniture from the drawing-room before he noticed it, but he had the whole lot replaced in position. This really exasperated the men, who declared that they would not do the job according to their given estimate if they were to be hindered in that fashion. As it was they were too late loading up to get to the town, and I had eight men to feed and sleep that night.

Altogether I reflected when at last I laid down for the last time in that house, I really had had a trying time all the fourteen months we had been there. First of all, perhaps, because it was the first house we had had during our married life with a bath-room, my husband must at odd and most inconvenient times choose that particular room in which to write. It faced south, I believe, that was the reason given, for it was warm without his having to keep up the fire.

Another time he insisted that the old gardener should remove all the plants from the tall stage in the glass house, that adjoined the drawing-room. Then he had been wont to appear at the door clad only in a yellow and blue striped bath-robe, a wet parti-coloured bath towel wound round his head, and his feet encased in a big pair of Moorish slippers. In this garb he would mount to the top of the stage, right under the glass roof, and armed with a book and a supply of cigarettes, take a sun-bath. It meant mounting a guard at the front gate to warn off any chance visitors, who had to be kept waiting while the strange figure beat a hasty retreat, usually voicing his displeasure and making uncomplimentary remarks on those visitors. If he declined to move, I had to be either indisposed or away from home, and unable to receive visitors.

CHAPTER ELEVEN

THAT last night was disturbed by a variety of strange noises. My bedroom was above a huge cellar, and many times I was awakened by the sound of coal being shovelled and a wheelbarrow being moved to and fro. Neither of the two children seemed to be affected, and I was almost too tired to trouble very much. That house was full of noises. I think that most probably the foundations had shifted somewhat, for sometimes a step upstairs would affect the lintel of the kitchen door, and the latch would turn in the most ghostly fashion, and the door open in such a natural manner, that failing some human agency, one could not help believing that the ghost must be walking.

In the morning my impressions were proved beyond doubt. Some of the cottage neighbours had indeed taken time by the forelock and had removed in the night every vestige of coal or wood out of that cellar. We waited without any means of getting a hot drink till the last of the furniture had been packed, and the trap came from the inn to transport us to the station.

I have a very lively recollection of the kindness of the good landlord of the Bell Inn in Luton. These good people had prepared a tasty little feast for us when we reached their hospitable house, and that without being asked.

Meanwhile as no S O S had reached me from Joseph Conrad by the time we were ready to start, I decided to keep my latest discomfort provided by the cottages, that of stealing all my fuel, to myself. I was thankful that the foreman of the firm removing us was such a decent fellow. I had to call upon him when the farm bailiff became very rude and insulting and persisted in speaking to me with his back turned and would not get away from the door. The result of my appeal for aid very nearly resulted in a free fight. Altogether that move was not a very pleasant experience to look back upon.

In the afternoon I left Borys at school as arranged. One of the moving men undertook the care of the cat in its basket as far as Smeeth, which was our nearest station in Kent. So with John, a little fellow of three, the old maid and Escamillo, the dog, we made the journey back into our favourite county. It was past nine when we left the train in Smeeth, and clambered into the open car that was at the station to meet us. It was impossible to feel very cheerful that night. I cuddled the kiddie up to keep him warm, for the short run, and he was asleep when we reached the little cottage. We had part of the one we arrived at that night to store the furniture, and another on the opposite side of the road, where we intended to hang out, as Joseph Conrad put it, till we found another house.

We literally stowed ourselves in that small space and it was little short of marvellous what a lot of quite big furniture got into those small rooms. I, in fact, had not realized how much there was until we moved again, and then I had the laugh of the removal foreman, who was exactly a van-load out in his estimate.

The thing that troubled me most while we lived in Aldington was the fact that there was no place for the small boy to play in. A tiny three-cornered plot of ground in front, leading on to the road, was all the garden, and I was anxious all the time for fear the boy got out on the highway by himself. There were several amusing little episodes that happened while we lived there. The little fellow with his long curls hanging to his waist would invite all and sundry of those people who passed to come inside. " Wouldn't you like to come in my house ? There's a nice fire in there."

Poor Joseph Conrad must have felt the cramped quarters very much indeed. The only room I could give him for writing was the big front bedroom. This I turned into a study sitting-room. It had a tiny little room opening out of it, little bigger than a cupboard. Here I had managed to get some book-shelves put up. There was a miniature registered stove for all heat and the old oak door scarcely kept out the view of the staircase, let alone the draught. Still some good work got itself written there. We had no modern comforts or conveniences of any kind. Once again the old maid went down with gastric trouble, and had to be removed to Folkestone Hospital.

But even here we had visitors, for whom we managed to get sleeping accommodation outside. Norman Douglas spent several days with us while we were living there. Sir Hugh Clifford came with a lady friend and many people from the surrounding neighbourhood, including Mr. Michael Holland, a man who had been much in Africa, and who was then living in Smeeth and was a member of the Hunt.

It was here that Captain Marris, an Australian sea captain, paid a never to be forgotten visit. A pathetic story lay behind the loss of his memory, and helplessness. He showed us photographs of his wife who was a Malay princess, and his little daughter. The partial paralysis that obscured his recollection, was the result of a collision in some Eastern river. He had some relations in England and had been brought over with the idea, perhaps, of recovering the use of his limbs.

Arthur Marwood was now a very frequent visitor and Joseph Conrad was often a guest at his house a few miles away. He had been bidden to take tea with us one day on the occasion of the first visit made to us by a young man, a native of Charlestown.

This new friend had been shooting big game with President Theodore Roosevelt and his son.

When he came first to us he had been instructed by his host to take the train to Smeeth Station. But the notepaper was misleading, having the postal address Nr. Hythe. Not being familiar with the district he had hired an ancient fly and been driven some seven miles out of his way. Of course, in Hythe he was soon put on the right road, but it meant some four hours' delay in reaching us. Truly a fiasco.

Joseph Conrad had given me very minute instructions as to the lunch, which was to be dainty as well as substantial and ready to the minute the guest arrived at the tiny cottage. But we had had our lunch some three hours before he arrived. I can still hear my husband's excited voice hailing me from the room upstairs as soon as he caught sight of the belated trap creeping down the steep hill above the cottage. "Here he is, Jess. Let's have lunch in again at once, let there be no delay."

The lunch was mercifully one that it was possible to re-present with a very short wait, and it was still on the table at five o'clock when Arthur Marwood appeared, as arranged, for tea. A change of crockery and the appearance of a well-laden tea-tray, that was all—a simple transition, but a little trying. Difficult too, with only a rough country maid. She showed signs of weeping before I was able to leave the table and soothe her ruffled plumes with the promise of a whole day's leave on the morrow.

Warrington Dawson, our delayed visitor, charmed us both by his ready friendship. He brought to my husband some warm words of greeting from President Roosevelt, and the three men enjoyed a long talk. Arthur Marwood was always interesting, and they found a great deal in common. To this day my own feeling for the young cosmopolitan continues as warm and steadfast as if I had remained always his near neighbour, but I am anticipating somewhat. We met many times between that first time and the beginning of hostilities, although fate has decided to keep us apart practically ever since.

F. M. H. had a cottage quite close to us in Aldington, which stood on the edge of the hill overlooking the Romney marsh. The intimacy was not now so great, and there was, I feel sure, some little jealousy on account of Joseph Conrad's great affection for that other neighbour, Arthur Marwood. I recall the following episode with some amusement now, although at the time I was almost speechless with anger.

F. M. H. was not very often at home in Aldington just at that time, but on this particular Saturday he appeared, and in his most grandiose manner imparted the following information: "Oh, by the way, my dear chap, Mackintosh and one or two others

REGINALD PERCEVAL GIBBON IN 1909

M. JEAN AUBRY, FRENCH AUTHOR AND CRITIC, 1911

are coming down to us for the week-end. We shall be coming here for meals, it is much too much for my wife to do to feed so many people." I waited, while Joseph Conrad gasped, this was surely a bit too much of a good thing. Then I found my voice and said very quietly: "Oh, wait one minute, if you please, Dr. Mackintosh is also a friend of ours. This being so, my idea is, that if they are paying a visit to you to-morrow you will do all the entertaining yourself. When they visit us, we shall do the same without involving you or your wife in any way. I decline absolutely to fall in with your suggestion."

It was the first time I had delivered myself at such length or indeed revolted against any plan in which I saw any chance of any pleasure for my husband. He showed his displeasure and disgust by going out of the room and slamming the door without taking any further notice of F. M. H., who then retired discomfited. It amused me to notice the friends did not appear at his cottage the next day.

That little incident is absolutely true in every detail, and shows the cause of a certain coolness between the two households.

Some time afterwards things seemed to get rather more strained between the couple and F. M. H. was absent more than ever. I bothered myself very little about them anyway. There were one or two uncomfortable meetings between the Marwoods and the Hueffers, and I managed to keep them from meeting in our house as much as possible.

One day, and one on which my husband was very reluctant to be disturbed by any outside influence, a message was brought to the house, worded in a very peremptory fashion, and asking that Joseph Conrad should go at once to their cottage. I decided to accompany him, and accordingly we drove the pony over at once. I can see the principal room of that cottage now. It was extremely picturesque, with its big open fire-place, on which some huge logs were smouldering. A faded and worn Turkish carpet covered most of the floor. Numerous books lay about on the tables, a big divan couch at one end of the room covered by some faded material, a few rush-bottomed chairs, a big pair of bellows lay on the hearth, reproductions of Ford Madox Brown's pictures hung from the smoky walls at odd angles. The centre of the low ceiling was propped up by two very high bed-posts, belonging to a big four-poster. The light filtered through the heavily leaded panes of the low windows, falling almost with the effect of a lime-light on the tall female figure of Elsie Hueffer as she came into the room purposefully.

She fitted her surroundings perfectly, and completed the old world picture. Slightly lame and clad in a straight, somewhat shapeless gown of a nondescript hue, with a girdle round her waist and some heavy wooden beads hanging from her neck. She greeted my husband with some impressiveness and ignored me. I had seated myself on the divan, and beyond a slight bow, I copied her indifference. I was not in the least disconcerted, because I saw quite plainly she had not counted upon my accompanying my husband. I sat silent and watchful.

Apparently her only reason for disturbing Joseph Conrad was to deliver a long tirade against the habits and manners of all literary people. She became greatly excited, warming to her subject and threatening to show up the whole literary world. It was not quite clear to either of us why she inflicted all this upon my husband. I allowed my gaze to wander round the room, and the next moment I was recalled to the present by hearing the name of John Galsworthy. In an instant my husband sprang to his feet wildly excited and stood shaking his finger within an inch or so of the lady's face. "Don't you say 'dat,'" he repeated two or three times. His English had completely deserted him in a moment. He turned aside, grabbed his hat and almost hurled me through the door. "Don't you dare say 'dat.'"

We were out of the house in the twinkling of an eye, and into the trap. No word of farewell had been spoken, but I fancy our abrupt exit did more to recall the irate woman to herself than any amount of protest could have done.

There was some connection between that incident and the cause of my husband's extreme agitation when he had to go up to town a few days afterwards. I knew the signs of certain exasperation, and invariably I was right in my surmise.

The manuscript of *The Western Eyes* was ready to hand to Mr. Pinker, and I was rather surprised when he declined to take it to London that day with him. He was very irritable and I felt sure this was a forerunner of an attack of gout. To begin with he elected to drive my pony to the station himself. A governess-car is, I think, the most uncomfortable form of conveyance ever invented. His nerves already frayed to tatters and his mind pre-occupied by something he would keep to himself, he drove the little trap over a bump in the road, and broke a spring. Fortunately he was just outside the station. He tossed the reins to Slingsby, who was to bring the trap back, and disappeared through the booking-office without a word. The old man led the pony back, rather hurt by the abrupt departure.

Arrived at his publishers, something further displeased him, and his irritability increased out of all control. At such times he did not know his own nervous strength. In the course of that heated argument, he placed his elbows against the arms of the big leather arm-chair and pushed the sides out. I am not sure what happened after that, perhaps such an exhibition of bodily strength had its effect, or the argument may have ended in his favour, but his irritation was renewed when he got to Mr. Pinker's office.

Here my excitable husband propounded some quixotic notion to his tried and trusty friend, making use of some foreign idiom. This greatly exasperated the other, and he turned upon him with a sharp demand that he should speak English, if he could!

After that he sought sanctuary with his friend John Galsworthy for the night, and incredible as it seemed, he pushed the foot out of the bed in an excess of nervous strength. I had a wire from his host telling me he was afraid my husband was in for a bad attack of gout, and advising me to meet his train myself.

I noticed at once that the storm had not abated when I met him at the station. I forbore to give away the fact that I had been told what train he would be taking. He thought it was pure chance that led me there to time.

He said very little, but I was thankful that he made no objection to my driving. He sat with his head sunk in his shoulders, a sure sign of some suppressed excitement, and I was very glad to get him back home as soon as possible.

When we got home he sat turning the pages of the pile of manuscript over, without appearing to notice what he was doing, and then turning to the writing-table, he rapidly wrote the following somewhat cryptic wire to his agent, J. B. Pinker: "Have you a complete copy of *Western Eyes?*" It was a prepaid telegram, and I was concerned to see his agitation until the answer came back. Only the one word "No." My wonder increased, for my husband seemed to be so unaccountably elated to know that there was no other copy in existence. I covertly but closely watched that pile on the table, afraid in my mind that he meant to destroy it. To this day I cannot say why I mistrusted his intentions. I knew by some intuition that some disaster hung over that mighty pile, that represented so many agonized hours for him and real hard work of typing for me. It taught me a lesson also and never again did I take only one copy.

But this was a very delicate situation, and called for the greatest tact and diplomacy. Under the pretence of tidying the table and while he seemed absorbed in his own moody reflections, I surreptitiously removed the package, and the next moment I had the satisfaction of turning the key in the lock of the drawer containing it. I was not a little disconcerted to hear his voice the next moment speaking in smooth, level tones from the window seat behind me. "Mind what you do with that key, don't mislay it."

I managed to answer easily, in spite of my surprise: "I will take the greatest care of it," and the next moment I tried to draw his attention from it by telling him of something that had happened in the village. I was trying to provoke an argument, but he continued rubbing his hand, and evidently not listening to what I was saying.

He remained idly fretting himself into a state of excitement, very difficult to please and to cater for. I was not surprised when next day he complained of pain here and there, and everywhere. But he was unusually subdued and unlike himself. He left my room very early in the morning, and curled himself up in an uncomfortable position on a big couch in a little room little less than a passage-way, immediately above the kitchen. His manner struck me as so very strange. I followed him very soon with some hot coffee, and suggested that he should have the doctor sent for there and then. I was met with such a decided refusal that I half persuaded myself that he was still feeling resentment towards me for reserving the manuscript. I left him and returned to finish dressing myself.

It must have been quite an hour later when I again came into the room, creeping past the couch. He had not spoken and I fancied he was asleep. I was startled to hear his voice strangely hoarse saying almost in a whisper: "I think . . . perhaps, you . . . had better let Dr. Hackney come . . . if he comes at once." I glanced quickly round and managed not to voice my dismay. Clearly he was very ill, and I was horrified to see his throat was swollen out level with the end of his chin, and in a moment more he rambled off in evident delirium, using his own language and muttering fiercely words of resentment against Mr. Pinker: "Speak English . . . if I can . . . what does he call all I have written? I'll burn the whole damned . . . let me get up, give me a looking-glass. I must look a pretty guy, with all this beard." . . .

His voice ended almost in a sob. I became the nurse at once. One thing he must not have was a chance of seeing himself. His speech and breathing was still without much effort, which convinced me that the swelling was mostly, if not all, external. I promised to bring him everything he asked for if he would only keep quiet and still a few moments while I fetched them. I hurried away and dispatched an urgent message for the doctor. Then seeing that he had fallen into an uneasy doze I set about my preparations swiftly and silently.

Clearly he could not be left where he was, lying in the draught. I prepared the big sitting-room as a bedroom, and soon had a fire burning in readiness, by the time the doctor arrived. It is astonishing how trifles impress themselves upon the subconscious mind. I was desperately anxious and quite aware that this attack was of a much more serious nature than any that had gone before, for a very long time. Yet with my mind so fully occupied I still noticed that the wooden uprights of the mantelpiece were far too near the grate for a fire of any size to be safe.

I made my way down into the yard where the landlord had an assortment of long slate slabs. I soon persuaded the good man to lend me two of these, and a length of stout wire. Quickly I fastened these between the fire and the wood, and had only just completed my task when the doctor arrived.

I was disappointed not to see our regular medical attendant, but his partner. This man was tremendously impressed by what he found, but not at all helpful. He flatly refused to stay and superintend the move from one room to the other. "He has a temperature of 104 and you move him at your own risk."

In vain I pointed out that the patient lay in a direct draught which I was powerless to shield him from, as most of it came through the old oak planks of the floor. The wind eddied under the carpet, billowing it out every time the kitchen door was opened beneath. He remained obdurate, repeating "at your own risk, entirely," as he left the house.

I looked round seeking in vain for some way to avoid that risk, but there was none, and I decided that things might easily get worse while I hesitated. Already he was shivering and his teeth chattering. I quickly decided that moved he must be, and at once.

I called three farmhands to my aid, who carried my husband gently on a sheet the few yards to the bed I had prepared for him. He was quite indifferent, apparently, to what might be going to happen to him. He offered no resistance and lay with his eyes closed and his arms folded, repeating snatches of orders in an Eastern language. His mind was evidently back in the past, and I suppose he was to some extent aware that he was being moved, and his mind connected that with his terrible transportation to the African Coast when he was taken ill on the Congo River.

My bearers made up in zeal and willingness what they lacked in skill. Not one of them would take the money I offered, but silently shook my hand and protested their readiness for any further help I might need. I think I suffered the most in connection with that move. I felt my responsibility, but I was also very angry with the doctor, who I considered had rather left me in the lurch. However, my patient, who recovered his senses for a few moments, smiled his thanks for making him comfortable, and then relapsed into his former restless state, muttering continuously.

He spoke all the time in Polish, but for a few fierce sentences against poor J. B. Pinker. That day seemed endless. I could get no one to help me but the old maid. I scarcely left his side for he was constantly calling upon me to sit on the side of the bed to make a rest for his back. Hour after hour I sat in that cramped position. Day and night I watched over him, fearful that if I turned my back he would escape from the room. I slept what little I could on the couch drawn across the only door. More than once I opened my eyes to find him tottering towards me in search of something he had dreamed of. If it had not been for Perceval Gibbon who came often and always, it seemed, in the nick of time, I feel sure I would not have held out.

The little cottage was half-way down a steep hill, at the top of which the grand old church stood, dominating the village. I decided that when we left there, never again would I live close to a church. I would wake from my few moments' sleep to hear the strange voice of my invalid repeating the burial service in hoarse gasps, and the church bell a few yards away tolling its lament for some other poor departed soul. And the climax was reached one night when I was really shaken out of my calm. The doctor, still the partner, had warned me that Joseph Conrad was indeed very ill. I tried to make some allowance for the fact that it was the first time this particular man had attended my husband. He was evidently greatly impressed. In the end I asked him for his card so that if necessary I could send it to the local doctor, who was well known for standing on his dignity, should I require medical assistance at night. He went rapidly through his pockets, then declared: "I haven't a card on me, but this doctor will attend if you should want help, we should do the same for him, it is quite customary."

It must have been some kind of premonition that led me to think of warning the local doctor, for that night I was in desperate need of help. I am not a trained nurse and I suppose I had overlooked certain signs that to a professional eye would have been obvious. I only know that by two o'clock the next morning I felt that my husband was very seriously and critically ill. He seemed to breathe once when he should have done at least a dozen times, a cold heavy sweat came over him, and he lay on his back, faintly murmuring the words of the burial service. At last my helplessness overcame me to such an extent that I roused the dear old gardener and sent him on his bicycle for the local doctor, begging him to come to me at once.

I watched the man walk his machine up the hill, and stood by the bed in an agony of suspense till he returned with the cheering news that he had given my message to the doctor himself. I waited, one, two, three hours, and the moon paled and gave way to early dawn. Still no sound of the doctor's arrival. The figure on the bed seemed to my anxious fancy to become more rigid in outline, the breathing more laboured and slower. Not a sound otherwise, outside or in, except the occasional hoot of an owl, or the faint crow of a cock in the far distance. I could bear it no longer. I rapidly left the room and returned with some whisky and hot water. Raising my husband's head on my arm I managed to get him to swallow the restorative, sip by sip, and then with great difficulty I turned him over on to his side. Trembling violently I waited till his breathing grew stronger and more regular. He was now asleep, I felt the warmth coming back into his chilled and nerveless fingers. I then put two or three hot-water bottles near him, taking care that they were not hot enough to burn him should he move, and then, having extinguished the lamp and made up the fire, I silently withdrew.

I felt that I must get out of that house if only for a few seconds. I placed a chair on the path under his window and I am not ashamed to say I indulged in the feminine luxury of a good cry. A few moments afterwards the old maid brought me a cup of coffee and announced that my patient was still sleeping quietly.

Five hours after my messenger had returned with the information that he had given my message to the doctor himself, and an hour after my urgent message had been sent to Dr. Hackney in Hythe, I saw the local practitioner coming leisurely down the hill in his car. Without any pretence of haste or concern he came towards me where I stood bursting with anger. I waited quietly. "Show me the patient, if you please, at once." I still stood motionless, looking him steadily in the face. "You sent for me," he began impatiently.

"Yes, I did, and you received my message yourself, asking you to come at once—five hours ago."

"I ought to have been warned that I might expect a night call, but take me to the patient now." I passed my tongue over my dry lips and then turned squarely to face the man.

"My husband is better now, thank you, and will not need your services, he is sleeping quietly." He was clearly taken aback. "Do you mean you will not let me see him ?"

I bent my head. "Precisely, I have no need of your services now."

He stamped his foot in a rage. "You understand that if you refuse to allow me to see him that the risk is your own ?"

"I shall not allow you to see my husband under any circumstances. My own doctor has been summoned, and here he is coming down the hill now," I added, and I was never in my life before, or since, more pleased and relieved to see a doctor, and that one our usual attendant.

The two cars passed each other on the hill. Dr. Hackney was furious, he extolled my pluck and after he had seen his patient he assured me quite seriously that my timely dose of hot whisky had undoubtedly saved his life. He would have slipped through our fingers very easily that night.

It was soon after that time that my wilful invalid was behaving in a very reprehensible way. I had been greatly troubled as to what course to pursue. Our good friend Dr. Hackney had been in close attendance and he was very puzzled as the patient appeared to make no headway at all. He explained the action that certain drugs should have had at length. He was not at all satisfied and asked for another opinion. At this I had no option, I had to play tell-tale, as the boys would have said.

I stood hesitating by the side of the bed, then decided that under the circumstances I must speak out, but evidently it had better not be in front of my husband. He was busy unloading a lot of fresh symptoms and pathetically appealing for something to cure this or that. I turned and left the room to await the doctor downstairs.

I had rather an unusual tale to tell him, and it took some persuading to induce him to continue his attendance after he had mastered the facts. I had some coffee and cigarettes ready when he came at last downstairs. With as matter-of-fact air as I could manage to assume I began my tale. I had to explain that there were two doctor friends coming each week, once or twice, each from London, and neither aware of the other's visits. In this way three different men were treating my husband, unknown to each other. Joseph Conrad displayed a craftiness that I had not given him credit for, it must have been due to his sick condition and his dislike to taking medicine. None of the drugs prescribed got further than the kitchen sink. Each bottle was solemnly emptied down as it appeared in the house by the old maid. She had simply followed my husband's instructions to the letter. When I had remonstrated with him the day before I made a clean breast of the facts to Dr. Hackney, he had declared that surely I must understand that there was a limit to his capacity for swallowing the beastly muck. He finished up by saying : " I know what is wrong with me, but I'm not going to tell them. I'm not going to do half the dam' doctor's work for him."

In the end it was arranged that I should write to the two friends and make an appointment for them all three to meet in consultation. We never let my husband know that all were aware of his offence to medical etiquette. Soon after this I discovered that the evening I had been in such distress and apprehension, thinking I had overlooked some serious symptoms in my ignorance as an amateur nurse, the old maid had been, according to his instructions, feeding him on aspirin. This accounted for some of his collapse, being in such a weak and exhausted condition.

As soon as he was able to stand the exertion I hired a fly and took him driving to see an old house I had discovered, which seemed to promise a solution to our difficulty at a rental of very little more than we were paying for our cramped quarters in the cottage. But this would mean paying rent for no less than three houses. I had not seen the agreement for the Someries before. Now I found that there still remained three quarters' liability for rent there, nearly a year at the cottage and there would be also the rent of the house I had taken a fancy to. "Not possible, my dear, I would need to be a millionaire. I knew there would be a 'nigger on the fence and a fly in the ointment.'" Joseph Conrad was great at quotations. For a couple of days I was nonplussed. Then I wrote a diplomatic letter to a tradesman in Luton and discovered that the Someries was again occupied by a fresh tenant. The half-quarter was about due, so greatly daring I wrote a reasonable letter to the landlord asking him which of his two tenants he preferred to pay the rent, as he had no right to both. That disposed of one hindrance. The landlord of the cottage agreed to accept a tenant which I found for him. Then I went to my husband and tried to coax him into a proper frame of mind for the purpose of signing the new lease.

The landlord and owner of Capel House was the most charming man and generous friend we had ever met. Not only did he forgo the house for his own occupation, but every repair I ever wanted done to it was done at once. He, himself, removed what furniture he had already placed in Capel House, to a tiny gamekeeper's cottage on the same estate, but right in the sixty acres of woodland. Thus he was our near neighbour. He allowed us the run over the woods and became a very real and trusty friend. His son, Mr. Roland Oliver, K.C., has Capel House now. We had some amusing passages with him during the rationing times. He generously sent me a good part of his bag of game one day. He was coming to eat his meals with us, and I further requested him to give me his ration tickets, just to be on the safe side.

All that happened at Capel House will fill quite another chapter or two of this narrative. It holds certainly the most, or some of the most, anxious and poignant hours of human suffering, mental and physical. The four years of war. But the last few weeks of that very heavy attack of gout, and the difficulties under which I nursed Joseph Conrad in the little cottage at Aldington were weeks that seemed endless.

Then the long convalescence, complicated as it was by the irritability and nervousness of my husband's unusual temperament. He was quite childish at times, and at the same time very tenacious of his point, that he would stick to even in the face of the most obvious reasons for relinquishing the idea.

There was also a certain secretiveness often very difficult to penetrate and often due, I am sure, to his super-sensitive nature. This trait belongs very much to his nationality. It was months after he had begun to live a normal life again that I dared to refer to his injudicious use of aspirin. One good thing, when the effect was made clear to him he was quite cured of the habit. But there were certain drugs that he pinned implicit faith upon. He had a favourite gout medicine given him by Dr. Mackintosh—I had the formula, the ingredients together with a small balance for mixing the dose always with me. I say always with me, there were one or two occasions when I had not packed my precious "first aid" for gout. I remember one time going to a big chemist in town with the request that he should mix me a bottle of four doses. The good man refused to do so without the prescription. He was undoubtedly quite right, but I wanted that medicine. I thanked him, and in the next breath I said "I will have so much of this, and that, and the other." I intended purchasing a new pair of scales and mixing the drugs myself according to the instructions which I knew by heart. The chemist climbed down and with a rather twisted smile gave me the mixture made up according to my spoken directions, without further parley.

Another time I had considerably more trouble to get what I wanted. In this case my supply was completely exhausted. This was when we were trying to get home from Poland in 1914. We had arrived in Vienna the night before my tragic discovery that I had run out of my supply. With the two boys I explored street after street in Vienna looking for a chemist with the cheering sign displayed "English spoken here," but every one had been removed, and when I had boldly entered several and made my request I had been shortly refused by a shake of the head. At last I entered one and I noticed an interested expression on the face of one of the men behind the counter when my small son addressed his brother in a stage whisper. He had been forbidden to say a word. Desperately I turned on the man who was very young and I said quietly: "It is of no use, you can understand perfectly well all I say. Your country and mine are at war. Be a sport and let me have what I ask for."

There was a hurried pow-wow, the two elder men mumbled something under their breath, and I waited until the three customers had left the shop. The elder assistant then stationed himself by the door, under the pretence of altering some advertisement displayed upon it, and in the twinkling of an eye, the three ingredients appeared wrapped in a neat little parcel. I had added two cakes of soap and some tooth paste. Without a word I tendered my note and received the change. With a slight bow and a perfectly straight face I took the little packages, which Borys slipped into his pocket, and we left the shop.

That bit of shopping had taken us exactly an hour and a half to perform, but my relief was out of all proportion. I had a queer little catch in my breast, until then I had not thought how the fact that we were indeed at war with the inhabitants of that wonderful town, might even now affect us.

In a narrative such as this it is extremely difficult to know exactly the best place to include matters that are so strictly related to each other as these last two little episodes, even although the better part of seven years lay between them. It is not my difficulty alone. I recall my husband's constant worry over the same thing, when he was writing his *Reminiscences*. Some critic complained that they did not always follow in proper sequence. But I do not think they lost much for that reason, and Joseph Conrad declined to reconsider anything he had written.

Speaking of reminiscences, we were very much amused when John, who was at the time about five or six, asked me quite seriously: "Do you think I am old enough to write my Reminiscences, mum?"

The boy's serious face and voice restrained my impulse to laugh outright, and I contented myself with the advice to wait until he had a little more to put into them. I wonder, will they one day be written?

CHAPTER TWELVE

THAT move from the little cottage in Aldington to Capel House was accomplished after my husband had been dispatched in Perceval Gibbon's care for the transition. I have since told Joseph Conrad that he was more difficult to shift than all the household goods. As before the vans stood empty waiting while he got in and out of the car, finding first one book then another that he simply could not be happy without, even although he expected to return to his new home in a couple of days. He had portioned out what I was to accomplish in the way of placing each article of furniture, pictures and books. Everything was to be in position within the next two days. It was done. Curtains, carpets as well, even to the filling of the lamps. Only the books remained still in drawers when the master of the house arrived.

It was a big undertaking as he had delayed the things so long by his tardy departure from the cottage. Then when we were all ready and the fly stood literally packed to its utmost capacity before the door, the dear old dog, Escamillo, could not be found anywhere. John, who was only a small boy of five, was inconsolable. Then after wasting two hours, and just as I had persuaded him that his old friend Mr. Slingsby should bring him over later in the day when he drove the pony over, the dog poked his nose from under some of the packages in the fly. He had made certain that he should not be left behind.

Our arrival at Capel House was some four hours later than I had intended, and my schedule time for completing my arrangements sadly depleted. But I had only the books left to arrange when the time was up.

Very soon I had become fast friends with the old farmer who had the land round the house He was a farmer of the real old school. He wore the old-fashioned rough leather gaiters, one or two top coats—according to the weather, and as he was very bald, an antiquated black skull-cap met the fringe of wiry grey hair round the base of his skull. He was a kindly man whose first wife had died and left him with a large grown-up family and a goodly number of grandchildren who troubled him very little. His hopes were centred in the youngest son whose chief characteristic, as far as I could see, was a pair of intense blue eyes. The bluest I have ever seen in any grown person.

I recall the old man's rather awed lament when one of his elder sons fell in the war. He had come into the house with his old tired eyes wet with tears that remained glistening on the sparse side-whiskers. These spread fan-wise over his chest, and blew behind his ears with each gust of wind. He sat himself down in an easy chair after removing two top coats and his shiny bowler.

" I'm in great tr'uble," he began as he changed the felt hat for the shabby skull-cap and passed his knotty fingers over his eyes. " You'll mind my oldest son, I 'prenticed him to a draper when he were a boy, he was that shy, he'd get under the counter when a wuman came into the shop. Too shy to serve 'er he were. An' thay send 'im to fight Germans. Terrible shy he were."

Many were the long talks we had and I chuckled to see the old man's interest in my small boy, and his power over birds and dumb animals. There was a big oak tree one side of the dry moat, by the side of the oast-house, and John's delight was great when his father bought an old rope ladder in Rye and fastened it to one of the branches. It dangled just clear of the ground in a tempting fashion and the boy would swarm up it in true sailor fashion and remain in the big tree for hours on end.

I can see the " scampie," his father's pet name for him, clad in his blue jersey and his favourite india-rubber shoes. A few years earlier he had worn blue cotton overalls, but by the time he was presented with the rope ladder he had discarded overalls for the close-fitting jersey suits. His father alluded to him as a little pagan and refused to let him learn any religion until he was turned six years old. Then he chuckled with delight because the boy's first words when he heard of the crucifixion were " It's disgusting, it ought to be forgotten, it's not a thing to be proud of." Possibly such an opinion is unique, but it would not have been possible if the child had been taught any religion whatever. The subject for some months stayed in the child's mind and he propounded several original notions before he was sent away to school.

One day I found him biting his pencil in great perplexity. His home lessons were spread out all over the table. Two cats sat one each side of the pile of books and croaking in a corner was a large frog. " Mama dear, it is difficult to know the truth. If there was only one kind of religion it would be much easier wouldn't it ? "

The next moment he was chasing the cat round the room as irresponsible as ever. Then as I stood watching him and wondering exactly what would be the next original remark, he came coaxingly against me and declared his intention of starting a " Cat-factory. You know old Mr. Hogbin sold a lot of cats for one shilling each."

That was the boy's idea of a good bargain. Joseph Conrad has told of his own one solitary bargain in the " Smile of Fortune."

At this time Borys was a cadet on board the *Worcester* training ship lying off Greenhythe in the Thames. That choice of a school had meant so much to the boy's father. I could put forward no objection. The education aboard the training ship was very sound and good. The nautical side of the life would undoubtedly bring father and son more in tune than any other college life could possibly do. And so it proved. The boy left at sixteen with a very good leaving certificate and with very real regret.

During the time he was a cadet on board, his father and I very frequently paid visits to the captain, Sir David Wilson-Barker, with our younger son in attendance. It struck me as somewhat strange, that my husband had no intention of placing his second son in the training ship. One reason for this may have been his inability to realise the passage of time, and for another the war came and altered everything.

The first few weeks we were living at Capel House my husband found it difficult to settle down to work at his new book. It was about this time that he wrote some few articles for the *Daily Mail.* He was somewhat shy of this undertaking as is shown by this extract from a letter he wrote to John Galsworthy on his first coming to live in Capel House. It is dated June 26th, 1910.

. . . " On leaving Ashford all alone, for the first time since the illness, I felt all of a shake and utterly lost without Jessie. (He had been staying with Perceval Gibbon and his wife in Trosley, some few miles from Maidstone.) Of course notwithstanding our good resolutions neither Gibbon nor I did a line of work while I was in Trosley. He rushed me about on his side-car motor-bike, storming up hills and flying down vales as if the devil was after him. I don't know whether it was particularly good for the nerves, but on return from these excursions I felt ventilated, as though I were a bag of muslin, frightfully hungry and almost too sleepy to eat. No other harm seems to have been done.

At the very moment of leaving Aldington last Tuesday, I had a letter from Bashford which I enclose here. (This letter from the editor of the *Daily Mail* suggested his becoming a regular contributor.) I need not tell you that it was totally unexpected. But here was the thing thrown at my head ; wonderful ! After hurriedly reflecting upon the miracle, I answered as noted, and now I am in possession of another letter offering five guineas per column and cheering me on to have a try. No formal agreement of any sort and liberty for either party to terminate the arrangement at any time.

I am very tempted. My view is that nothing unfair to Pinker will be done if I accept. I shall take one day a week (or its equivalent in snatches) for that article. If I find I can't do it in that time I shall throw the thing up. *Voilà !* At the same time I must consider him entitled to his commission on everything I earn, for that, I believe, is the 'custom of the trade.' What do you think ?

I am writing to Bashford accepting provisionally and asking him to send me a couple of books in the course of this week. Should P. object I shall simply leave off after an article or two. . . ."

The amusing sequel to this undertaking came not long afterwards when five reviews had been written and four paid for. This fifth one became the bone of contention. Why it was never published we never knew. But when number six was required Joseph Conrad became very irate and without opening the package of books, he wrote across the paper wrapper: "Your price doesn't even cut the string," and returned it unopened.

Arthur Symons was another friend who came often to Capel House. He and the small boy John became very fast friends. One day the poet arrived in one of his most mystical moods and I watched him walking round the house with the boy several times. I came upon the two standing together by the side of the moat that on this one side was still fairly deep with muddy water. Presently Arthur Symons said in a perfectly matter-of-fact tone: "Let us try walking on the water, John!" "All right, Mr. Symons, you try first," returned the boy and skipped off to safe distance to watch the result.

I include here a short extract from a letter written to the poet by my husband in 1911 which shows a very real regard and appreciation for that poet's work. Joseph Conrad is speaking of a translation Arthur Symons had just completed.

. . . "If you can do such things as your translation of *Crimen Amoris* out of despair—then take my word for it, you need not despair. One survives everything—disaster—annihilation itself, absurd as it seems to say it. Your *désir de vivre* is the best proof that you deserve to live. And you must not forget that you exist *pour les esprits d'élite* which is the best sort of existence.

To recommend forgetfulness to a man so profoundly tried as you have been tried, would be folly. Yet, as has been said, life is a dream, or, as I should say, a successions of *songes doux ou terribles*. Well, and if it is so, then even in terror we may find inspiration once we regain courage enough to turn our eyes away from it. Don't look back, for indeed the only way to overcome injustice whether of man or fate is to disregard it."

I recall my husband's pleasure when Arthur Symons sent him the following lines as a motto for the book, *'Twixt Land and Sea*:

"Life is a tragic folly
Let us laugh and be jolly
Away with melancholy
Bring me a branch of holly
Life is a tragic folly."

A. Symons.

The great dissimilarity between the two artists, Arthur Symons and Joseph Conrad, may have been the reason of the close bond that existed between them. I believe Symon's verse was almost the only verse that my husband ever read, I mean with any real appreciation and pleasure. Usually I had to read any manuscript in this form—and he would, quite unblushingly, put forward my opinion as his own, when acknowledging its receipt.

Arthur Symons' writing-table was a model of tidiness and every scrap of manuscript was docketed, and the place noted in the most orderly manner. Very surprising in a poet, I always thought. My husband, on the other hand, had a rooted objection to any kind of order as regards his work-table. This was a mass of dis-related matter and in a constant state of chaos. Long over-due accounts, tax demands, invitations jumbled together. When I took over the care of the papers when he had gone to America, I discovered enough stamps, stuck on envelopes, and unused, to keep me going for some months, had they been those of the ordinary postage rates. But most, if not all, were 6d. or 1/-.

Joseph Conrad had a curious habit of annexing anything that was given to me personally, to his own use, if anyhow possible. Thus, for instance, a small silver pin-tray, given me as a birthday present—became an ashtray.

A parchment note-book, an address-book, and the trouble I had to preserve a writing-table for my own use became laughable. At one time he had in his " torture chamber " no less than four of these useful pieces of furniture. At last I found one that brought forth his scorn to such an extent, that he refused to have it in the house, much less in his room.

Every time he caught sight of the " horror," as he called it, he threatened to set fire to it. " Wait till the next 5th of November, John, and you shall have a proper bonfire." But fortunately for me he had forgotten his threat before that date arrived. But many times soon after I had bought it, he would point the finger of scorn at my purchase and lament my want of artistic taste.

He had a disconcerting habit of returning again and again to a grievance, although it was a failing he deplored long and loudly in anyone else, references such as " chewing the cud " were always made in rather a biting tone, if either the boys or I indulged in a renewed growl over anything.

Capel House came in for a good share of bitter grumbling, on account of its enclosed position. As Richard Curle describes it . . . " A typical Kentish Farmhouse "—but here he was a bit severe. Pent Farm had a wide view from all but one side, that which tucked itself under the side of the hill called the Pent. Richard Curle goes on to say . . . " This low house standing away by itself in the midst of flat fields, and bordered by woods of dwarf oak-trees, in its very isolation, infused with homeliness, had something symbolic, to me, of Conrad's aloof genius and friendly personality." Perhaps, but that " aloofness " had another side, one that was known only to his wife and sons. There were times when his passion for his own company alone, made it extremely difficult for the usual run of life. If he desired to see no one, no matter how much room the house allowed, none must come within its doors.

It happened once that my dear old friend Miss Capes came at the time when he wished the house closed. She arrived in the late afternoon and he only saw her at the evening meal. His manner had no cordiality and he resolutely kept silence, rising directly after the feast was over, and disappearing into his study. He even made a point of wishing the dear old lady a more than irritable " Good night " as he rose.

To make what amends in my power I invited her to retire early, declaring I had something upon which I wanted her advice. As a matter of fact I had hard work to find anything with which to claim her undivided attention, and judged myself fortunate in remembering a new dress that was a little ill-fitting.

Dear Harriet saw through my subterfuge, I knew perfectly well, and she was too intelligent for me to deny his bad temper, but I managed to coax her to remain and overlook his want of cordiality. I produced the dress and we retired to her room, a long way out of earshot. We had been chatting for not more than a short half-hour, when we heard his restless pacing up and down the corridor outside.

" Hadn't you better go and see if he wants something, dear ? " she asked me in the middle of our discussion. I obediently opened the door and looked out. Joseph Conrad beckoned me across the passage dividing our room from that occupied by our guest, and said in a most peremptory fashion, " Aren't you going to bed ? " he began irritably, " I want to work. I must get that manuscript off by to-morrow, you know that very well. I want the house to myself." I gazed at him, not a little perturbed. " But," I began, " I . . . am not disturbing you. You cannot hear us talking in that room, and you know dear Harriet never likes to turn in early." My protest only made him more insistent that I should undress at once. I shrugged my shoulders and, half-amused at his insistence, I quickly disrobed and began to brush my hair. All this time he had said nothing, but when I had actually got into bed he came over and kissed me and left the room. I listened for his step going downstairs. A moment afterwards I heard him laughing heartily in the room opposite. I had dozed once or twice before I heard the door open and shut and he departed downstairs to finish the work that had to be finished.

He hesitated a few seconds outside my door, but did not come in.

I allowed a few more moments to pass, then seizing my dressing-gown, I cautiously crept out of my room and into the one opposite. To my relief our old friend turned to me a serene countenance and began to exclaim at the wonderful charm of her host. She finished up with, " My dear, what a blessing you understand him so well—and he is a little difficult, at times. Go to bed, it is past midnight." How I blessed her for her patient understanding. But the next time he had one of those peculiar fits on, we happened to be dining with her at her club, and she could not overlook his ill-humour in the same way. My grief is that this misunderstanding was never cleared up; they had not met for some years when my husband died.

The other laughable, but exasperating incident many years after was rendered the more ridiculous because this time it was a man guest, dear Edward Garnett, and I had not had anything to do with his invitation. The old friend was very surprised, and not disposed to let it rest at mere eccentricity on the part of his host. Although at the time he followed me from the room and upstairs to the small boy John's bedroom, and sat on the bed for more than three hours talking to us both, he intercepted Joseph Conrad on his way to bed, and I heard their voices raised in a heated disagreement until late in the night. I did not allude to the matter again until after the friend had left. But when the next one was invited I remarked very quietly: " Are you feeling equal to having anyone staying for a long week-end?" My husband gave me a quick look, and began pacing the room restlessly. I waited, his letter of invitation in my hand, and presently he patted my arm and subsided into his chair with his favourite " dam," lit a cigarette, and puffed at it for a few seconds, then he said in a quiet tone: " It will be quite all right, Jess, let him come, post the letter."

This friend was none other than Richard Curle, and I knew perfectly well that it was very unlikely that he would repeat the scene with him. Still, I had to sometimes assert myself in a quiet way, and he could hardly expect me to submit to that treatment often.

Richard Curle refers to this visit when he speaks of the many times they had sat in deck chairs on the rough lawn above the old weedy moat, enjoying the solitude and the sun. He says, speaking of Joseph Conrad: " I can see him now, waving his hands at the oak woods beyond and saying, ' How I hate the feeling these woods give me of being shut in.' " Richard Curle goes on to say that his happiest recollections of my husband are bound up with Capel House. He declares that there was an informality about the life there, a warm comfort, which were never quite caught in the grander surroundings of Oswalds, where he spent his final years.

My version of the reason for this is I think pardonable, because it is an acknowledged fact, that it was due to my personal care and cooking ability that our guest's creature comforts were so much better looked after when I was able to take an active part in making them so.

I can never forget one Sunday morning during the time we lived at Capel. It was certainly no day of rest, but of travail—work is too mild a term to use. Joseph Conrad appeared that morning minus his high stiff collar, and he wore no tie, a sure sign of excessive energy. I knew at once what the omission of the "boiled rag" would mean, some strenuous hours before us both. There are two very wonderful dry point etchings by Muirhead Bone which were to the two boys and myself unfamiliar somehow, until Borys suddenly spotted what was unusual. "He has no starched collar on, mum, that's what makes it so unreal." And that is a fact, the absence of "the boiled rag" was all that was wrong.

His old-time sailor expressions still came out at times unexpectedly. I was greatly puzzled in the early days by this remark: "It means a square-mainsail coat and a gaff-topsail hat" for that entertainment. It was a long time before I understood this to mean a frock-coat and tall hat.

But the Sunday he descended the stairs after having eaten his breakfast in the solitude of his bedroom—which breakfast had perforce to be cut up in order that he could read while he ate, a favourite habit of his when the fancy took him. That particular morning I had planned something widely different before my husband appeared and claimed my undivided attention.

This demand was rather unusual and in this case quite unexpected, but I was quite ready to assist and we gave the two boys their lunch to take out in the woods and prepared for some real hard work. I had to give careful instructions to the serving maid as regards our midday meal, which was of necessity to be a very elementary one. Even so I had to leave something of that to her initiative because of the insistence of my husand's call from his room: "Come at once, let everything else go. I must finish this before to-morrow morning. I shan't want anything to eat, I couldn't swallow a mouthful." He had only just had a good breakfast!

I sat down at my typewriter in the next room, ready to copy each page as it was thrust through the door dividing the two rooms. The boys had taken their picnic lunch and faded, with strict injunctions to keep away from the house. A little after eleven I saw an antiquated motor-car come lumbering up the rather long drive, closely followed by my two boys, and come to a halt with a wheeze—apparently bronchial—before the front door. My husband heard it, too, and appeared at the communicating door with a grunt of exasperation. Who was it who had dared to disturb his peace? He must be sent away anyhow. Even as he spoke there was a shrill peal at the bell and the maid came hastily through the room to answer the unusually peremptory summons. We heard a short parley, diffident on the girl's part but insistent on that of the visitor. Meanwhile Joseph Conrad stood at the dining-room door biting his nails and glaring at me. In less time than it takes to tell, the maid retreated backwards into the room closely followed by the caller who made straight for the door my husband had flung to at the moment of the stranger's entry. My protest was not more efficient than that of the maid, for the man, hat in hand crossed the room, determined to fulfil his mission. "I have been sent to fetch Mr. Conrad to Ashford to speak on the telephone." "The devil, you have," exploded Joseph Conrad reappearing rather like a jack-in-the-box. The man fell back a pace or so, then plucking up his courage, and raising his voice, began insistently: "Let me explain, please, sir. I was in my bath when my barmaid called to me telling me I was wanted at once, London call on the telephone. I am the only one on the ''phone' in that part of Ashford," he added fatuously. My husband interrupted him in a somewhat derisive tone: "Yes, yes. You were in your bath, but I don't see how that affects me, my dear sir, or why it should induce you to come here interrupting my morning's work, a damned sight more important than your bath let me tell you. What do you want anyway, now you are here?"

The visitor became almost incoherent with excitement. "I was in my bath," he repeated, while my husband raised his hands in a gesture of despair and the two boys and I exchanged a smile. "It was the *Daily Mail* office that directed me to hire a car and come here to bring you, sir, to the 'phone to speak to them." "And you don't know why?" Joseph Conrad's tone was surprisingly gentle.

The man admitted he had no notion what the editor wanted, but concluded that the matter must be of vital importance by reason of the direction to hire a car. "Very well," muttered my husband at last, in an ominously quiet tone. "But you will send me back if I go. You have done enough damage as it is. Come along you boys."

I watched the car proceeding ponderously away and I smiled to myself picturing the boys' critical judgment of the machine. In an incredibly short space of time the party returned, and contrary to precedent, the driver after a short wait for a tip that was not forthcoming, turned his car and departed as he had come. Joseph Conrad entered the house followed by the boys, their eyes wide with wonder, for they had not apparently heard a word as to why their father had been carted off in such a summary manner. Joseph Conrad flung his hat to them and retreated to his study.

We sat down to the next meal in silence, and the boys noting signs of some sort of explosion, had left the table and the house to resume their birds'-nesting. Then I glanced questioningly at my husband's angry face at the other end of the table, and he answered my look with a peal of exasperated laughter, a sure sign of irritation, rose from the table and lighted a cigarette. "The damned cheek," he flung round and banged his fist on the table, making the cups leap in their saucers. "I couldn't say half of what I wanted to, I was completely taken aback. Imagine, Jess, all they wanted when I got there was an article on the books Crippen had read on his passage home, after he was caught." He walked rapidly up and down the room, flinging his arms out, then said more quietly: "As if I knew, or cared what he read. Very likely nothing; and anyhow what did it matter to me? They wanted it telegraphed too, this evening. I gave them a price of £20 and the ass at the other end began to stutter, 'Isn't that a bit stiff?' Then I let myself go and . . . he rang off pretty soon after that." The late Archibald Marshall quotes this episode in his book, *Out and About*.

We were very discreet when there was any chance reference to anything connected with that Sunday morning drive. I heard the boys' description of the ancient vehicle which had borne the brunt of the irate author's exasperation on the passage back, later in the day.

One other event before our visit to Poland in 1914 was a journey I made to town alone. I cannot now recall the reason, but it must have been something important and the date a fixture or I should never have gone alone. Borys was by this time a cadet on board the training ship *Worcester*, and I have a vague idea that my journey had some reference to that. I had had to hurry to catch my train back, which was to be met in Ashford by Joseph Conrad and the car. A certain ease of mind was mine because I knew that owing to a somewhat severe attack of gout, he would not be driving the car himself to meet me.

I have often wondered what satisfaction people get from the fictitious form of lying. Such as, for instance, claiming an intimate acquaintance with some person more or less in the public eye at the moment. I imagine many well-known writers have been victimized in this manner, but this day it was my unique experience to overhear a most romantic version of my own husband's life and habits, related with every appearance of truth and conviction.

It happened, as I have said, that I travelled down from town unattended by either my husband or the boys. I was rather late for the train at Charing Cross and was somewhat agitated by the time I was settled in the corner of a first class carriage. My porter, who from an excess of zeal had hurried me rather unnecessarily, announced triumphantly as he opened the carriage door: "'ere you are ma'm, ladies only, fust stop Ashford." I gasped my thanks and tendered him my tip, and as I waited then for some minutes till the train started, I regretted that I had not the good fortune to have fallen to the care of one of the many officials known to me on that line who would not have hurried me so much. However, I had caught the train and as we drew out of the station I glanced across at my fellow-travellers, two ladies no longer in their first youth. They were in an animated discussion at the time of my entry and after favouring me with that apprising glance which seems to value your garments and intimate how very insignificant a person you are, they turned their gaze away and resumed their former conversation. I, in my turn, subsided in my corner and watched the fields and the country-side slipping past the carriage window with restful interest. I had a book with me, but I have never been able to read in a train. We had just cleared the outskirts of London when the mention of my own name, or rather I should say my husband's, arrested my attention and I heard one of my two fellow-travellers asserting that he was known to her intimately. I half rose in my seat, but the next moment a rather shrill voice declared that the man to whom I had then been married for twenty years, was still a bachelor. I gasped. "Yes, dear," the voice continued, "I should have thought you would have heard something from someone in our set. You remember the time when I was staying with Lady M——, I met him there. He is a near neighbour of hers. There was even . . ." she lowered her voice and there followed a whispered confidence too low to be audible to me above the rumble of the train. "But, Agnes, my dear," interrupted the other, "isn't that a trifle indiscreet of you. He's a foreigner, he may have a wife in his own country?"

"Oh, as to that, I can assure you it is perfectly safe. I was reading in the paper only a few days ago that he left his own country when he was seventeen and has not been back since. He is a most charming man with the most wonderful manners. I am simply devoted to him."

Here followed a pause and I longed to proclaim the fact that I was the wife of the man they were discussing. Then I reflected

TWO OLD POLISH FRIENDS IN 1914

JOSÉF SPIRIDION KLISZCZEWSKI

KONSTANTIN BUSZCZYNSKI
Consul-General of Poland to the U.S.A.

JOSÉF TEADOR KONRAD KORZENIOWSKI IN 1914

that to at least one of these women I might appear to be lying and I hesitated. Meanwhile the conversation began again and I listened appalled to a tissue of fibs. The good lady now fairly embarked on the tale of the conquest of my husband, began to enlarge freely, but as she now mentioned dates in order to convince her friend, I was quite unruffled. From time to time she favoured me with a somewhat hostile glance while her friend indulged in a haughty stare. I perceived that quite unwittingly some of my interest must have appeared in my face. I half turned my back and kept my gaze fixed on the landscape. I was wondering how on earth I could proclaim myself with any show of truth for my fighting spirit was aroused and I felt a passionate desire to speak out before I left the carriage. Just then the train slowed down and I had a sudden brain-wave. . . . I would manage to make the railway official address me by name. I knew that my husband would be at the station to meet me and I knew also that owing to his gout he would not leave the car. I was also perfectly certain that some official would be told off to assist me from the train. Everything happened as I had foreseen, only the man greeted me with a cheerful: "Good morning, ma'm" without the prefix of my name. For a moment I was stumped, then I questioned: "Is my car here, do you know?" "Oh, yes, Mrs. Conrad, and Mr. Conrad is here, too." This was all I wanted. With what I hope was becoming dignity I turned to the lady who had claimed such intimate acquaintance with the man to whom I had been married for over twenty years, and trying to keep my face straight, for the official still held open the carriage door, I said: "I am Mrs. Joseph Conrad, madam, and have been now for nearly twenty years, and I am the mother of Mr. Conrad's two sons."

The expression of those two faces I shall never forget, and I chuckled inwardly at the recollection as I made my way to the car. It was about that time that a neighbour of ours returned from a short holiday in Switzerland, and during an early call informed me with much apparent satisfaction that she had met, in a Swiss hotel, my husband's sister. "Such a charming woman, and immensely proud of her brother. We saw a lot of Miss Conrad. She had a complete set of his books with her and she was quite thrilled to know he was our near neighbour."

I gasped in amazement, then found my voice, and said indignantly: "Indeed, that was remarkable, for, you see, my husband was an only child and has no sister." The lady's face fell for a moment, then she smiled an indulgent smile that said as plainly as any words could have done: "That is what he has told you," and I longed to shake her I remarked quietly: "You see, her name would not have been Miss Conrad as this is only my husband's

Christian name. His surname is, as I thought you knew' Korzeniowski."

There was distinctly a chill in my neighbour's manner when she bade me farewell. The lady in Switzerland had evidently had a good time, sailing under false colours. One other incident occurred when our boy Borys was in France during the war. He had been dining with some brother officers in Paris and had noticed that three American officers seemed a good deal interested in his little party. At last he heard distinctly the elder of the three remark to his companions : " Wal, I guess most people would find it hard to believe that Joseph Conrad, the author of *Victory*, looked as young as that young man over there."

CHAPTER THIRTEEN

JOSEPH Conrad had a curious craze for house-hunting, even when he knew that he was settled, and would be held to the remainder of a lease that might have two or three years to run. "Let's pretend" was a fetish of his.

He once indulged in his queer pastime, and truly it provided one of the strangest and most amusing adventures I ever experienced in our search for a home.

My husband had possessed himself of a local paper and had there seen advertised a house directly on the lowest level of the Romney Marsh. That the paper happened to be more than a fortnight old had evidently not struck him, and one afternoon after lunch he announced his intention of going off to inspect the place. He ordered the car, at that time an open touring Cadillac, and with his secretary and our small boy John we set off. There were five of us counting the chauffeur. In due time we arrived before the house, which to my mind had little if any attraction. I had not seen the advertisement, but concluded it was recent enough to account for the fact that curtains adorned most of the windows, and apparently the old tenant had not yet left. It was characteristic of the great author that even before he had even seen the inside of a house he would start fussing and fuming over the abominable colour or texture of the curtains, if the exterior appealed in the smallest degree. He seldom heeded my remark that they were not likely to be fixtures and that if everything else in the place pleased him the curtains could soon be changed.

This afternoon he was a little difficult to manage, and in spite of the fact that I was still forced to use crutches he insisted that I should also view the premises.

The house stood below the road, with a small sunken garden on each side of the stone path that led up to the front door. In size and shape it had certain amenities—but, and this was a big but to my mind, a short flight of stone steps without a rail led down to the garden. The place must have been at least five feet below the level of the street.

Unmistakable signs of activity, even agitated activity, buzzed from the interior as my husband swept down the steps with the cape of his haverlock overcoat swinging around him. This style of dress suited him in every way, and one would never have taken him for an Englishman when wearing it. The door was opened by a somewhat startled maid still in her morning dress and grasping the handle of her broom tightly in her hand. Behind her, at the door of what I concluded was the drawing-room, the mistress of the house appeared, looking flustered and not over pleased. She came forward a few steps, Joseph Conrad bowed low, hat in hand, with a smart military click of his heels—this was his most ceremonious greeting. Her evident intention was to shepherd him into the drawing-room, which was possibly the most furnished room in the house. With another bow and a wide sweep of his hand he declared that " as his wife was at the moment very lame, he would examine the bedrooms first."

The lady gasped and the maid all but dropped her broom in evident consternation, while my husband moved a step or two nearer the staircase. From the vantage point of the car we looked upon the little comedy in wonderment. Just then a youngish man appeared on the stairs, half-way up, and for a moment he hesitated, then, overcome with mirth, subsided on the step above him and stuttered out : " I . . . I imagine, sir . . . that you were under the impression that . . . that this house was still . . ." he controlled his inclination to laugh outright by a mighty effort . . . " to let. We only moved in the day before yesterday. We . . . we thought you were callers."

He descended the remaining stairs and came forward protesting that any apology on our part was quite unnecessary as my husband bowed himself out, considerably disconcerted and not too good-tempered. The rest of the drive was somewhat uncomfortable, and for the life of me I could not think of anything mildly intelligent to say to break the spell. However, a little further on we had a burst tyre and the tension was relaxed.

As was usual after one of these abortive attempts to change houses we settled down again, and perhaps months would pass without any dissatisfaction being voiced at any rate. It was generally some small defect, either in the matter of draught or light that brought the matter of a change being desirable up again.

Jean Aubry provided a unique interest in the author's somewhat hermit-like existence. This affection was caused partly by ill-health and partly from a natural indolence. He was shy of going to fresh houses but always ready to make new friends. There was also the reason that nothing pleased him more than playing host. He used, so to speak, his intimate friends as scouts. I think it was a bit of a pose sometimes, and I was often disappointed when he refused to go out with me, when I had set my mind upon a particular call. And he did not approve of my going out much alone. I can hear him now telling Aubry: " Bring him to the lion's den," he would say. He seldom liked to entertain more than one or two people at a time, for he was easily tired and somewhat irrational. In the early days he would hold a whole room-full enthralled by the relation of some personal experience, and I have often heard him tell the same tale totally differently. At first I had the temerity to break in, correcting some date, or other discrepancy, but later on I found it more discreet to hold my tongue.

That manuscript of *Karain*, in the margin of which appeared his creator's conception of that character, was one of my favourite short stories, and one day I came upon my husband bending absorbed over the pile of papers on his desk and ruminating deeply. His thoughts were far away from me and the object of my intrusion; these moments of complete detachment were very familiar to me before I had been married a year. I made as if to leave the room, but he turned in his chair and, with that courtesy of which he was usually past master, seized my hand and carried it to his lips. "Don't go away for a moment. What do you think of this?" He bent over the desk on which lay the first page of my beloved *Karain* and made some few rapid strokes with his pen, hiding the paper from my sight with his other hand. "What do you think of him, Jess? Do you recognize Karain?" I gazed on the sensitive face that had appeared in those few seconds, and mentally resolved to cut it out, if possible without damaging the page of writing. Not that I had then the most remote notion that there could be any such adventure in the future for that particular manuscript; it was years later that we heard of possible collectors and the fantastic prices even a signature might obtain. I put that sacred pile away very carefully when I had finished typing it, and only a year afterwards my husband flatly denied that he had ever drawn on that narrow margin a face that had such a haunting quality of strength and pathos. Karain must have made a deep impression on his creator subconsciously for him to be able to portray such a vivid, living likeness with those few strokes of his pen.

One of the strangest and most profitable friendships we ever made in the years we were together—I mean profitable in the sense that the money Mr. Quinn paid for the manuscripts was not in a sense earned as it was paid for—was with Miss Agnes Tobin, who was introduced into our household through Arthur Symons, and managed to interest Mr. Quinn enough to induce him to buy the manuscripts—all of them for £2000 inclusive. The items were hard at the moment, and in addition to our Bank breaking and dissolving—there is no other word—our small hard-earned capital, the work had dragged and the great author was depressed and ill.

Miss Tobin spent a great deal of time with us, appearing unexpectedly out of the blue, sometimes alone, at others with some stranger for whom she claimed our friendship and hospitality. It was she who first brought André Gide and Valery Larbaud, two French "boys" as she said. My husband was delighted to welcome these two artists. Our house was not big enough to house them for the night, and I well remember our rush to secure accommodation for them in the old inn in the village. This inn boasted of some very fine old oak beams, which intrigued the two French "boys" very much, and the inn-keeper's daughter had the shock of her life when they invaded her bedroom in the very early morning bent on a tour of inspection. She confessed to a real thrill when she raised her pretty curly head and surprised them into the most abject apologies and instant retreat.

Jean Aubry amused me once very much by the following anecdote, which he told me in the simplest manner possible. It was his habit when in London to take a pension in some small out-of-the-way hotel and to keep himself very much to himself. His habits there were well known and his privacy seldom intruded upon. But one day the place was extra full and with an apology the waiter placed an elderly lady at the same small table in the restaurant where Jean Aubry sat enthroned.

As usual he took his meal with a book propped up before him and his attention far away from his fellow diners. The lady gazed at him for some time, then catching a wandering glance for the moment in her direction she leaned forward and said, cupping her ear with her hand, anticipating his reply:

"I'm so sorry, sir, that on account of my deafness I am not able to entertain you." His answer must have surprised her considerably. He raised his head with a jerk and rapped out: "Madam, it is well known here that I am very nearly dumb."

And the next morning, descending the stairs somewhat exasperated by the fact that his rest had been much disturbed by the persistent crying of an infant in the next room to his, he met the mother with the child in her arms. She paused a step or so above him and said with an ingratiating smile: "I am so sorry, sir, I fear my little boy must have disturbed you very much during the night." Jean Aubry made her a formal bow and said in a crisp tone: "Pray don't mention it, madam, I hate children."

The lady was decidedly disconcerted and gazed rather resentfully after the Frenchman, who continued his way downstairs quite unmoved.

It was almost immediately after *Victory* was finished that we prepared for the visit to Poland, which might have ended so tragically had it not been for the intervention of the American Ambassador (the late Mr. Penfield). The journey there held plenty of excitement and not a little anxiety for Joseph Conrad at least. I knew nothing of war, except what I had read. Then it had seemed far away. It was all so different here. Our arrival, the strangeness of it all seemed part of the agitation that surrounded us on every side. I would watch, not a little exasperated, the long talks between my husband and the young man who had been our fellow traveller, and to whose wife's home we were invited to spend that month's holiday. War? It seemed impossible. Everything was quiet, until a few days later in the space of a few moments when all was bustle and confusion. What became of all the small money ? All change disappeared in but a few short hours, everyone seemed to have altered. In place of courtesy and gentleness one sensed only watchful care. Each for himself—if God is for us all.

The Austrian mobilization was wonderful in its quick response ; troops poured into Cracow in such numbers that many had to be sent back, for a time at least. We were actually on a visit to an old school friend of my husband's that afternoon. We had been sitting at lunch when we noticed a man with a fine head of white hair staring hard at our table. Presently he caught my husband's eye and the two rushed together in close embrace. I felt not a little embarrassed by the scene. Then after the somewhat incoherent introductions had been made, nothing would do but that we must go that very afternoon to this good man's home a few miles from Cracow. He was Joseph Conrad's oldest school friend. In a few moments he had telephoned for his carriage and pair, there being too many of our party for his car to accommodate. It was during this drive that I think I first understood some of my husband's—till then unaccountable—reluctance to keeping things in repair. This friend's car had a hole in the hood, through which a regular cataract of rain water poured. I turned my head this way and that to avoid the stream, but without avail. I do not object to a little rain as a rule, being, as the wag said, " warranted to wash and keep my colour," but this was more than a little wetting. At last one of the sons of our host noticed my discomfort and opened an umbrella with the remark, " We may have to hand the car over any day, and it is hardly worth repairing it, if that should be so." It struck me then that here was the keynote to my husband's dislike for repairs. In Poland there was always the possibility that property might be confiscated, and that tradition still remained in the mind of Joseph Conrad, even after dwelling for so many years in free England. The drive was not a long one, and we had not been able to go very fast on account of the poor surface of the roads. The gutters each side needed some very careful negotiation as they were deep enough to break the springs if crossed too quickly.

Arrived at the house one's heart went out to those people with their old-world courteous greeting. A comfortable seat was found for me on the wide stone veranda and immediately refreshment was forthcoming. Here again I recognized my husband's national characteristic. Something in the way of refreshments would have to be produced, even in the middle of the night if, as sometimes happened, a guest arrived. Here each member of the family vied with the other to make me feel at home, and although I could not speak the language, I hope I managed to show my appreciation.

From where I sat the flat fields of sugar beet stretched as far as the eye could see. The sun shone brilliantly and the horses harnessed to the wagons in the distance swung their tails rhythmically to keep off the flies. All was peace around us, and only the two old school friends talked anxiously together in the corner, making a significant gesture with their hands from time to time. Already we had begun to think of our return journey to the hotel when we noticed our hostess coming hastily towards us. "It has come, that war we all of us tried not to believe in," she gasped. "They are commandeering the horses; already the soldiers are taking them out of the ploughs." She flung her hands out hopelessly.

There was something so helpless and despairing in that gesture, a mute surrender of everything that one had counted one's own. In a few moments the shafts of the laden wagons rested on the ground, and the horses, unconscious of their ultimate fate, stepped without haste by the side of the soldier who led them through the fields and out on to the road.

CHAPTER FOURTEEN

TO the last day of my life I shall see that proud, lonely figure of our hostess as she stood at the door when we took our sympathetic farewell and entered the car for the return journey. A short conversation between the eldest son and his mother and an ominous whisper "perhaps," and we slowly drove away from the hospitable homestead. All along that road we passed horses being led along, and every now and then a large field close to the roadside resembled a horse-fair, such as one might see in some parts of rural England.

In the far corner of that field, surrounded by helpers, we saw an officer, a blue-grey clad figure, seated at a small table, commandeered from some farm-house hear at hand, making a tally of the animals that were passed before him. Empty carriages, their occupants in various stages of distress and despair, stood along the roadside. Their appearance incongruous because of the empty shafts, either rearing up to the sky, or resting on the ground in mute dismay.

We had one vacant seat in the car, and our host rescued an old white-haired lady from one horseless carriage and transported her into the town. Her daughter appeared at the hotel the next day. to thank us. She appealed to the officials for permission to keep firearms. She intended with her younger sister and two trusty servants to defend their home as long as possible. She spoke a little English, and I talked with her for an hour or more. Their fate in the end was tragic, because of those very firearms. In another house close by a prospective bride had the heart-rending experience of seeing all her trousseau handed out of the windows by some unfriendly natives, who gave everything to a crowd of roughs. These people made short work of the poor girl's dainty underwear. I heard afterwards that the bridegroom fell early in the war in a frontier battle.

The night that hostilities were declared between Austria and Russia was one that will for ever live in my mind. Early in the evening I had seen my eldest boy Borys and our young married friend leave in the hotel car; they were trying to get word to the latter's wife to come to him at once. The manager stepped forward and offered the boys and the chauffeur a business-like pistol; it was really the first time our own personal share in the possible trouble came home to me. I happily was able to persuade them that they were probably considerably safer unarmed, for I distrusted their discretion in the first place, perhaps they might fire either unnecessarily—or, more likely than not—unadvisedly. And the mere fact that they had the wretched pistols might lead to trouble. Even our war-like hotel manager readily saw my point and replaced the pistols in their cases.

They reached the frontier, guarded only by the Austrians; the Russian guard, having blown up all the bridges, had retired from any possible contest. The peasants had deserted the farms and taken to the woods. The doors of the guard-house on the Russian side stood open, the post forsaken. Only an old peasant woman, the mother of one of those men already netted in, sat on the steps with her head lowered, lamenting loudly all through the night. The Austrian guard made the two youths welcome and shared rations with them. It was a bitterly cold night, and in the end they returned discomfited in the early hours of the morning. The chauffeur would have driven them over the frontier but for the fact that he could not have returned, and would have been virtually a prisoner.

I spent that night by the window watching for their return, listening to the ceaseless tramping of the men and the loud sobbing of the women. Little children lamented in a ceaseless wail, partly because they were frightened and partly, I suspect, from sheer bodily discomfort. For the next two days we waited for the young wife who had been promised a safe escort across the frontier. During those days the time seemed long and tense, almost as if the next happening, no matter what, must end the strain somewhat. Everything in the hotel was changed, strangers came and went. Then on the third day our rooms were requisitioned, and we had to make up our minds quickly, whether we should make a dash for home by the last civilian train or seek sanctuary elsewhere. Suddenly Joseph Conrad decided that he would take us up into the mountains to a health resort, Zakopane, where some connections of his were at the time living, and who housed us with many other refugees much more unfortunate than ourselves. We were at least all four together, and in that house we found parts of families, many of whose children had been lost in the wild rush for safety. There was there a mother and her two daughters, the three younger children and their trusty nurse had been swept aside and there came no word of their safety all the two months we stayed. I heard afterwards that only one of these three had survived to be re-united with her family. Train loads of refugees would steam into the station, there to remain full to overflowing. Ladies suffered from various complaints or shock. None could leave the train because there was not enough food to feed those who had already arrived, and after a while the train ran on to the next village. It cut one to the quick to know that there were human beings within a stone's throw, hungry, sick and hopeless. Yet among so many it would be impossible to try to relieve even a few, from the little food available. We were fortunate in more ways than one that we met some good friends in that pension. One man, a Dr. Kosh, who was there with his wife and baby girl. A baby! Needless to say that a very great part of my time was spent in ministering to her. She was just four months old and her mother had been ill in bed for a long time. The village girl who acted as nursemaid had about as much notion of the little one's needs as one of our own untrained girls of the same class. It was bitterly cold in the mountains by this time, and the bright attendant would undress the infant down to a little cotton shift, then, leaving it lying almost in a state of nature, would begin to prepare its bath, put a thermometer into it, and even when the child was wailing a protest against the cold, would wait for the water to be just the right heat, before she attempted to cover the poor shivering little mortal. I had heard the child cry many times and I had hesitated to intrude, but one day the cry was so insistent that I boldly entered the room. On this occasion the tiny mite was already out of her bath and, blue with the cold, lay on a bed, out of her mother's reach, clad only in her vest. The nurse had left her while she retired to the kitchen to iron a gown. Our good friend Madame Zagorska stood over the mite making little friendly cooing sounds while the little face remained puckered up in distress. I took a large shawl and, wrapping it closely round the poor baby, held it against me to get some warmth into it.

After that I always attended to her toilet and never again was the ironing of the gown left until just when it was required. Those parents showed their appreciation in a very practical form indeed. By the end of the first fortnight our little stock of money was nearly exhausted and there was no possibility of getting further supplies from England. It was not, as this statement perhaps suggests, that we had been either extravagant or had miscalculated the amount needed, but Joseph Conrad had been bearing all travelling expenses for both parties, which were to be repaid on our arrival at the country house in Russia, and also further supplies were to come to us from England. Now every arrangement was cancelled and no post came to us and none of ours ever reached our friends and relations at home. Dr. Kosh was indeed a good friend, for he financed us until we could get into Italy, the only stipulation he made was that we should not speak about it to anyone as he would be besieged from all sides, since no one in the pension had any money. Even what he lent us he knew he could not get until after the war was ended. I have a great feeling of thankfulness for his aid, although I knew nothing of the arrangement at the time. Our journey from Cracow to Zakopane had been indeed a momentous one, and can never be forgotten. The morning we left our rooms was a farce indeed. My husband and the boys had gone down to breakfast and had left me to finish dressing and do the packing. I was barely clothed at all when without any preliminary knock or warning of any kind an Austrian officer entered my room, followed by four private soldiers carrying his baggage. Apparently he had thought the rooms empty, and in response to my urgent appeal, directed his men to dump the things on a bed and retire. This they did somewhat unwillingly. They were all more or less under the influence of drink, and anxious to be released from duty. Their clothes barely hung on them, buttons were unfastened and belts hanging loose. My dressing was finished with all possible speed, and the rest of my things flung into the trunk pell-mell, for I had no fancy to be still in the rooms when those men returned.

At the station the crowd was appalling, and no one knew which platform our train might start from. I had some stout safety pins, with which I fastened the small boy's coat to my dress, and keeping my hand firmly on his shoulder, I stayed close to an open space protected by a low wall to guard my sick knee from the crush as much as possible. After what seemed an interminable time my husband and Borys fought their way towards us, and with a Polish friend succeeded in shepherding me to the carriage in which they had secured the seats. Even then for a time in the turmoil, we were not quite certain that the train was right. Scores of less fortunate travellers remained on that platform when at last the train puffed out of the station. I was feeling sick and faint with anxiety and hunger, and my anxious enquiries as to the fate of our luggage were met by my husband with an exasperated wave of the hand. "Who could say?" It had been enough of an effort to get what hand luggage we had and ourselves into the train, without worrying about what might have happened to the other blamed stuff. I might make up my mind to its loss, anyway.

Characteristically, Joseph Conrad saw the gloomy side of things from the first, and continued to do so. I had seen one of the trunks go into the van, but whether that van remained attached to the train in which we were travelling was another matter.

"Then it was only one trunk we saw go into the van," remarked the small boy, his lip quivering. "I don't think that was the one that had my new engine in." The boy caught his father's very decided scowl and subsided into his allotted corner.

There was something pathetically sinister and alarming in the groups of peasants at every level crossing. Large crowds of women and girls with small children pressed themselves against the bars of the crossing gates as the train thundered over the points. Sometimes it stopped and more often than not it rumbled by. Everywhere handkerchiefs were waved or hats solemnly lifted, and there were tears and lamentations all the way. Many times our train remained stationary on some short line while heavily laden troop trains passed. Here the men's faces seemed piled one on top of the other, moisture pouring down their cheeks. A few women's figures would detach themselves from the cluster at the gate and bring to the side of those open trucks pails of water with an iron dipping cup. The men drank thirstily, but often the train moved on before all had had the chance to drink. The two men of our little party would smother their cigarettes out because they had not enough to hand out to those hot, tired, dusty men who were to be made into soldiers. Some were old, others pitifully young, and none looked anxious for the great adventure before them.

It always strikes me how close on the heels of tragedy, comedy can creep. Hardly had that long train, loaded with depressed humanity, vanished from sight and our train in turn drawn up at a wayside station, when the truly laughable spectacle of the fattest man I had ever seen in plus-fours descended from a carriage a little nearer the engine than ours, and waddled slowly across the intervening railway line to a refreshment stall. His comical gravity was heightened by the fact that the dog he was towing behind him, obstinately refused to use his legs for the legitimate purpose for which nature had intended them. At every two or three steps he sat down and refused to move. The boys and I watched them from our window, stifling our merriment with our pocket-handkerchiefs. My husband called us severely to account. No doubt our mirth was misplaced, but it was the first thing we had found to laugh at in all that melancholy long journey. It ended in the fat round man bending low enough to pick up the little animal—and thereby nearly losing his equilibrium, which caused us to laugh outright. The gentleman was very irate and as soon as he was again in an upright position turned and shook his fist at us, and let fall a stream of vehement abuse, but as it was in some foreign tongue we were still able to smile, yet it sobered us nevertheless.

We had been some fourteen hours in the train when it ran into Zakopane and we discovered to our disgust that indeed only one trunk had travelled with us. No one could help us and it never came to hand during our two months' stay. I was able to assure the small boy at first sight that the one we had, did contain his engine, which seemed the only thing that troubled him. When we got to the hotel we soon discovered that the trunk contained no complete suits; white flannel trousers and dinner jackets only. I don't believe either Joseph Conrad or Borys had a whole suit other than what they were wearing, and I was even worse off. I had just two nightdresses, and one of these was to be commandeered by the young wife of our friend who was following by the next train. I did rebel that night when my husband in an excess of politeness, to which he was rather prone, rebuked me for having fallen asleep while he and Borys had gone to the station to meet Madame Retinger. I was quite ready to be awakened, but I thought his scolding rather beyond the limit, for I was desperately tired, bodily and mentally.

The next day our young friend joined her two sisters who were staying in another part of the place, and we sought the home of my husband's distant relative, who was living there. Here our troubles were as nearly at an end as they could be under the circumstances. Everyone was kindness itself, and I like to think I was able to make myself a bit useful to the dear lady. The people in that house had a great affection for Joseph Conrad, an affection that was freely extended to us all, and which is now a treasured memory. It was here that I learned a great deal of my husband's early life and of the trials and tribulations of his unfortunate parents. Madame Zagorska was the widow of a doctor whom my husband had known very well years before, and the visit we made had been in contemplation ever since we were married. For me it was indeed fortunate that both she and her daughters spoke English and understood it. Here we met many influential Poles, and had it not been for the terrible anxiety for the country of his adoption, I feel sure Joseph Conrad would have enjoyed the time we spent in that household. Often I would not see him all day except for meals, and then only with the width of the long table between us. Without being greedy, my good man was distinctly fastidious about his food, to put it mildly, and sometimes about twice as many people appeared at the meals as were expected or catered for, and everyone went short.

The weather for the most part of our stay was fine, and to look at a cloudless sky and hear no sound of a gun made it very difficult to believe that war, terrible and menacing, was taking its toll of life, of the lives of those near and dear, with such ruthless rapidity. Now and again a train-load would be expected, and one saw a little band of nurses trying to look—and feel professional. The nursing movement there was in its first infancy, and perhaps fortunately for the wounded, none reached Zakopane—at least, while I was there, for the valiant little band to try their apprentice hand upon. I suppose it was a long way from any base hospital.

Many men who were fighting came and went ; they brought stories that scarcely served as a comfort to those refugees. I remember a man who was a wonderful amateur photographer coming many times, and one night he went away wearing General Pilsudski's furs to take them to him at the front. " May as well be warm for once," he had remarked as he left the house. His lady friend and her two young daughters were left to the tender care of our good hostess. One girl was truly beautiful ; the other warped in form and mind—and neither had a right to the name they bore.

When we first arrived the pension boasted of a man-servant, but in time the machine of war drew him into its toils and Zakopane saw him no more. One evening not long before he left, the younger children, of whom our boy John was one, were playing on a wide wooden veranda when suddenly they all disappeared into the depths of the foundations of the house. The man's curious outcry: "Wounds of our Saviour, what have they done?" brought us all quickly to the scene. Fortunately, none of the children were hurt, although all were very frightened.

For quite a long time I had noticed the extreme moderation displayed by my husband and Borys at breakfast-time. They scarcely seemed to eat anything. I was becoming quite concerned when chance took me into the principal street where there was a large café. Chancing to raise my eyes as the little trap passed, I saw the two with one or two other resident refugees sitting before a well-laden tray, and the secret was out. I carefully refrained from any comment and I soon found that I had passed unnoticed, but my anxiety as to the restraint of their natural appetites was a thing of the past. I had often wondered at their energy, taking a walk so early in the morning.

By this time there was an urgent need for some kind of suit of clothing for the eldest boy, whose arms and legs seemed to protrude through the ends of his garments in a more than grotesque fashion. We found a shop and a suit which became possible with a few alterations made by me, and we also purchased a reversible Burberry. This useful garment figured a good deal in my recollections later on. Joseph Conrad and the small boy John were the only two of us who boasted an overcoat. I was minus a vest and many other equally necessary garments, and so frequently I had to go without while the necessary washing was done, I had begun to think kindly of a complete suit in but one garment. Then as the weather grew colder and our hopes of ultimate release from exile grew less and seemed to recede further and further away, it became increasingly difficult to continue philosophical. One other purchase we made to meet my needs, and that was a long grey woollen cloak. I had brought with me a thick woollen brown cardigan, unmistakably a feminine garment which fastened in the orthodox fashion from right to left. Very early in our stay in Zakopane my husband annexed this and wore it constantly. The day after we purchased that cloak, Joseph Conrad had arranged that I should return a rather ceremonious call a few miles away. The requisite trap was ordered and he came into my room with the last messages of greeting and goodwill. I had said that I had no overcoat; what was my surprise and amusement when my husband appeared wearing the cardigan, his own overcoat—and the cloak. Evidently he had felt the need of warmth and had forgotten that, driving, I should need it. I forbore to call his attention to the fact and hoped the drizzle that was falling would have ceased before the time came for me to pay that call. I wished to arrive dry at any rate—it was an open trap. This is only told as an instance of his complete absentmindedness. Like a child, he was quite irresponsible, and I know well that he would have been terribly distressed had he stopped to think that he was wearing literally all the outdoor clothing we had.

Our patience was getting greatly worn and our anxiety about our friends and relations in England almost unbearable, when by some lucky chance we managed to get permission to leave Zakopane ; just a few words written on an officer's card, a friend in Cracow. Once in Vienna we were assured of the good will and the power of the American Ambassador, the late Mr. Penfield. That journey was timed to begin some few days after we secured the card, and in preparation for it I furnished a big suit-case as a miniature kitchen, for we had been warned that our chance of getting food on the way was very unlikely and that the journey to Vienna was certain to take three or four times as long as normally. It behoved me, therefore, as the caterer for the party, to make my preparations as complete as possible. I also did the one and only day's washing I had ever undertaken. All the garments not actually in wear I laboriously washed, rubbing my fingers raw in the process, and then like a bolt from the blue came the news that we must start at least twenty-four hours sooner than we had intended. I gasped, for all my washing hung before the closed stove, and clouds of steam testified to the fact that they were still dripping wet. But there was no help for it, wet as they were they had to be packed away in the trunks ready for the journey an hour or so later. My husband was more than anxious that all those garments should be left behind. "I am certain everything will be lost on the way," he muttered angrily, "and we shall have enough to do to get through with what we have on our backs." I smiled to myself ; no doubt he would turn out to be right, but . . . perhaps he wouldn't. Anyway, I said no more, and the trunk containing those garments was stowed away in its allotted place in the back of the roomy trap, and I am certain Joseph Conrad soon dismissed all thought of it from his mind.

The last meal we ate in that house full of friendly refugees who came there to speed us on our way, was indeed a scrappy one. With the best intentions in the world, our sorely tried hostess was hard put to it to produce even the resemblance of a meal for the great number of people who poured in that night, their desire being merely to say farewell to the man who was their loyal countryman and whose wonderful writing achievement they one and all desired to honour. That Joseph Conrad was as good an Englishman as a Pole was known and recognized, but that night it was not to him as a man of world-wide fame that those Poles wished to render homage, but rather as a man of their own nation and tradition. I knew so well how much he felt his powerlessness to show hospitality. I had to point out to him that our meagre provision of eatables and the solitary bottle of cherry brandy that I had somehow managed to procure for our journey would have been hopelessly inadequate to offer to the vast number of friends gathered there to see us depart. I did at last convince him. For weeks before that night, when the household provisions had become very scarce, I had by some means, either pure luck or perhaps a little personality, managed to buy some few provisions in readiness for my husband's well-known demand for offers of hospitality in our own room. Long after the pathetic little notices appeared on the dinner-table attached by a cord to the water jugs or similar utensils explaining the absence of this or that article of food, I could produce for the few that very thing. Almost every night after the first few weeks, after Joseph Conrad and the boys had retired to bed, our room would be invaded by six or seven anxious country men and women.

From his vantage-point in bed, even when gout had claimed him for a victim, my husband would enjoy those visitations. Through a haze of tobacco smoke and the fetid odour of many humans confined in a tiny space, humans who must have worn the same clothes for days on end, I have made quarts of tea and provided small piles of sandwiches and biscuits. Far into the night I have sat on the side of my bed in the far corner by the window, sometimes half-dozing, but ready and alert directly a fresh brew of tea was wanted or some mislaid paper required. Then, when those people went, each kissed my fingers with every sign of homage. I piled my bed-clothes on top of Joseph Conrad who was often already asleep and having guarded him as far as laid in my power from any draught, I opened the door, and sat shivering for an hour or more until the atmosphere was purified sufficiently for me to get to bed. Then often I retired in the best part of my clothes, for I had not the heart to remove any of the covering from my sleeping husband. Twice while we were in that pension a love-sick mountaineer, who had an appointment with one of the serving maids whose quarters were immediately below our room, roused me quickly from my sleep. With the knowledge that we were, so to speak, in an enemy country, it was distinctly alarming to hear rapid steps coming directly up the flight of wooden steps that led to the glass door of the room. Once I had just time to fling myself against it and turn the key in the lock as the intruder appeared sharply in silhouette just outside. But Joseph Conrad, who was awake the second time the amorous mountaineer sought his quarry, could not bring himself to undertake the defence of the flimsy stronghold alone and must needs summon his son to his aid. For a moment I was inclined to crow, until it struck me that in my ignorance alone I had been bold and brave.

When we left that hospitable wooden habitation, with its lights faintly glimmering in the windows, (for here there were no regulations as to curtained windows), the trap that was to bear us on the first stage of our adventurous journey was some hours late. Already it was long past midnight and various special constables had gone in different directions to look for any sign of it. We stood ready, our baggage piled on the steps together with that of an influential Polish friend who was to be our companion as far as Vienna. A heap of ineffectively dressed sheep-skins lay by the side of the trunks, our *kitchen* case with a large cardboard box containing a cream cake, the farewell gift of the cook, and jealously watched by the good dame, completed our preparations. A borrowed fur-lined coat had been wrapped round me, and was to be entrusted with the sheep-skins to the coachman to be returned when he had left us at the little railway station which was the first at which we could hope to catch our train to Cracow. At last the carriage came slowly along the sloshy road, the hedges along the roadside bending with the weight of half-melted snow, and the mountains standing out in the moonlight in austere grandeur. One, higher than the others, had an iron cross placed on its summit in such a position that from where we stood below it had the appearance of a gigantic figure lying full length with a cigar in its mouth. There was in that pose something ineffably dignified and restful. As the trap drew abreast of the gate and the two unshod horses came to a halt, the moon swam clear of the clouds that had somewhat obscured my view, and I took a silent and sad farewell of that familiar effigy high above me.

The next few moments were filled with sad good-byes. Who could say when next we might meet even one of those friends now clustered round the open door. At last we were packed into our seats, our luggage secured in what seemed a most doubtful fashion. Under the carriage in a sort of sacking sling was the food for the two horses. The number of packages that hung about that vehicle was truly miraculous. After the last handshake and tearful wave, the coachman climbed on to his seat and with a swing of his long whip the horses started with a jerk. One by one the now familiar landmarks appeared and receded as we headed for the next village. The coachman seemed surly and morose. Every now and then he would let out a loud shout as we thundered across a wooden bridge and our progress would be barred by a single pole slung over the road. A tiny house stood as it were at the head of the pole, and in response to the shout a thin, almost naked figure would detach itself from the obscurity and with a blanket flung over its head, step indifferently through the mud and with an answering shout raise the pole and allow us to pass on our way.

These obstructions became more frequent as we neared a town, and at each entrance to them three or four uniformed officials appeared at the side of the carriage and examined its contents. I use the word contents, because they seemed supremely indifferent to the fact that we were human beings. They paid no heed to our proffered papers, and only gave a cursory glance at the formidable wad produced each time by our fellow traveller, who told us when we reached the station that he had all that was necessary in that collection to ensure our safe transit to Cracow.

CHAPTER FIFTEEN

SOME of that road to the small railway station, whence we got a through train to Cracow, stands out crisp and clear in my mental vision, eclipsing events of much more recent date. The slip-slop sound of the two unshod horses going through the mud and slosh, or the even stranger beat of their hooves on the cobble-stones as we passed through towns, had nothing of the rhythmic beat we associate with the trot of horses.

That thirty-mile night drive through village after village was monotonous and exasperating. It seemed endless and was terribly uncomfortable. Four grown people were packed in the small carriage, and the warmth of our bodies brought to life those which were inhabiting the improperly dressed sheep-skins. My stiff limb was laid across the division between the seats, and so tight a fit was it that my foot felt as if held in a vice. Joseph Conrad and Borys sat under the one hood that I would consent to being raised, while our more than portly Polish friend and I occupied the back seat. The small boy, John, lay equally distributed upon our knees. For long periods the child slept in spite of his far from comfortable position. None of us spoke, and from time to time it was only a slight pressure of Borys' hand on the ankle, that was jammed so tightly against him, that told me I was not the only one awake. Yet even that drive came to an end at last, and we alighted, just as the dawn was breaking, at the little wayside station. The train thundered in, ill-lighted and sadly depleted in official staff. Our Jehu stole all the straps off the luggage, and before I could stop him, kissed my cheek. My husband and our friend, that all-efficient Pole, found seats in a carriage where lay a wounded officer on his way to hospital, occupying one side with his soldier servant. This poor fellow had lain for many hours exposed on the battle-field and he was very ill. His batman gratefully accepted some hot coffee, which he induced his officer to swallow drop by drop, and his own eyes watered with eagerness at the sight of the few thick sandwiches which we offered him from our little store. The two boys and I had places in a half-compartment in which we found seated despondently the chauffeur of a Grand-duke. He was either too preoccupied, or from some other cause too indifferent, to take any notice of us, and we remained quietly in our places until at a junction where we changed trains for Cracow.

The next stage of our journey we five had the carriage to ourselves, and the many hours we spent in that train tried the small boy's patience very much. Borys had somewhere discovered a book which interested him ; Joseph Conrad and the influential Pole were for the most part deeply engrossed in some mighty discussion in their own tongue, and I could think of nothing more interesting to amuse John than counting the telegraph posts, taking care, each time we compared our record, to be some five or six posts more or less than his number. This for the sole reason of getting some interest for the tired child. From time to time he helped me get ready a meal from that conjurer's case. It amused both of us to see the smile of satisfaction that crossed the faces of the three others as the tea or other eatables appeared. I had tins of spaghetti and tomato which I heated over the spirit lamp, chicken in jelly, tins of sheeps' tongues, and corned beef. It is true that our bread got very dry towards the end, and our little stock of sugar diminished rapidly, but on the whole our hunger was satisfied, and the collection provided both variety and interest to the end. Even when we left the train in Cracow, one of the guards climbed into the carriage and gathered the meagre remains into a piece of newspaper, remarking : "There is enough for one meal for me in these few scraps." Joseph Conrad himself translated this remark for me.

We had left Cracow only two months earlier, but it was difficult to recognize it as the same place. All around the station ran a thick maze of wire, through which one saw blue-grey figures of Austrian soldiers getting into or out of the long trains drawn up in the station. The effect of this was that of a gigantic caterpillar. Here we were successful in getting one meal, but we had no permission to leave the station. Our friend, who had numerous matters to attend to, barely finished his much-needed coffee before he vanished unostentatiously from our sight with a single tight grip of the hand. His mission was a secret from me, though not from my husband, and I sensed its importance by the anxious watch he kept for the other's return. We sat uncomfortably in the buffet waiting-room for hours, while trains thundered into the station to discharge their human freight of sick and wounded as well as closely guarded prisoners. At a long table near the door a number of volunteer nurses sat in animated conversation, seemingly enjoying a scrappy meal. Scores of wounded were borne across the floor of that buffet, so that it became slippery and stained with blood. Little attempt was made to clear away the evidence of horror. Now and then an old man would appear with a bucket of some strong disinfectant and a few shovelsful of sawdust. We remained in that place for eleven hours, awaiting the return of our friend and the train which was to take us on to Vienna, and they were, without exception, the worst and the most distressing of the whole journey. When at last we were all five ready to board the train, it was nearly midnight. Joseph Conrad, our fellow-traveller and Borys stood at the very end of the long train, guarding the seats they had managed to retain for our little party. John, who had remained with me, opened very wide eyes indeed, and I felt him shrink closer to my side as we moved down the platform. A double row of Austrian Infantry drawn up at attention filled the whole of the space between the boy and myself and the three waiting anxiously at the end of that long vista. Their forms seemed misty and vague in the dim light. I had one hand on the small boy's shoulder and the other grasped my trusty stick. My consternation, when we issued from the station doors to see our way absolutely blocked by the double row of soldiers, is better imagined than described. The officer in charge was shouting orders to the men in German, his tones sufficiently menacing to my unaccustomed ears, yet when I glanced at the steep drop on to the railway line, which was to be my path to the goal at the end of that train, my heart sank into my boots. I stood a moment hesitating, then with what I intended as a most disarming smile, I began to walk down the middle of the double column of men. The officer stood still a moment then, his moustaches bristling, he stamped his feet and approached me angrily, protesting.

Clearly I was in the wrong, but I pointed to the railway line and indicated the stick in my hand. That did not in the least appease him, and he walked backwards in front of me, a stream of invective pouring from his lips, while he gesticulated wildly. I had never feared a soldier, and possibly my ignorance of what he was saying saved the situation. I continued to smile and proceeded to the end of the column. As I drew nearer the others, the expression on two of their faces made me realize that my passage had been an anxious moment for them both. "Good God, Jess, you have scared the life out of me. Anything might have happened. Didn't you remember that we are in an enemy country?" Poor Joseph Conrad gasped rather than said the words as he helped me into the train. A grip of the hand that he raised to his lips was the only comment our friend made, but one felt his sympathy and relief that the incident had passed off as well as it had. My husband later on explained in detail what a serious situation might have arisen for our helpful friend, if the officer had really made trouble. But I could afford to smile, the danger was past—and walking on the railway-line itself had appeared to me at the moment much the greater danger.

My first effort when we were at last in the train and it began to move was to induce John to lie on the seat and use my lap for a pillow, the other three sat on the seat facing me, huddled in various uncomfortable positions. The train was stripped of even the most elementary comforts or conveniences. The carriage and the corridor reeked of blood and phenol, alarm cords were disconnected and the cushions ripped from the seats. Straps had been torn from the windows and even the windows themselves were in many cases either cracked, broken or bodily removed. It was not an easy journey and we knew not what might happen after we got to Vienna. There was the grim possibility that our homeward journey might end there. It was intensely unpleasant to know that we should be under police supervision while we stayed in the city. I glanced across the carriage at our good friend and was reassured by his smile and the two words he had learnt in English, "Don't worry," while he kissed the tips of his fingers to me. I pondered for a long time wondering exactly how much power he had to help his distressed compatriot and his family. With great difficulty he had made me understand that if it were at all possible he intended to stay with us until we left Vienna. He was a host in himself and his name—as I soon found when at last we reached the hotel—was one to conjure with. It was a great shock to find when the train ran into the big station that our second trunk had been mislaid by some cruel mischance and my husband and our friend stayed a long time trying to locate its whereabouts. The two boys and I were despatched in a taxi in advance, and for the nonce my husband had evidently completely forgotten that neither the boys not I understood scarcely a word of Polish or German.

Fortunately I knew the name of the hotel and, as I have said, the name of our travelling companion was one with which to conjure. But beyond that, I was hopelessly at sea. I felt sure the two we had left at the station would have a bad time of it when they came to think. Meanwhile, I forebore to voice my anxiety, for I knew both boys were very tired and they could could do nothing to help me. We reached the hotel and by signs and many references to our good friend, I had got settled into our rooms and the boys had already indulged in much-needed baths and were ready for bed when Joseph Conrad arrived in a very worried condition. I really think he was as really surprised as relieved to find that we had reached our destination. We had a meal and prepared to retire. I say prepared, for that night it was a lengthy business. The bandage I had been wearing round my sick knee had cut so deeply into the swelling that I felt sick when I first removed it and the room then seemed to me insufferably hot. It had a stove let in the wall from the outside, you could not see the fire, and I could find no means of regulating the heat. The double windows were hermetically sealed, as far as I could judge, and had draught cushions laid along the openings. The two single beds stood some little distance apart and my consternation was considerable when Joseph Conrad announced while I was still trying to restore the circulation in my limb, that he felt a twinge of gout and must have a dose of his usual medicine prepared. I did not think I could force my limb to perform its allotted function and I felt for the first time faint and literally unable to move. A somewhat irritable repetition of his request roused me to action and I managed to mix the dose, and bandage the tender ankle. Almost before I had finished he was asleep, but I knew that I must not put out the light.

A book close at hand—any book—was an essential in case he might wake. When John—then a little over five—had been having a surfeit of scripture lessons I remember his father's exasperation on finding one of the boy's story books (a different one each night) laid on the bedside table. I had been puzzled by the child's persistence, for each time the book had been returned by his father to its home on the boy's own book-shelf. At last he told me that the local schoolmaster who was acting as tutor to him after school hours had told him that everyone should have a Bible by the side of his bed, and he had thought any one of his books would serve the same purpose. I glanced all around and noted that in place of the dressing-gown that was now lost somewhere in Austria, Joseph Conrad's overcoat hung behind the door. It was some time before I closed my eyes, and when I did I must have slept soundly. I woke suddenly and at once looked across the bed which I had last seen containing the thin figure in rather gaudy pyjamas. (These we had been forced to purchase because of the loss of our first trunk.) To my surprise, and I had almost said horror, that bed contained what looked from the distance a burly figure clad in dark brown. I gasped and trembled, for a moment I was incapable of action. There on the door hung the overcoat, but who was the stranger in place of my husband? I raised myself cautiously and at each movement my heart almost stood still with apprehension. I must be careful not to wake that person, whoever he might be. My intention was to get outside the room as quickly and quietly as possible, then to summon help and find Joseph Conrad.

I suspect my recent adventures had impressed themselves on my mind more than I had been aware at the time, for I was definitely scared stiff. I crept softly round the room, keeping as great a distance from the stranger as possible, and had almost reached the door when a startled exclamation in the familiar voice brought me up all standing (as a sailor would say) and the figure in the bed sat up with a short laugh and an irritable demand to know what all this "play acting" was about. I was past finding an excuse and to Conrad's consternation I burst into tears and it was some time before I could make him comprehend what had caused me to "play act" as he called it. When I came to examine him closer I found that he had been to the boys' room and annexed the Burberry because, incredible as it

ALFRED BORYS CONRAD KORZENIOWSKI ON OBTAINING HIS COMMISSION, 1916

IVY WALLS FARM, ESSEX, 1898

CAPEL HOUSE IN 1916, WITH CONRAD AND JOHN, AGED 10

appeared to me in the insufferable heat of that room, he had felt cold. For a moment I was tempted to remind him that only a couple of hours before he had declared it to be impossible for him to put his foot to the ground. He looked at me with a quizzical smile which I knew meant as plainly as words: "Do make me a glass of tea," and as I had the spirit-stove and everything needful in the room, I carried out his implied request as quickly as possible. Whilst he was contentedly smoking and drinking it I managed with great difficulty to throw open the window and I sat as close as possible to it, my head resting against the sill.

It was characteristic of Joseph Conrad that he should always go out of his way to meet trouble, and this morning he declared his conviction that we should soon find ourselves in some remote village, away from any friends or influence.

The day after my fright I was just in the middle of my morning toilet when our travelling companion came to the door of our room demanding instant admission. Hastily flinging on a dressing-gown, I admitted him, almost sick with apprehension. But his early visit was only intended to show his friendliness and to inquire how I had slept. He proposed that as my husband intended to stay in bed resting until such time as he was due to present himself at the office of the police, I should accompany him with the two boys on a short tour of inspection of the city. It was at once quite apparent that this suggestion did not meet with approval. The quick frown and curt direction I received to go as soon as possible and send some breakfast to the bedroom and the manner in which the offer was declined soon sent our friend away. I finished my dressing as speedily as possible, and went downstairs in quest of the food. With the exception of the few occasions on which he had to go to the police station, Joseph Conrad kept his bed for the eight or nine days we were in Vienna. Our good friend had evidently quite understood my husband's unwillingness to allow him to be my escort at any time and never repeated the invitation. One day I discovered a guide, a man who spoke every language under the sun sufficiently well to make him useful for all practical purposes, and having secured a taxi, accompanied by the two boys, I made a round of every railway station in Vienna until I found the trunk we had lost two months before in Cracow. The guide who was a typical "Don Q." in appearance—a little man with round cloak and hat—hopped about officiously and made my pose of a distressed American citizen very difficult to sustain. It had seemed to me to be essential to do nothing to annoy the officials or give them an opening for any antagonism, but I was desperately anxious to get possession of that trunk.

At last I was shown into a big warehouse and on the very top of a pile that reached to the lofty ceiling, lay the trunk. Those on the floor and for a long way upwards were squashed flat, their contents bulging out and having the pathetic appearance of wanton destruction. By the time I had secured the precious trunk and parted with the charge demanded by the custodian, the taxi fare had mounted alarmingly high. Old Don Q., who took the full credit for everything and spoke as if the recovery of our property had been due to his efforts alone, was a little difficult to satisfy in the matter of a tip. At last I managed to explain to him that we should need him again when we were ready to leave Vienna and that without doubt his good services would be remembered—and rewarded—more liberally on that occasion. Two or three days later we did indeed employ the old ruffian to find corners, or least least comfortable seats, Joseph Conrad had been having a bad time trying to get things arranged for crossing the frontier into Italy. Mr. Penfield, the American Ambassador, had done everything in his power, but he could get us no written permission—the most that could be done was a promise of assistance should we find our way stopped. "In that case send me a wire, using these words: 'short of cash,' and I will manage to get the permission through to you." Evidently there was some final pressure he was reluctant to bring to bear upon the authorities unless absolutely forced to do so. We knew that he was pretty certain that no difficulties would be raised, but my husband was in a more than usually distrustful mood that day and the worst seemed to him bound to happen.

The train was filled to overflowing with young officers and their belongings. One young man, evidently of considerable importance, had his mother with him for part of the journey, and one and all appeared very much to resent Joseph Conrad's irritability. His fear was that my knee might be knocked or hurt and he kept on trying to find some manner in which I could put my foot up out of harm's way. At last, when the occupants of the carriage seemed inclined to show their teeth, a curious chance put it in my power to render a slight service to the mother of the important young man. I saw her handbag slip from her knee on to the floor and with my most disarming smile I called attention to the fact, taking care not to move from my seat. In a second all was changed and the son, with a few words to his brother officers, cleared the carriage in the twinkling of an eye. They left us in possession of all the seats except that occupied by the lady. She moved to the door leading into the corridor where she still kept up an animated conversation with her son who stood just outside. In his relief Joseph Conrad closed his eyes and for a good hour slept peacefully in his corner. A sudden grinding of the brakes and the accompanying commotion of the greater portion of the travellers leaving the train, woke him with a start and he returned to his lamentations. These were uttered in such a long-suffering tone that a fresh traveller, a young officer—who seemed to have indulged a little freely—flung an insult in German across the carriage. I trembled for the result, although it was only by the tone I undertood an insult was intended. Some intuition must have made it plain to Joseph Conrad that a countryman of his own was speaking. In the next second they were clasping hands and exchanging facts that proved that the young man was the son of a landowner from the same province. He was greatly awed when he discovered that he was travelling with the great author, for Poland reverenced the name of my husband and the Korzeniowski family had been well known to our fellow-traveller.

A few stations farther on the youth, for he was little more, left the carriage with every gesture of homage and respect. Another man sprang into the carriage and removing his sword fell asleep immediately. I sat opposite him and once when he opened his eyes he caught my glance and such an appalling scowl spread over his pink and white countenance that I hastily looked through the window. But I felt my mouth twitching and I longed to laugh, only I could find no tangible excuse. I was really afraid to be amused by the sulky looking youth ; having the recollection of his predecessor, I could hardly hope that he, too, might come from the same province as my husband. A few seconds later we ran into a large station and my *vis-à-vis* hastily roused himself and left the carriage. Now came my opportunity. I stretched out my hand and touched him on the shoulder sharply. He swung round with the same appalling scowl, but I simply pointed to the sword he had forgotten, which still stood in the corner of the seat. Then I permitted myself to laugh outright, and he had the grace to smile and salute before he disappeared in the crowd.

The next big station we had to change, but for a friendly Hungarian I am convinced I should never have contrived to board the train. As it was I was gasping long after we had started and the man who had rendered me such signal service stood by looking rather anxious. Fortunately for me it was a corridor carriage, the dining-car next to ours, and my new friend quickly procured me a glass of water. Then, in my turn, I produced from my dressing-bag soap and a towel, and the men-folk gladly retired and had a much-needed wash. I was a little dismayed when I saw the state of the towel when they returned, and my toilet had to be very elementary. The Hungarian proved very interesting and he travelled with us as far as Milan. He was hoping to get back to his destination on a Chinese Station. He had got to the Austrian frontier once before and had been sent back because some paper or other was not quite in order. There was once chance in a hundred that he would accomplish his journey, but if he did he promised to write to us. We never heard any more of him.

In Milan I had the first opportunity of unpacking that trunk of wet clothes, and the pile of washing was truly appalling. Baths were the most expensive luxury and as usual Joseph Conrad, who had a passion for doing contrary things, must have one, if not two, in the day. One of his most outstanding characteristics was a habit of doing the very thing you would—quite reasonably—wish him not to do, even when he must have known very well that what he did would cost him both money and inconvenience. I had only to remind him that he had left one electric light burning, for him to fly down the stairs and put on every light in the house. I grew wise at last and would never call his attention to the fact, only when able to do so, creeping down the stairs myself to extinguish them when he had retired.

The eight or nine days we spent in Milan were days of relief, for it was only when we reached this stage of our homeward journey that we were able to get real news of our friends and of England, not from a German source. From Milan we proceded to Genoa there to wait for a passage to England. We received our first letters in Italy and it was over a week before we left on the last stage of our homeward journey. During the week's sea trip Joseph Conrad grew more and more lame. He was evidently feeling the result of the long strain. One day he decided to seek the advice of the ship's doctor. As so often happened, he unloaded his symptoms on the first man he met, who listened gravely and then remarked concernedly : " I should consult the doctor, sir, if I were you." The mistake disturbed the invalid not a little, but his next venture was still too impulsive. This man was apparently in a hurry : " Pardon me, sir, I am the purser, the doctor is below."

By this time Joseph Conrad was discouraged and instead of asking again for the doctor he retired to his cabin in high dudgeon. Then he sent for me and instructed me to find the " blamed " man, and see to it that he was the doctor.

But the day we reached the Thames was the worst of the voyage. We were all shepherded into one of the main saloons and confronted by a most formidable body of interpreters, who spoke all languages, and subjected one and all to the most severe scrutiny. One or two of the passengers were invited to retire for the purpose of being searched and followed the men or women detailed for that duty greatly discomforted. Suddenly one of our inquisitors turned to me and said sharply in English : " Mrs. Conrad ? " I assented calmly, but the next moment my heart leaped into my mouth, and I remembered some letters and papers I had concealed in the neck of my dress. "You have letters for a Mrs. Gielgud?" I gasped with relief while my husband made a startled movement towards me. I dived into my bag and produced a letter of introduction to Mrs. Terry Gielgud. This seemed to satisfy the good man, and I thankfully made my way out of the saloon. I did not then confess to Joseph Conrad that I had other letters and even a newspaper article which had been entrusted to my care. It had been written by some young girl from the confines of a Russian prison. I dared not think what might have been the result if those papers had been discovered. But I determined that my first task when once I got to town should be to deliver the papers. To this day I have puzzled my brains as to how my questioner had discovered that I had letters for anyone of the name he had given.

CHAPTER SIXTEEN

OUR arrival in the Thames, just below the pontoon-bridge which showed up plainly in the bright moonlight, seemed to mark a fresh stage in the long and tiring journey that had taken just two days less than two months. November 3rd, 1914, was the day we arrived. The big steamer lay in mid-stream, while a fussy little tender lay alongside waiting to transport passengers and their baggage to the quay at Tilbury. Our luggage, the whole of it, everything we had taken with us, had been amongst the first to be placed on the tender. Then for some unaccountable reason it was all carted back for some further formality. There were a good many passengers and all were extremely anxious to get ashore. Exasperated beyond all endurance and very much resenting the extra scrutiny as a personal afront, Joseph Conrad became quite incoherent when demanding an explanation. Then he almost spoilt everything by declaring that the damned stuff could be left altogether—this after my almost superhuman efforts to preserve it intact.

I was forced to laugh even under these trying circumstances when a lady, a fellow-passenger, turned to me greatly irate, and said in a shrill, penetrating tone: "Look at that excitable old gentleman, a foreigner, making all that fuss about his luggage." I turned to her, keeping my face as straight as possible: "Madam. that excitable old gentleman, as you please to call him, is my husband." "Then for goodness sake calm him down if you can, he is wasting time kicking up all that fuss. He won't get attended to any sooner. Or let him get away and leave your beastly luggage behind altogether." At last we were allowed to go, and my feeling of quiet satisfaction, I fear, showed rather plainly on my face when it was discovered that the disagreeable lady's own luggage was short by two cases. I permitted myself a smile as I remarked audibly: "One has to make a fuss at the time, after all."

When we arrived at Fenchurch Street Station my husband's nerves were so frayed that he absolutely refused to negotiate with the luggage porter for my transport down in the luggage-lift. I was incapable of attempting to descend the interminable flight of steps to the street level. "Do it yourself, my dear, a word from you will be much more effective than an hour's speech from me," was all I could get out of him.

He was by this time so worked up by the difficulties of finishing the journey that he was almost exhausted and I was thankful when we reached the hotel—the Norfolk Hotel, Surrey Street, where we were known—and I persuaded him to go straight to bed.

It was by this time well after nine, and although the possession of those letters and papers worried me, and I longed to deliver them to their destination, I had the sense to see that I must await my opportunity if I did not wish to give a full explanation of the matter, and caution urged me to keep my own counsel. I waited until some of our many friends in town had heard of our safe arrival and I could leave my sorely tried partner with some one of them. It was past six the next evening before I got my chance. The understanding was that I was going to deliver in person the letter of introduction to Mrs. Terry Gielgud. Joseph Conrad sent many warm messages to her, for we had known her husband's parents and many of her relations in Zakopane. I managed to get rid of the other letters first, also the article. I breathed a sigh of relief when it was out of my possession. By this time I had realized a little of the risk I had run.

The next morning I was busy arranging for our transport by car to Capel House when James B. Pinker sent word that he wished to see my husband and that he had Edmund Candler with him. Joseph Conrad's excitement was intense. "The one and only Edmund, Jess. Clear out all that paper and stuff, never mind anything else. Come back presently, any time, never mind I say. Let them in."

I smiled to myself and left the room, but I completed the arrangements on my own, and when we met again I was able to tell him that everything was ready for our return home the next day. I had wired for the old retainer we had left behind and I had been able to provision the "ship" by letter from the hotel. The next day saw us on the road.

On the journey, our old maid-servant, who had joined us in town, gave us details of the extraordinary kindness and generosity of Sir David and Lady Wilson-Barker, who had indeed shown a more than Christian spirit. He was at that time Captain of the training-ship *Worcester*, where Borys had spent part of his school-days. There had been a warm friendship between us. These two friends had sought out our maid and paid her wages all the time we were away. They had, moreover, made themselves responsible for the rent of the house for the whole of our absence—even had we been, as we feared, detained till the end of the war. How nearly that was the case we knew soon afterwards when Mr. Penfield explained his embarrassment as to our crossing from Austria into Italy. We had just slipped through by the greatest good chance.

When we arrived at Capel House late that afternoon, its familiarity and its peaceful surroundings made the idea of the terrible strife appear like a fantastic dream. It was only later, with the ceaseless passage of troops past the house, that the truth came home to us in grim earnest.

Everyone we knew, with hardly an exception, was in training. Sons of old friends would appear either full of importance and optimistic or the reverse. For all one had that feeling of pity and anxiety.

One evening soon after our return a big Zeppelin passed so low over the house that I could distinctly see the heads of men leaning out of the gondolas. For a time it remained above us, nosing about for Ashford Railway Station. Capel House stood right in the fair-way and every raid passed over us coming and going. So little were we impressed by the fact that here was death hovering only a little above us, that Borys quite unconcernedly suggested getting the car out, in order to get to the nearest post-office to get them to telephone through to warn Ashford, our nearest big town. How soon was this indifference to be turned into terror, and the fact borne in upon us that a war—and a very fierce and nasty war—was going on all round us.

About this time we made many new friends and renewed old friendships. The war seemed to have dislodged people so very thoroughly, and brought many distant friends into the most unexpected close contact, some of whom one had not seen or heard of for many years.

Among the new friends we made during the years immediately preceding and following the Great War, taken in order of their appearance on our horizon, I think the following are easily the most outstanding. In 1912 Richard Curle first came to the house and this acquaintance began through an article he had written for a (now defunct) periodical called *Rhythm*. And his unstinted praise for a book my husband had written and had a great affection for, cemented a friendship from the first. A friendship that was to be as close as is usually supposed to be possible only between blood relations. And it was Edward Garnett who brought the article to the notice of Joseph Conrad. His delight is best expressed in his own words which were contained in a letter written to Richard Curle as follows :

" That criticism is something and no mistake. All that went before seems mere verbiage in comparison "—and Joseph Conrad expressed his eagerness to meet his critic. And this first meeting took place in the restaurant " Mont Blanc " in Gerrard Street. It was a meeting place for many of our friends among whom were the following: W. H. Hudson, Edward Thomas, Perceval Gibbon, Stephen Reynolds, Norman Douglas and many others. The other friends of this period were M. Jean Aubry, Major Gordon Gardiner, Sir Ralph Wedgwood and Lady Wedgwood ; Sir James Lithgow, and last but not least, Hugh Walpole. I quote from a letter I came across this morning written to me from Iowa in 1930. This passage means so much as showing how true friendship endures, even at a great distance both as to time and place. Mr. Walpole writes hurriedly, excusing himself for his use of the hotel note-paper, and explaining how constantly he is on the move. And speaks of his hope of one day retiring to his fastness in Cumberland, where he need see nothing more exciting than a shepherd and his dog. He ends up with the warm-hearted remark, underlined: "Of course my friendly feelings never change. I seem just now to be involved in so many things, but that will pass. . . ."

I remember so many occasions when he made week-end visits to us both in Capel House, and afterwards in Bishopsbourne. Many visits, too, that he made to me in the Nursing Home. And one occasion when he came to see me and told me of some friend who might like to have some baby shoes I had been making. He did, in fact, pick several pairs out of the drawer, and carry them off in his pocket. The sequel to that was his omission to mention the matter to his man-servant, who subsequently found them in his coat pocket, and must have been greatly puzzled.

There is a short biography written by Hugh Walpole and dedicated by him to a man who was a very dear and valued friend of both of us: Sir Sidney Colvin, in 1918. My husband was very pleased with his book, and the copy I have by me is marked with sentences written by him in the margin, testifying to his pleasure and satisfaction.

The Last Twelve Years of Joseph Conrad, by Richard Curle, bears Hugh Walpole's name on the dedication page, and proves the fact that these two met first in our house. Further facts and happenings belong to a later part of these recollections.

As soon as Borys was seventeen he joined up and a new phase of horror began for me and for his father. Neither of us would have said a word to deter the boy from serving his country, but as his mother, I plead guilty to the wish that he should wait awhile. And to the sneaking hope that hostilities might be over before my son should have an active part in them I should have felt an overbearing shame had he even appeared to hang back, but I could never understand the woman who could lament that she had no *son to give to the war*. Only wives and parents, and in a lesser degree, sisters, could know the terrible dread and the anguish of those awful four years of war.

It was due to that old friend Mr. Cunninghame Graham that the boy obtained his commission. I felt certain that apart from the dreadful apprehension his father felt, there was also a great feeling of pride that his son should risk his life with others of his age and station. The wording of the dedication of the *Shadow Line*: "To Borys and All Others who like himself have crossed in early youth the shadow-line of their generation. With Love."

Very many friends and acquaintances misread those words and forbore to write fearing the shadow-line must mean the shadow of death. I pointed out the possibility of such a misunderstanding to Joseph Conrad, but he was set on just that phrase and would not alter a word. He agreed afterwards that I had been right. It is a beautiful dedication and if it were to me, I should treasure it very highly.

On the day on which Borys received his commission, together with his first cheque book, the two, father and son, were coming home from town in an ancient Ford, Borys driving. I heard the vivid story of that drive from Borys, who has all his father's power of picturesque exaggeration. Still, the mental picture was certainly very dramatic. It had been a wet day and the road was very slippery in consequence. Coming down the long hill into Farningham the car skidded and turned completely round, hitting a gate-post hard enough to snap it clean off.

The car had made three complete backward circles before finally coming to rest facing the way it had come. Before it was actually stopped Joseph Conrad was out and Borys in amazement beheld him already bowing low before two flag-sellers on the opposite side of the road, with the familiar flourish of his arms and military click of his heels. The two girls' faces were very pale, they had seen the car strike the post and its subsequent performance, revolving round and round. They were greatly surprised when one of the occupants appeared before them in such a gallant fashion.

That Ford, shabby and much damaged by hard usage, figured in yet another adventure that might have been very serious a few days afterwards. This time a hired man was driving, and he was greatly impressed by the fact that he was driving Joseph Conrad. Most men from that garage were impressed if my husband happened to be their passenger. He had rather the habit of reducing their nerves to a thread by a show of harmless ferocity if the slightest thing happened to upset him. In this case the man had called forth a sharp rebuke for standing in too close to the kerb, and was very nervous in consequence. He swerved suddenly, struck an old man who was crossing the road, and scattered his parcels all over the roadway. Then, completely losing his head, struck the kerb with his offside front wheel and tipped his passengers on to the side-walk, a few inches from the church wall. He followed himself helplessly as the car turned over and then being very high on its wheels, righted itself and went off driverless down the road. Borys, who was the first to regain his feet, chased the runaway and caught it just before it did further damage against a car drawn up on the side of the road.

Numerous soldiers who were close by picked up the old man, and assisted my husband back into the car. The old man they had knocked down was taken to hospital and the rescuers in their zeal placed all his parcels in the Ford. I discovered amongst the parcels of grocery, etc., which belonged to us, one extra that for some time puzzled us all very much. It was not, in fact, until I called to enquire for the injured man at the hospital that we discovered that in addition to knocking him down we had unintentionally robbed the poor old fellow of a coloured shirt, some socks, and a pair of braces, the contents of his parcel. The zealous soldiers must have placed the parcel in the car when they retrieved ours.

Only a short year after the boy had joined up he was sent to France and more than a year passed before I saw him again. About this time we received a letter from a very mysterious and attractive American girl who wished to visit us on an introduction from our friend Lord Northcliffe. Her letter arrived on a bad day, a day immediately preceding a bad attack of gout. Had it not been so, I am sure that the bare fact that Lord Northcliffe sponsored her would have been enough to induce my husband to admit anyone. We had both of us a very sincere admiration and personal liking for the man. But as I have said, the time was ill-chosen and Joseph Conrad wrote to Miss A —— declining courteously to receive her on the grounds of ill-health.

But here a curious coincidence intervened. An American artist, Mr. Joe Davidson, had made a portrait bust of my husband which was to be on view in London, and in due course we received cards for the private view. My husband, still true to his pose of ill health, decided that I must go to town alone to see it. An American lady friend, Mrs. Grace Willard, who had in fact introduced the artist to our house, offered to meet me and also accepted an invitation from Mr. Davidson for lunch in my name. This lunch was to be at the Café Royal.

For me the journey to town by myself had all the elements of a great adventure, for I seldom went anywhere alone, as I was even then very lame. But on the promise that I should be met at Charing Cross I ventured up. Instead of the familiar friendly face of "Mama Grace," as we affectionately called her, the only persons I saw who could be awaiting me at the station turned out to be a tiny, doll-like creature, my friend's secretary, and the biggest member of the police force I had ever seen. The enormous minion of the law paced beside us down the long platform, the secretary looking smaller than ever by force of contrast. I was so much taken aback by his presence and so much at a loss to understand the need for this attendant that I forgot to show my appreciation in the most welcome and tangible form. It was only as the taxi moved away leaving our escort on the kerb, that I noticed his disappointed countenance.

Some five or six guests lunched with us, and afterwards we broke up into parties and proceeded by taxis to the picture gallery. Here, after I had viewed the bust, whose most striking resemblance to Joseph Conrad, was the back of the head, the face is too much fore-shortened, although I have seen my husband's face wear such an expression, I was introduced to Mr. Voynich, and he I have since learned suggested to my husband the character of Vladimir in the *Secret Agent*. I met also another American, who was very charming, and who told me that he was flying over to France. When he heard I had a son over there he offered to take any special message I might have to send him.

This offer I repeated to Joseph Conrad when I returned and the upshot of it was that we wired him an invitation to come down for lunch the following Sunday. It was at once accepted if we could allow him to bring a young lady with him, who had been going to lunch with him before he received our invitation.

The moment they entered the house, and almost before he introduced her by the name of Miss A——, I had guessed the identity of our visitor. I was both amused and apprehensive, for my husband was somewhat difficult to appease if he considered he had been affronted in any way, and judging by the very great impression the lady appeared to have made upon her host, I judged it well for the moment to keep my own counsel. It was well on in the afternoon before the lady herself deliberately let the cat out of the bag.

Miss A——'s next visit was with Lord Northcliffe himself, who brought her down for lunch.

Lord Northcliffe came many times alone after that particular visit. His great affection for his mother was a great bond between us. He has talked of her by the hour and every time he had some fresh story of her love and devotion, of which he showed himself very deeply sensible. He was very kind to our small boy, John, too. Once he placed a sum of money with a model maker and John's great delight was to spend against it.

One Sunday Miss A—— was staying with us and a French Red Cross officer and his wife came down to lunch. I watched the little comedy in a detached fashion and had further food for reflection. Our American friend was at once aware of the Frenchman's interest—and incidentally so was his wife. Miss A—— seated herself before the fire like an idol. M. Paul Vance immediately seized a pair of tall vases full of flowers and solemnly placed them before the figure on the rug, making at the same time a deep obeisance. There was a sniff of disgust on the part of the wife and a rather vexed laugh from Joseph Conrad, who at once held out his hand to assist his guest to rise, and upset both vases in the process.

Lord Northcliffe by now was quite a frequent visitor. He would appear for lunch with baskets of wonderful fruit—declaring he had gathered the grapes with his own fair hands—spend a long afternoon seated in the garden and telling me of his mother. He was never tired of that subject, and it is one I could listen to all day. Meanwhile he had lent his Rolls-Royce and good-natured chauffeur to the boys, Norman Douglas's youngest son and John, who would career round the countryside for an hour or so.

Lord Northcliffe was always exceedingly kind to me. He once offered me the loan of his house in St. Peter's when I was beginning to recover from an operation. It was there during a call that we met Mr. Wickham Steed and the New York correspondent, Mr. Bullock. And last, but not least, Mr. Scott Moncrieff, whose wonderful translation of *Swan's Way* was such a delight to Joseph Conrad. The last direct communication we had from Lord Northcliffe was a cable from Newfoundland, where he had a large hospital for his workpeople—paper-makers. It was addressed to me, and contained a very kindly and courteous enquiry as to my health, and the hope that he would soon again be sitting in the garden talking to Joseph Conrad and to me. Also a special reference to his young friend John.

Borys was in France a month after his eighteenth birthday and a year and some odd months which passed before he got any leave were filled with dread and apprehension. Only very rare letters reached us and news was very scarce and scrappy. Field cards are not much, but at least brought some little comfort. Meanwhile, people came and went, some never to come again, others to return wounded, blinded or even worse with their minds terribly distorted and their affections blunted as a result of the horrors they had witnessed.

It must have been some time in 1918 that we first had Hugh Walpole under our roof. He came often in those days. His cheery presence and ready sympathy made him a delightful friend and welcome visitor. No trouble was ever too great for him to undertake in the interests of friendship, and he kept his belief in the goodness of human nature, long after he might have been justified in doubting it. He was a true philanthropist and I suppose must have got a certain amount of satisfaction from his generosity. That is a form of reward that is greater than mere gratitude.

I have been told that during the war, there was in a V.A.D. hospital in France a wounded hero who indulged in a flight of fancy and amused himself in giving copies of Hugh Walpole's books signed by himself as the author, to all and sundry. In time, he was, of course, unmasked. When the real author was told he made the characteristic remark: " Perhaps he is more proud of them than I am."

It was after Borys's first leave that Joseph Conrad felt the urge to take up some active work in connection with the war. I suppose this was only natural, for it was difficult to settle down to writing in those times of stress and strife. The sole topic was war, the one great dread and fear that the next victim might be one's own husband, brother or son.

Several times during the early months of 1916 my husband made tentative attempts to do something active, and great was his satisfaction when the Admiralty sent him to Dover, and other ports on the East Coast in an official capacity. I used to watch that ancient Ford, our car at the time, leave the front door, with apprehension, and spent anxious hours before the horn sounded its usual impatient toot, which heralded its return. We had a curious echo, a single voice would carry clearly from a distance of over two miles by road, and I heard the note of that horn plainly long before the " machine " turned in at the gate. Long enough to have hot coffee, or a repast of some sort ready on the table. He would always return tired and nervous, and generally two more days would elapse before he made another journey. I tried to persuade him to take someone with him, the youthful chauffeur even, for fear of a flat tyre, but always to no purpose.

Between these excursions many letters got themselves written and I include one written to F. M. H. who had begged the loan of an old pair of binoculars that had belonged to the sea-faring days. As Joseph Conrad points out, they would not be much use on active service:

. . . " I answer at once the question of glasses. The pair you may remember knocking about at the Pent has in the process of time (and by some help from John's hand) dissolved into its primitive elements. But even if these glasses had been still in existence they would not have been good enough for your purpose. They were my watchkeeping glasses, just sufficiently powerful to pick up a ship's lights at night. You would want something much more efficient.

" You won't be surprised to hear that you have been much in my thoughts of late. It must have been an enormous change in your mental habits; but I know your wonderful intellectual adaptability and your letter, most welcome, is very much what I expected it to be.

" Yes: *mon cher!* our world of 15 years ago is gone to pieces; what will come in its place, God knows, but I imagine doesn't care.

" Still what I always said was the only immortal line in

Romance; 'Excellency,' a few goats, survives—esoteric, symbolic, profound and comic—it survives. . . ."

This extract shows that my husband had a really high opinion of the intelligence of his one-time collaborator, and also a great affection for the child of their joint fabrication, *Romance.*

There is also this extract from a letter written in 1916 to the Editor of the *Sydney Bulletin.*

It begins: "Why apologize; it is always a pleasure to hear from Sydney, the town of my youthful affection—not to mention the *Bulletin*, where the Torch of Letters has been kept burning at the Antipodes for so many years.

"My Frenchman without hands I knew in December, 1878. He kept a small tobacco shop in George Street, not very far from Circular Quay. Both his hands were gone. He was then 75, if a day, and didn't look like a man who would live long. He used to spin long, Melanesian yarns, but he was not very interesting—except for the pent up store of energy one was aware of in that maimed body. For all I knew he *might* have been the model of all the virtues—but I doubt if this accident then was not very recent; the stumps were always neatly bandaged; there was no question of any hook or mechanical contrivance. I am sure he was not M. Pierre of your correspondents.

"Apart from the physical appearance, everything about him in the story is 'all same one piecie lie.' . . ."

This extract is interesting as showing how slender a fact might be that the story-teller could hang a story upon. There had to be always some slight truth as to a personal experience, but so much had but the smallest truth as to a real happening, at least to him personally.

It was about this time that Edward Thomas made his last visit to us on his way back to the front. I had seldom seen this Welshman apart from that other, Perceval Gibbon, whose dominating personality instead of dwarfing the other's slow quietness, seemed only to throw it into sharper relief. On this occasion Edward Thomas, of all those men present in our home that night, seemed to be marked out for some special enmity of a cruel fate. His calm was ominous and hopeless, yet with all he was not by any means dismal or dull. He stayed that night and remained sitting late into the night talking of every subject except one, the cause for his change of garb, from loose-fitting rough tweed and flowing pinkish-red tie. His khaki was worn without ostentation, but correct in every detail.

A few days later my husband was travelling down from town with a friend. They occupied two of the corner-seats and in a few moments two more acquaintances boarded the train and their friendly greetings were hardly over when the door of the carriage opened to admit the fifth. Edward Thomas, for it was he, subsided into his seat without haste and turning, addressed my husband: "So we meet, at least once more, my dear Conrad." The words once more struck on the ear of the others with an ominous ring of finality. None of them continued to speak, and the animated discussion that had but just started died out in utter silence. When they parted with just a handshake, and no word of farewell, all watched the doomed figure wending its way down the long platform and disappear from sight. Three days afterwards we heard that he was dead. But there was no sign of a wound anywhere. It was indeed only "once more."

It was a few days later when certain papers having been completed, Joseph Conrad made his final preparations to leave me alone and fulfil his undertaking. October, '16, became a memorable month in those four years of horror. Even now, reading the letter my husband had written to his friend J. B. Pinker, I feel a catch in my breath. This letter I knew nothing of at the time. I was simply to stay and wait for his return, and I had only the general feeling of apprehension because of my ignorance of the extent of his proposed adventure. This is best told in his own words:

"MY DEAR PINKER,

"The expenses of hotels amount to more than £15, you will find here the slip with the exact amount and the receipted bills.

"I enclose here for your edification the letter from Sir Douglas Brownrigg. He's a good fellow. Hurrah! So that's settled. I am going—you know on that errand. Should the ship fail to report herself for more than ten days after the time fixed for her return (by wireless)—at night there will be no use hoping for her return. I shall ask Ad: Startin to communicate with you then.

"I have no nearer friend on whom I could lay the painful task. I believe I have your approval; Borys isn't likely to be angry with my memory; Jessie understands and John knows nothing of course. As to these last I know you will do all you can to make their fate as tolerable as it can be made.

"That much had to be said, tho' don't imagine I have gloomy forebodings, nothing of the kind. Still it is no use ignoring the fact that the vessel has made three trips already and she may have been spotted. Also there are spies about. The prospect of an expedition of this sort gives a curious force to the idea of spies. It drives home to one's conviction that they do exist. Our service is pretty good too. The raid before last was noted to the Granton command 10 hours before the *Zepps started* from

Germany. This is fairly smart work. I shall see you next week early, as I may get 'the call' towards the end of it."

The first intimation I had of this expedition was contained in a letter written from Granton the day before my husband was due to go on this dangerous service. I had barely time to catch the post for him to be sure of receiving my letter before he left. I felt a great temptation to beg him not to go, and fearful that my desire would get the better of me, I sent him a long wire, urging him to be careful not to take cold.

This injunction, I heard afterwards, provoked much merriment when read out at the breakfast-table. But it had the effect also of inducing him to go into the town and purchase a thick jersey.

CHAPTER SEVENTEEN

THE twelve days that followed were each surely twenty-four hours twice over; I lived in terror, and I was ill at the time. I had only John with me and the old maid who seemed to be more feeble-witted than ever. My one friend at that time was Doctor Atkinson, who came as often as his big practice would allow him, cheering me by every means in his power.

All that time I had one or two scrappy lines from Joseph Conrad posted by the greatest difficulty, and secretly. No word the whole time from Borys in France. And to crown my anxiety John took it into his head one afternoon to disappear with his bicycle for several hours, an unheard of thing, as usually he stayed close by my side. Some tradesman saw him miles from home and brought him back. I was so relieved that I forbore to rebuke the boy, and only extracted a solemn promise from him that he would not go away again.

During the time that the boy and I were alone together he tried to fill the place of his father, and brother, most faithfully. He was always at hand, never leaving me for more than half an hour at a time. His chief activity at this time was gathering big baskets of apples and cycling with them to the end of the road where the various troops were generally to be found at midday eating their rations. The boy and his machine were a welcome sight to the thirsty men, and the fruit was greatly appreciated.

Then came the day when the wire came announcing Joseph Conrad's return. Hours of waiting at Ashford station, and the return to the house, in disappointed anxiety. Four hours later another wire from town giving the time of a very late train, with directions to await him at home. When he arrived just before midnight, I could see that he was nearly exhausted and in a state of terrific excitement.

For some time he paced to and fro the room, flinging his hands out dramatically, but without giving any explanation as to his delay or why he could not settle down to eat anything. He was, indeed, so unlike himself that I was becoming alarmed. I had heated his soup twice before he suddenly began to eat ravenously, and immediately afterwards resumed his restless pacing to and fro.

When he had finished everything on the tray I felt emboldened to suggest that he must be very tired. At this he turned and then flung himself into his chair, lighting his cigarette with trembling fingers.

I waited patiently, too excited to feel fatigue, and rather reluctantly at last retired to bed. All he had said was: "You go to bed, Jess, I will be there in half an hour or so."

It was not until the third or fourth day after his return that I learned the real reason for his intense excitement, and then not directly from him. I was startled one day when a policeman appeared and quietly but very firmly, demanded to see my husband without delay.

He had perforce to wait some few moments, for Joseph Conrad had been in bed ever since his return. I sensed some difficulty, but not what was actually to happen.

The officer rose as we came into the room, and at once produced a formidable looking paper and began: "You are Mr. Joseph Conrad?" A nod was the only answer. The man cleared his throat and proceeded: "You were instructed to forward your private papers to the Police Office in Ashford, up to the time I left this morning we had not received them, I must ask you to produce them at once."

I looked from one to the other. It was the first I had heard of any trouble with regard to private papers. Then I indeed felt a glow of pride. Those precious papers that I had so patiently patched and mended on our honeymoon, when I had found them literally in strips, soaked many years before with sea-water, and crumpled amost out of all recognition. I came forward eagerly: "Oh they are in the care of the Bank of London, but I will write at once for them, and let you have them as soon as I receive them, meanwhile, I can show you Sir Edward's (Lord Grey's) passport we had when we went to Poland in 1914."

The man took it civilly enough and pored over it for a few seconds, and then said: "That is in order, but I must have the original private papers, at least the Naturalization paper, within two days. Pray attend to it." He took up his helmet and left the room and the house.

I turned questionally to my husband, who began immediately to explain at length, in a quiet, rather subdued tone.

"You see, Jess, when Commander Sutherland signalled to those drifters that he wanted to put a sick man ashore and they landed me at Bridlington—I hadn't gone a dozen yards before I was stopped, arrested in fact, and taken to the police station. I wasn't detained very long, only long enough to lose my connection, dam' it, and I forgot all about the blamed papers. Thought they were here in the house, in fact." I smiled: "You sent them to the Bank yourself when you knew you were going away three weeks ago, dear. But it will be all right, if you send them in two days' time. Better write now, shall I type a letter for you to sign?"

When the precious packet arrived within the specified time, I decided to take them to Ashford myself. There were continous raids over the town and I had now a very clear idea of the importance of those documents I had tended so carefully so many years before. I announced my intention only after the car was waiting at the door, thus leaving little time for any argument, for or against.

This turned out to be quite a little adventure. When I arrived at the police station, the Superintendent was out and his understudy was busy shaving himself. He appeared in answer to my urgent summons with one side of his face still covered with soap, and somewhat shortly told me I could leave the papers on the table.

Greatly daring, this I refused to do. It was sheer bluff, for I had no knowledge whether or not I might be running foul of the law. Fortunately for me, the man was disposed to be obliging, and excusing himself for a few moments, retired to finish his shave. Those moments seemed hours, for I began to have some anxious qualms, and sat shivering by the side of the fire. However, my friend of the soapsuds reappeared in due course, and laboriously waded through what papers he could read. The foreign ones he seemed very glad to pass over with only a cursory glance, and accepted what explanation I was able to offer as to their meaning. Altogether he appeared rather pleased that I had remained instead of obeying his mandate and leaving my precious papers on his office table.

Joseph Conrad's impatience when I got back and he met me half-way down the drive, was as usual quite out of proportion. But with a little judicious management I coaxed him into a calmer state of mind, and in the end he laughed heartily at my description of my interview at the police station. "You women will do anything," was his final comment as he disappeared into his study.

Not very long after this rather trying episode, our American friend paid us a rather long visit. She had been ill in London, following some extra activity. There was so much she had seen of the horrors of the war, and under circumstances few women, other than those engaged as nurses, could have dreamt of. She had made a passage across the Channel in a hospital ship, been present at least once very close to where a German machine had come down in flames.

Her own story of this incident was that she heavily bribed a taxi-man to drive her to Cuffly, following the track of the fated 'plane. She had made many flights and been to and from Paris. She told one tale of when she was lunching in Paris and artlessly asked: "What is the difference between lobster and *homard*," and the quick reply from the waiter standing just behind her: "Exactly thirty francs, madame."

When she came to us after a spell of these adventures she spent a month practically in bed. Her nerves were decidedly ragged, and she made an interesting invalid. There was not much done in the matter of writing, but there was a decided interest for us both accruing from that prolonged visitation.

First of all, she was very intelligent and amusing, even when she was most indolent. For the month she showed herself sympathetic to our anxiety on Borys' account. It was just then that his letters and field cards were so far apart. I remember in particular one night I came into the room just in time to hear her declare her intention of looking the boy up when she next went to Paris. And I brought myself up short, when I heard the short, terse tone in which Joseph Conrad replied: "None of that, you let the boy alone."

A few days later saw the departure of our guest, and the promise, quite eagerly given by my husband, to meet her for lunch in a day or so in town. His next activities were in course of preparation, and during his absence I was to take John to Folkestone to recover from a feverish cold that had left him weak and languid. It was arranged that our American friend should join us there for a week or ten days. She was very fond of the boy, and he of her, and as I have said, I was sufficiently interested in her to be glad of her company, and anything was better than having no one to talk to.

CHAPTER EIGHTEEN

I MANAGED to argue myself into a curiously detached mood on my way to the station, and I had myself well in hand by the time the train ran into the station, a little late. I had noticed my husband looking eagerly out of a carriage window well in the fore part of the train, and I missed his wave of the hand as he passed the place where I stood, although I was sure he had seen me. It seemed an age before I made out the well-known figure coming towards me, preceded by the obsequious porter carrying an armful of literature, a new model engine for the boy and some chocolates. He had hardly come within speaking distance when he asked: "Where is your stable-companion?"

I was quite unprepared for this question and he had time to repeat it in a decidedly irritable tone before I recovered myself. Fortunately, John had by this time received his parcel and the two, father and son were locked in a close embrace. I managed to say: "She did not come with me," and in my turn received my greeting.

Joseph Conrad turned to walk by my side, and I caught a disappointed expression on his face. For the life of me I could not have spoken just then. In silence he put up his stick to hail a taxi, and then said in a tone of stern disapproval: "Have you nothing to say?" At this I stopped short and said quietly: "A great deal, but I do not think this is the proper place, I had intended to say nothing, it hardly seems worth while." "What on earth do you mean?" The hand he laid on my arm was by no means gentle, and I began to feel really angry, it was rather like adding insult to injury. Then he went on: "I don't understand you at all. You had my message when I went to Lowestoft, and you must have seen and read my wires. I kept you posted up all the time."

This way of receiving my magnanimity, for I was very conscious of my efforts to be generous, and indulgent to the little back-sliding, struck me as overstepping the bounds of endurance, and I bit my lip in silence. This provoked a stream of hurried words in which he wished he had not come to Folkestone, or even survived his recent experiences. "My flight was every bit as dangerous as any other observer's might have been, and yet you greet me like this. I am disappointed in you, very disappointed." "Your flight—of fancy? do you mean. I heard a great deal about that, but she told me she had destroyed the letter, and we will say no more about it, but I don't think I want her to stay with us any longer—at least not at present."

His face still wore a puzzled expression and he flung himself back in the corner of the taxi and tossed his cigarette through the window unsmoked. For a few moments there was silence, then he said very quietly: "You have been so reasonable before and a real sport, I had no idea you would have taken my flying in such a tragic manner?" I interrupted him quickly: "Flying, what do you mean? It is the first I have heard about it. This is really a bit too much, you said you had had my message. I sent the wire directly we got out of the machine." A light fell on the situation, and almost in a flash I saw that our fair American had been amusing herself at my expense. The seriousness of that deliberate attempt to spoil our long understanding affection had probably never struck her and more than likely would not have troubled her if it had. Something of this I made Joseph Conrad understand before we reached the hotel. I was not present when the first interview took place, but I gathered that it had been more than a little stormy. We stayed two days longer at Folkestone, and when we left our lady friend elected to return to town. One curious thing might be said in extenuation and that which possibly originated the idea in the lady's mind in the first place, came into my hands after the war. I was packing some books which was all that I could do towards helping the preparations for the move. I had the piles brought to the side of my bed and the cases put within my reach. We were obliged to store these books while we lived in Captain Halsey's house, Spring Grove, Wye, and during my task of sorting the volumes I dropped one and a letter fluttered on to the floor out of my reach.

The last book placed in its case, and I rested a few moments while my gaze fell on the letter lying tantalizingly just clear of my reach with my stick. I saw that it was undoubtedly in Joseph Conrad's own handwriting and rang my bell for someone to pass it back to me.

The fair American lady had told a little white lie when she said she had burnt the letter she had received from my husband. The letter that would have proved all she had said. It was a very high flown epistle, without signature or superscription, but there was no mistake who had written it. At that distance of time, between the time I had been told of it in the first place and my actually holding it in my hand, I had more than once proved its worth. But the sentiment expressed came to me as new, as addressed to another woman. I think that had I been the original recipient I would have treasured that piece of paper for the sheer beauty of language, and style of expression. I still held it in my hand when my husband came into the room.

"What have you got there?" I held it out in silence. Before I could say a word he had flung it on the fire, and turning to me suggested a way of procuring something I had expressed a wish for. A usual form of any penitence, that followed no accusation and no apology. But we understood each other well enough to dispense with any such formality.

This last episode anticipates matters somewhat, jumps a few years, so to speak. The first weeks after we returned from Folkestone were as usual taken up fighting an attack of gout and full of intense anxiety for the boy. It was at this time that we saw a deal of Richard Curle, who was on sick leave from the Anti-aircraft Service. Those days are now a confused jumble of pain, physical and mental, through which passed friends new and old, almost like figures on a screen. Some, one could help if only by sympathy, others there were whose despair was too complete, their loss too overwhelming.

Then came the day when it was decided that some further advice must be sought for the trouble in my knee, and we decided to take a flat for a time in town. We found a roomy one in Hyde Park Mansions. Here we were soon installed, and for three months we lived in London. In a way it had some beneficial effect on Joseph Conrad's work, in fact it made work possible, and the frequent intercourse with his fellows was helpful, too. During those months I was wearing a long Thomas' splint, as my dear friend, Sir Robert Jones, hoped by this means to avoid an operation. Many were the evenings when Edward Garnett would arrive for supper, and the anti-aircraft guns begin to boom, as if heralding his arrival. The two men would eat, talk far into the night, almost indifferent to the sound of gunfiring. Very often our flat would be full of friends and acquaintances who had been calling, and who were forced to remain by the raid. If the firing got very close we would all repair to my bedroom, which faced a small stone court-yard, and there remain drinking endless cups of tea to fortify ourselves. Here one night we sheltered Cecil Roberts, Allan Wade, Catherine Willard, Miss Harriet Capes and one or two more. Our rooms were crowded. It is wonderful how close one comes to one's fellows when a common danger is present. We felt we had known each other for years, and only one person was a friend of more than a few months, if that.

Once during Borys's leave, we four, Sir James Lithgow, Joseph Conrad, Borys and myself, met for dinner in Verrey's Restaurant. In thevestibule there stood resplendent in full uniform an American Admiral. Joseph Conrad jammed his hat on the Admiral's outstretched hand, and flung his coat over his arm in the most unceremonious manner, thinking he must be an attendant. "Take that, will you." The expression of the American's face was too outraged to be comic, and only Borys's prompt removal of the offending garments and tactful apology saved a scene.

We went after dinner to the theatre, and there we had my one

JAMES B. PINKER, JOSEPH CONRAD AND THE CORSICAN SKIPPER IN CORSICA, 1921

JOSEPH CONRAD AND SIR DAVID WILSON-BARKER IN THE BOWLING-GREEN AT "OSWALDS," 1922

CAROLA ZAGORSKA AND JOSEPH CONRAD IN THE STUDY AT "OSWALDS," 1922

JOSEPH CONRAD AND HIS NEAREST POLISH RELATION IN THE GARDEN AT "OSWALDS" IN JULY, 1924

and only experience of a raid while the performance was going on. It was long after midnight when we left that theatre and packed ourselves inside an old four-wheeled cab. Both the horse and the driver appeared indifferent to the din and bursts of firing. The horse plodded along, never altering its pace all the way back to the flat. The streets showed long empty vistas incredibly deserted, except here and there a flying figure running in the centre of the road, and the sound of the fleeing footsteps echoing in a ghostly manner.

That first leave passed much too quickly, and it seemed only a dream afterwards. The knee did not improve and in July, 1918, it was decided to operate. When all was ready Borys was allowed leave again to be with me for the ordeal. I had already been installed in the Nursing Home before the boy got to London, but he came in to see me the night before the operation, and was thus able to help and sustain his father through the next day's ordeal, but it was not until a week afterwards that I heard how very nearly that particular leave had been stopped. The telegram signed by Sir Robert Jones had arrived and the leave had been granted (special leave) and as the boy left by one entrance to the mess, an orderly arrived at the other with papers " cancelling all leave."

That time in the Nursing Home my husband and the two boys came every day to see me. That was my one consolation, for my pain was intense and the seven weeks I lay, or rather reclined, with my sick limb held in a vice, were the most nightmarish I can remember.

When the first few days were over and people were allowed to visit me, things became a little more bearable. I had discovered that my dear old friend, Sir Robert, had two granddaughters who were of an age to like a new doll, and I got my old maid to to buy me two and also the material to dress them. It was the day upon which I had completed their outfits that he paid one of his unofficial visits, that I was to grow to appreciate so much as time went on.

With his usual calm courtesy he dismissed the nurses who had rushed to attend his inspection of the poor limb. A quiet " No, thank you, nurse, I do not wish to see the wound, I came to pay Mrs. Conrad a friendly visit, not an official one." This kindly speech had the effect of dismissing them all, and he then seated himself by my side, and began talking about everyday happenings. When he saw the dolls he expressed himself as very pleased, and then made the following detached but characteristic remark: " Do they disrobe." My amused answer that they certainly did, afforded him some satisfaction, and immediately he began to " disrobe " both very thoroughly. There was something tenderly pathetic in that uniformed figure with his skilful fingers busily unbuttoning those tiny garments, and laying each as he removed it in a neat little pile on the bedside at his elbow. When the last garment had been removed, he laid the two realistic nude forms on the bed by my side, and surveyed them with a puzzled frown. He was still looking at them in comical dismay when Joseph Conrad entered the room, and having greeted him with effusion bent to kiss me, muttering under his breath loud enough to be overheard by the surgeon : " A most unseemly display, my dear. Most unseemly, let me tell you." He turned away in disgust and made one or two hurried walks up and down the room. I could see his exasperation in the set of his shoulders, and the movement of his hands. " Dam', isn't it time you began to grow up." He seated himself close to the chair occupied by Sir Robert, and irritably swept the little heap all on the floor.

With the same patient kindness the great surgeon picked them up and put them in a pile by the side of the dolls. Then, patting my hand, he suggested I should clothe the young ladies when he chatted with my husband. I had nearly re-dressed one when he leaned over, and interrupting the weighty discussion between the two men, he said quickly, " Blanche has Rosa's undies on." It was such a characteristic thing for him to make such minute observation of anything, however trivial, that I was hardly surprised at this, but Joseph Conrad turned a very angry face towards me. He could not understand Sir Robert's interest in such a trifle as a doll, and was disposed to call me to account in a rather peremptory fashion. But here again came the calm tones saying quietly, " Your good wife and I understand one another, my dear fellow, don't get worried over our little jokes."

This was just a week before the death of Lady Jones and I did not see him again until just before I left the home.

There were several air-raids while I was there. I would hear the warning, followed by some unusual sounds of activity in different parts of the home. Then the night-sister would appear quietly efficient, and after giving me a drink, or putting my pillows comfortable, and lowering the lights, would seat herself against the dark curtained window. I grew to connect her appearance with the warning of a raid. It was such a pleasure to have someone at night to speak to, and I knew that when she came at that time she usually stayed more than an hour. I felt a little guilty sometimes when I thought that were at least some sixteen other patients as suffering as I, who might be needing her.

After the second time I had prepared a little feast of chocolate and fruit within my reach with which to be hospitable, I was quite distressed when she shook her head each time I offered anything to her. She was usually very voluble, but that night she surpassed herself. Her usual topic, in fact her only topic, was the unfaithfulness of the poor man. I always contradicted her, trying to put in a good word for the lords of creation, partly for the sake of argument and because I am fond of the opposite sex generally. This particular night she held forth with such purpose I literally had no chance to get a word in edgeways. This night she had not thought fit to lower the lights, and I saw to my surprise the big drops of moisture shining on her forehead. As it sometimes happens to me I can sleep in a din and the noise that night was continual, and sounded, as I noticed particularly, very close at hand. I can see that room now, after a lapse of time. My bed seemed isolated, although the room was not very large, the figure in the chair against the dark curtain sat as motionless as if carved in stone. Only the hands betrayed the strain she was under that night. I was dozing once, and I opened my eyes at the sound of whispered words addressed to another nurse who had entered. "It must be nearly over now, surely." I turned the words over and over in my mind, and almost without any attention, I said in a scared whisper, scarcely audible to myself, "I am not going . . . to die, am I ?"

Both the nurses turned a smiling face towards me. "Better explain to her," muttered my faithful companion. It was almost my last night, as I was to go home that week, and I suppose they thought I might not even then understand. I heard that I was the only patient in the home they could not move into a downstairs room when there was a raid. That wonderful woman, the night nurse, had elected to share what risk I might be running and had sat each raid through in my room. Why she talked always on the subject of a man's shortcomings was for no other reason but that it was a subject in which I had betrayed a real interest, always taking the opposite side of that argument, anyway.

Borys's leave was prolonged because he caught influenza, and for three weeks at least had to remain in England. Even this incident provided an amusing episode, although it did not act quite in the way my husband had anticipated.

He came to the home one morning, and meeting the Matron in the hall, became voluble on the subject of his health, declaring that Borys had influenza and that he himself was suffering from the same complaint. He was greatly incensed when the good lady, mindful of her sixteen patients, flatly refused to let him come up to see me. "Indeed, no, Mr. Conrad, and the best thing you can do, if you have influenza, is to go back home and go to bed. And stay there until you are better."

In spite of all his arguments she remained obdurate. And at

last he flung over his shoulder: "Then you will please tell my wife that she will see no one from home. If I am not allowed to see her, no one else shall." And the Matron was so angry that she repeated word for word this message.

Two days afterwards Borys, although still feeling shaky, returned to duty. John went back to school, and it was only my husband who came now to see me of my little family. Many friends made a pilgrimage to the shrine of friendship; amongst the most faithful was Hugh Walpole. One evening he remarked: "Do you know I have known you nearly two years, and I have never seen you dressed, or with your hat on. Always in bed."

We returned in due course to Capel House, and I took up my quarters in a small room downstairs, the boy's den, in fact. And here I remained for months on end, waiting with the best grace I could the time when I could once again move independently. I had a wheel chair in which I made the passage from the little den into the dining-room. Once there I occupied the window recess until the time came for me to remove myself again to my bed. I grew a dark brown on the window side, and remained a pallid white on the other. My only outings were rare excursions to town in a big, hired car to see Sir Robert Jones.

At the time the Armistice was signed Borys was already in hospital, and after a time we managed to get him home. The change in my boy was a painful one. He had always had moody fits, but now these seemed to be continual. He would sit silent and listless till some sudden noise would cause him to jump from his chair, and look wildly round. Many were the nights when he would appear clad in pyjamas and dressing-gown, startled from his sleep by a noise that recalled some of the horrors to his half-conscious mind, and he would leap from bed and come to spend the rest of the night in my room in a big chair. I think those times we were nearer together than we had been since his boyhood. Possibly because of his need of sympathy, and understanding without the medium of words, which he would have been hard put to find capable of expressing just what troubled him. Sometimes he would fall asleep at once, and I would watch him silently, grateful to a Providence that had thought fit to let him return to me whole, at least in body. I tried unsuccessfully to persuade Joseph Conrad to send him on a voyage, to rouse him from the state of moody indolence, but my dear ostrich could not, or would not understand exactly what I was driving at. "He has been away from you long enough. Surely you are not anxious for him to go away again?"

Life was somewhat difficult during those months of forced inactivity and helplessness. The wound would not heal satisfactorily even on the surface, and my dear friend Sir Robert decided that when he returned to England something more must be done. Meanwhile, I waited and tried not to anticipate worse than was likely to befall me.

The two boys were as good friends as ever, and Borys seemed to be very dependent on the younger boy to take him out of himself. He would, as I have said, unbend more during those midnight hours when he came to my room and slept on my chair. Often he would make tea and I would coax him to eat something, and then when signs of activity began in the house he would retire for his bath and breakfast. But the gloomy fit invariably returned unless I had been fortunate enough to hit upon some plan which held some interest for the young man.

Father and son were very much alike. Some quite ordinary change in the domestic staff disturbed Joseph Conrad greatly. The maid had been ill a long time, but when she eventually went into hospital my husband had to take my place and visit her. His appearance at the Cottage Hospital was fraught with some confusion. He refused his name, and the name of the person he desired to visit, and returned in high dugeon.

When the poor girl died he betook himself to a bedroom upstairs, and there remained for weeks on end. He and his son were consummate actors. Both liked to live in the world of make-believe, both were fond of crying wolf. I see similarities between the two all the time. Joseph Conrad would play at having the same complaint—if he heard of or knew someone was ill. The following letter was written just after the maid's death, which had very much impressed him. He confessed the day after he had written it that there was nothing really wrong with him—but he had stayed upstairs for nearly three weeks.

"DEAR HEART,

"My soul is weary for the sight of you. I hope you will have a possible night. What a comfort it is to have the two kids with us in these trying times—and especially the big kid, who twines himself round my heart even more than when he was a small child.

"I worry about you all, and I fret at being laid up on his twenty-first birthday. What must be will be—and after all, I have all possible confidence in the future. Good night, dearest, and give me a friendly thought before you go to sleep.

"YOUR BOY."

This letter would give anyone the impression that he was ill miles away, whereas he was only lying in a room upstairs in the same house. I knew him so well that I let him stay there until he elected to join again the family circle. But the strangeness was more marked because of my own real helplessness. Beyond being able to call a greeting from the chair wheeled to the foot of the stairs, I had not heard his voice. This was the only time he had indulged his fancy in quite the same way, and it was not until I had reasoned with myself to some length that I could quite forgive the mood that allowed him to hold himself aloof from me for so long.

It must be plain that my household was one of some difficulty in the matter of organization. I had judged it best to avoid all discussion as to the "illness" that kept their father upstairs, but I am convinced that neither of the boys believed it to be sufficiently severe or serious for this strange and prolonged isolation.

I was very thankful when a few days after we were reunited, Jean Aubry made one of his rather frequent visits. My husband was always delighted to see this friend, and he was greatly stimulated by the long talks the two had together. I have much reason to be extremely grateful to this good Frenchman, whose ready courtesy never failed and who has remained to this day a friend indeed. I was seldom present at those meetings, except at meal times. The rather inefficient cook we had left me a good deal of conjuring to do in the matter of producing the meals. I had hit upon a plan for the "fancy-work" part of the menu, and besides the pleasure of doing something I really loved, there was the satisfaction of knowing that my efforts made all the difference to Joseph Conrad's enjoyment of his food.

I would have a thick sheet of brown paper spread over my counterpane, and a large iron tray brought with a powerful spirit-lamp and the frying-pan or necessary saucepans and ingredients for the dishes I proposed to fabricate. Only once disaster in the shape of a tray of flame nearly ruined the dish and my inspiration. The maid had clumsily poured the spirit more on to the tray than into the lamp, and had neglected my express warning to wash it thoroughly if she had spilt a single drop on it. I sat with the flaming tray on my lap, keeping perfectly still and waited for it to burn itself out. I dared not even move enough to press the bell within my reach for fear the bed might catch fire. The bottom of the tray was beginning to get uncomfortably hot when the last flicker of the flames subsided. I was rather proud of my fortitude under these circumstances, and I finished my preparation when I had obtained a fresh lamp and necessary ingredients.

By this time our dear old landlord, Mr. Edmund Oliver, had died, and we had decided to leave the house that had sheltered us during those years of war. This was when Joseph Conrad optimistically believed in the possibility of my being able to walk at the end of six months after the operation. But alas! the spirit, however willing, could not influence the flesh, and I remained helpless as far as independent movement was concerned. Because of this disability I wrote to Mr. Roland Oliver, who had inherited the property, explaining my difficulty. His answer amused us somewhat. He wrote saying that he did not think that we could have realized that he had intended occupying Capel House himself. I resisted the impulse to remark that that was the reason I had asked to be allowed to stay some months longer.

In the end we managed to hire Captain Halsey's house for the few months that must elapse before we could find another house to our liking. My greatest regret was that I was going so far from my friend, Lady Millais. We had found very real friends in her and her son, Sir John. Joseph Conrad and this young man had so much in common, both were real sailors at heart, and the friendship between them was built on the very firm basis of mutual esteem. It was one of the very few houses, practically the only one, in fact, that the author would visit in a neighbourly fashion after the death of his friend Arthur Marwood. However, Wye was not very much farther in the matter of mileage, and as we both had a car we looked forward to still paying and receiving visits.

The actual move was accomplished with the usual farcical formality, but the distance being small, and my husband's unconfessed reluctance to leave the Capel House when it came to the point, caused him to be extra difficult to please. From my wheel-chair I assisted to pack a complete lunch that would be heated, and one maid went with them—Joseph Conrad and his secretary. It seems hardly creditable, but he was an absolute mule that day. A coal strike made it extremely difficult to get any supply of coal in the least adequate for warming a house as big as Spring Grove.

By dint of some wangling I managed to get a little extra for my "invalid husband." I directed the maid to get a good fire in the study, and to serve the lunch in there. But my dear man insisted upon a big fire in the dining-room as well. He was not going to pay £400 a year for a house and live in one room.

There was nothing to say, and in fact it saved time to hold my peace. I have very grateful recollections of Captain Halsey's kindness while we were there. We had a great many visitors to that house, and catering, or rather, cooking for them was rather difficult. I made several journeys to town, travelling like a package in a big hired car, for the purpose of interviewing the great surgeon. But we had left Wye before the date of the next operation was fixed. That move was managed entirely by Borys, who proved that he had learnt to handle men in the army if nothing else.

At this time there was a general strike, but the boy managed to procure a box van that had come over the channel and which, because of the strike, could not be returned. From somewhere else he obtained the hire of a lorry chassis. The somewhat precarious combination was secured by none too stout ropes, and the proprietor of the lorry was so intrigued by the success of the first journey that he—with an eye to good business—hired the combination to other people desirous to shift their household goods immediately, making the different moves dove-tail into each other in such a manner that he did not lose any, but prolonged all. In all, the move occupied three times its intended time, and I am inclined to believe would have occupied a dozen times longer if Borys, with the wisdom of experience, had not procured a big cask of beer with which to lubricate the workers, and our move was declared the most popular, and finished first.

I made my first entrance in a carrying chair. There was a tremendous lot to do before Joseph Conrad decided that he could settle down to write. Oswalds has a store of memories and remembrances, which belong to the next chapters. But before the first Christmas we went to Liverpool and the third operation was performed.

CHAPTER NINETEEN

I HAVE forgotten the address of the nursing home in Liverpool, and also the journey there from London. Only Sir Robert Jones and his wonderful kindness and patience lights up what would otherwise be but a grim and painful memory. November is a month that shares with February an equal dislike in my mind. I can only remember that opposite that place of torture a chimney-pot continually bowed backwards and forwards in the wind, and that it was held to the rest of the stack by a frail length of wire rope.

It is curious how small a trifle will remain fixed in one's mind during any time of great physical suffering, and attain an importance above the most outstanding events. That chimney-pot and its weird habit of bowing seemingly, to me as I lay in bed, became the great feature of each day's programme.

Would it fall even as I watched it? My dreams were filled with it, and my half-delirious fancy made of it in time a positive fetish. I remember to this day trying to persuade Sir Robert that I had been catapulted across the road into the stack and had clung for hours to that very chimney-pot as my only frail support. Even when he explained the reason of my fancy, I still inclined to retain my delusion. My patient friend had explained that my impression was due to the powerful contraction of big leg muscles that had been cut across my knee.

My husband and two sons had rooms close to the Home, and it happened that during the time we were there, M. Jean Aubry was also in Liverpool, although I have no recollections of seeing him myself. Joseph Conrad spent a great deal of the weary time actually in Sir Robert's house, and he, too, came to see me every day when he was in Liverpool. This unusual procedure on his part, I found afterwards, had the effect of making me rather unpopular with the matron. I have discovered that these people do not like favourites; or is it that they object to any change in the hard and fast rules laid down in all institutions? I had several passages of arms over trifles when I was there.

However, two days under the three weeks after Sir Robert's delicate attention saw me on the road to town once more. The great surgeon himself came to the station to see us off. We spent two nights in a London hotel where Richard Curle awaited us on our arrival from Liverpool. I was only equal to getting to bed, where I remained the next forty-eight hours. My journey down to Canterbury was made by road in the charge of a maid. When we arrived I literally fell into the doctor's arms. I was still faint from loss of blood and feeling greatly the reaction. I had been "mulish" according to my husband's definition of what I had tried to persuade him was determination, in taking the journey so soon.

Thus the first part of our tenancy of Oswalds was passed by me in a big front bedroom. Here I received everyone who came to see us for coffee after lunch. Some work got itself done and the months sped along.

My pain and discomfort remained in spite of all my determination to ignore it, and little more than three months after my Liverpool adventure, I once again prepared for the ordeal of meeting the surgeon's knife. This time I went to a nursing home in Canterbury, and here it was that I first met Dr. Whitehead Reid, who became one of my closest and most sympathetic friends. Sir Robert this time elected to travel from Edinburgh by night, and prepared to "do business" in Canterbury as soon as he arrived.

The short drive from Bishopsbourne to Canterbury held all the elements of a complete farce. We had made perhaps half the journey when Joseph Conrad stopped the car in the middle of Bourne Park, and suggested that we should turn back. But although I anticipated a lot of pain, I could not show the white feather, particularly as I knew the long journey my great friend had undertaken in his desire to ease me. My husband shrugged his shoulders in his characteristic fashion and remarked in a grimly exasperated tone: "Very well, you want another operation, and you shall have one."

I can recall my first meeting with Dr. Reid, who had taken me over for the time from our old friend, Dr. Tilbery Fox, with all the professional ceremony. My levity was provoked by his extremely professional manner, and when at the end of his preliminary examination he paused, note-book in hand, and said without looking at me: "What age, Mrs. Conrad?"

"Seventy-four," I replied quietly, thinking he would surely reverse the figures. I was quite unprepared for his next remark, however, and I perceived that I had met my match here. He simply gave a look at me and made a quick movement while he remarked blandly: "I suppose I needn't ask what religion, after that?"

I don't think I ever enjoyed crossing my wits with anyone quite so much as I did with him. He got the best of it every time, and was never caught napping. But he was a real and trusty friend for the rest of his life, and my admiration and affection for him will never fade. His power of giving courage to others, his ready understanding and patient sympathy must have been a great drain upon his own personality. The very evident appreciation for the skill and understanding that those two surgeons, Sir Robert and Dr. Reid, had for each other, was always a matter of extreme pleasure and satisfaction to me.

During the months that followed I grew to love Oswalds very much, although now, because of that tragic Sunday morning in August, 1924, nothing could induce me to return to live under that roof. Every turn in the garden path, every corner in that house is fraught with memories that I dare not dwell upon. Other houses, where we have lived together, do not hold the same horror as that, but I suppose this is due to the fact that it was here that he died.

After many months I was once more able to move on crutches, and we made our plans for that long-projected visit to Corsica. This visit to the birth-place of Napoleon had been a cherished dream of Joseph Conrad's for many years. The visit had become an obsession of his since his early childhood. He always declared that he was no admirer of Napoleon, but the fact remains that this tragic personality exercised a spell over the author, that, as I will show, had a certain reason as an explanation.

My husband in his *Reminiscences*, tells the tale of an ancestor of his who was one of the officers in Napoleon's army at the time of the retreat from Moscow. This officer, whom he alludes to by the name of Mr. Nicholas B., was an uncle of my husband's. His unpleasant experience is recorded in the extract I include here :

" It is a good forty years since I heard the tale, and the effect is not worn off yet. I believe this is the very first, say realistic, story I heard in my life, but all the same, I don't know why I should have been so frightfully impressed. Of course I know what our village dogs look like—but still . . . No : at this very day, recalling the horror and compassion of my childhood, I ask myself whether I am right in disclosing to a cold and fastidious world that awful episode in the family history. I ask myself—is it right ?—especially as the B. family had always been honourably known in the wide countryside for the delicacy of their tastes in the matter of cating and drinking. But upon the whole and considering that this gastronomical degradation overtaking a gallant young officer lies really at the door of the great Napoleon, I think that to cover it up by silence would be an exaggeration of literary restraint. Let the truth stand here. The responsibility rests with the man of St. Helena, in view of his deplorable levity in the conduct of the Russian campaign. It was during that deplorable retreat from Moscow that Mr. Nicholas B., in company of two brother officers—as to whose loyalty and refinement I know nothing—bagged a dog on the outskirts of a village and subsequently devoured him. As far as I can remember, the weapon used was a cavalry sabre, and the issue of the sporting episode was rather more a matter of life and death than if it had been an encounter with a tiger. Near here a picket of Cossacks were sleeping in that village lost in the depths of the great Lithuanian Forest. The three sportsmen had observed them from a hiding-place making themselves very much at home amongst the huts, just before the early winter darkness set in at four o'clock. They observed them with disgust, and perhaps with despair. Late in the night the rash counsels of hunger overcame the dictates of prudence. Crawling through the snow, they crept up to the fence of dry branches, which generally encloses a village in that part of Lithuania. What they expected to get, and in what manner, and whether this expectation was worth the risk, goodness only knows. However, these Cossack parties, in most cases wandering without an officer, were known to guard themselves badly and often not at all. In addition, the village lying at a great distance from the line of French retreat, they would not expect the presence of stragglers from the Grand Army. The three officers had strayed away in a blizzard from the main column, and had been lost in the woods, which explains sufficiently the terrible straits to which they were reduced. Their plan was to try to attract the attention of the peasants in one of the huts which was nearest to the enclosure, but as they were preparing to venture into the jaws of the lion, so to speak, a dog (it is mighty strange that there was but one), a creature quite as formidable under the circumstances as a lion, began to bark on the other side of the fence. . . .

" At this stage of the narrative, which I heard many times (by request) from the lips of Captain Nicholas B.'s sister-in-law, my grandmother, I used to tremble with excitement.

" The dog barked, and if he had done no more than bark, three officers of the Great Napoleon's Army would have perished honourably on the points of Cossacks' lances, or perchance escaping the chase, would have died decently of starvation. But before they had time to think of running away, that fatal and revolting dog, being carried away by the excess of his zeal, dashed out through a gap in the fence. He dashed out and died. His head, I understand, was severed at one blow from his body. I understand also that, later on, within the gloomy solitudes of the snow-laden woods, when in a sheltering hollow, a fire was lit in that hollow by the party, the condition of the quarry was discovered to be distinctly unsatisfactory. It was not thin—on the contrary it was unhealthily obese ; its skin showed bare patches of an unpleasant character. However, they had not killed the dog for its pelt. He was large. . . . He was eaten. . . . The rest is silence . . . a silence in which a small boy shudders and says firmly:

" 'I could not have eaten that dog.' "

I have used this long quotation in order to show the great impression this story made upon the mind of the child. Also the lasting effect on the mind of the man. This episode is partly the origin of one of the last short stories, " The Warrior's Soul," I mean as to the setting, and it certainly was the beginning of my husband's interest in Napoleon, an interest that has been remarked upon so many times. It is certainly strange that such a pitch of interest should have lasted through all those years, when it had no sympathy or admiration to sustain it. To the end it remained merely critical—and not a little resentful.

This visit to Corsica which had been in dreamlike contemplation for so many years actually became a fact in 1921. As a journey, it held all the nightmarish qualities of our visit to Naples. It was an extravagant venture to say the least of it, and a venture, that having to be made under the conditions such as they were, seems to be, on looking back, more than a little insane. I shudder now to think of the amount of money that must have been expended upon it.

Had Joseph Conrad lived to complete the book, *Suspense*, the local colour for which a great deal of Corsica has, or rather, was to have been used, there would have been ample justification for the cost of the trip. But *Suspense* remains just suspense. No one could finish it as the author intended to finish it, much less F. M. H., who dared to declare that his book, *Little Less than Gods*, was that book completed. He knew perhaps less than most people in the literary world what my husband intended to be the finish, because, for the years from 1909, the two had been as far apart in thought as in actual personal contact.

Joseph Conrad had always the intention to go to the island of Elba, but this he meant to do alone. While we were in Corsica he made one or two abortive efforts to go to Sicily, but his health at that time was indifferent. I would have been quite willing for him to go if Borys had been at hand to go with him, but alone —I discouraged the notion, and as I have said his health was not sufficiently robust for him to set my opinion aside. He contented himself with the idea that his visit to Sicily was only put off.

I have a good deal to say of *Suspense*, but not here. When we went to Corsica we left one Sunday morning, a little late, and on that Sunday morning every conceivable obstacle was on the road to delay us still further. The various personal difficulties caused by my helpless condition, and my clumsy manipulation of my crutches were matters that chafed and tormented the author very much. My nurse was not very helpful, and the chauffeur was a raw yokel and unused to travel. If it had not been for Borys, who was to accompany us as far as Rouen, and show us a part of the battle area, the part on which nearly all his Service had been passed, I hardly think we should have embarked at all upon that adventure.

There was considerable difficulty getting the car aboard. With the luggage still as we left Oswalds, the poor car was hoisted by a crane on a lighter. This broke adrift and we watched our faithful old Cadillac careering around the harbour in Dover. At last it was lowered on board and with his feathers decidedly ruffled poor Joseph Conrad prepared for his little party to disgrace themselves by being sea-sick. But only my nurse fulfilled his predictions.

In Calais the rest of us devoured a good meal, and then, crutches and all, we left, preceded by a motor-cyclist to guide us on the right road. I sat with Borys, my limb shored up on a dressing-bag and cushions, the crutches secured against the side of the car. My husband greatly disapproved of the unavoidable display. Many were the half inaudible "dams" and wide gestures of despair that almost brought tears to my eyes on that first part of the journey. It was cold comfort to tell myself that I could not help it. Or that I had been perfectly willing even at the last to wait until I had recovered some more of the use in my limb. My argument had been met by the firm declaration, "We are going at once or not at all." This was unanswerable. I said no more, but schooling myself to rather a brazen disregard for his objections, I intended to see all that I could and enjoy what was possible. Perhaps the word "enjoy" is not quite the one I ought to use. But having the boy by my side, seeing with my own eyes the places, and hearing first hand the happenings at each and every turn of the road, I allowed my imagination to fill in the rest, and I sat awed and silent.

I was amazed to find how clear a recollection my son had retained of the way, never a wrong turn. Every small village we passed through held some poignant story of human grief and suffering that he had witnessed. Here a post office had been blown into atoms, a nice little girl had been serving there, here a small café—where he recalled some extra kindness the proprietor had shown to him and his column, during those years of war. These stories lost nothing of picturesque detail, for the boy is a true son of his father, and one day I feel convinced the power of portrayal will make of him no mean author.

Details were often too vividly described for his father to endure, and always there would come these words: " Enough, boy, it is past and over, let us forget that part of it. Have a cigarette." He, Joseph Conrad, had forgotten that he had asked for those very details. Still, the two had a lot in common, and I, knowing my husband as I did, could understand that he had a very great satisfaction in the boy's power of observation. He used often to say: " Some people have a lot to say and no power of expression, that is tragic, you know, and others fill pages with nothing more than mere verbiage."

In Armentières we stayed two nights in an hotel that still bore the marks of the bullets through the big folding doors of the salon, and the plate glass of the wardrobes showed big cracks from end to end. Little rivulets ran across the floors when we tried to use the hand-basins. There was ample evidence here of the havoc wrought by the war.

From here we intended to go through Rouen, but when we were ready to start in the morning we found that some mischievous person had stolen our R.A.C. badge and radiator cap. The hotel could, or would, give us no assistance, and in the end we had to have another rough cap made.

Borys, who went with his father to the post office, to wire to the R.A.C. reporting the loss and asking for another badge, was most amusing in his report of his father's uncomplimentary references to the hotel management. So much publicity was given to the theft that when we were in Rouen and in the small hours of the morning a messenger arrived with the missing badge. Joseph Conrad was so irate that he refused to reward the man or even pay the fare from Armentières to Rouen, and the fellow returned disappointed.

Here Borys left us to return home, after spending a few days in Paris. I had tried hard to persuade my husband to keep him with us for our trip, to take him, in fact, instead of the chauffeur. It would have made an enormous difference to me, and would have certainly had the most beneficial effect upon the young man's nerves and outlook on life. I could not persuade his father to listen to me when I tried to induce him to send the boy on a sea voyage as soon as he was out of the Military Hospital. All the answer he would make was: " No. Let him get settled in his job."

I had pleaded hard for the course I advocated, knowing that the boy would have had keen pleasure on a cruise because of his *Worcester* training. It is a very real regret that my dear " ostrich " was so decided in this, but, true to my resolve, I never returned to the subject again.

In Rouen Jean Aubry joined us, and stayed with us until we reached Lyons. I had now my seat beside the chauffeur, a poor substitute for my son, the other three sat behind in the tonneau. The journey was much more interesting for my husband with his good friend by his side instead of only my nurse. I think this friend was a little apprehensive with an English driver, for every time we approached a level crossing, even before we saw the sign of a gate swinging over our heads on the tall post by the side of the road, the official warning, Jean Aubry would rise in his seat and say nervously, " Railway, railway."

On the whole, except for the weather, and a sneaking longing for Borys, I enjoyed the trip. I shrank rather from the look of disgust that my crutches always brought forth whenever my husband's eyes fell upon them. Time after time he tried to stow them out of sight within the body of the car, and more than once he half suggested that I could manage with two sticks.

We were on the way to Orleans when the first trouble came with the car. This was due to a misunderstanding or rather to an incautious assertion on the part of the youthful chauffeur. The man had been beguiled into saying exactly how many miles he was doing to the gallon, one of my husband's little foibles, and there had been, of course, no allowance made for the many times we had missed a turn " backing and filling," in sailor parlance. It was useless to argue. We were only so many miles from the town we had left and that should have meant so many gallons of petrol.

The man at last grew sulky and muttered that he " hadn't drunk the blessed stuff," and matters were distinctly strained and unpleasant. Jean Aubry, anxious for peace with honour, walked the two miles from where we sat in the car, high and dry, to the village we had just passed through, to try to procure the necessary *essence*. Meanwhile, every cart that passed along the high road was hailed by my husband, who began: " Monsieur. . . ." In nearly every case he got no further, for the driver, with a courteous " Bon soir," passed on. How was he to understand that the stranger was trying to get a lift back to the village to help transport the *essence?* In the end we had to man-haul the car round and get back to the tiny village for the night.

My irate husband led the way walking and waving his stick excitedly each time the car stopped, and it did that every few yards. It was a weird passage between the two rows of tall trees bordering the road. No single light showed from any friendly window and our head-lamps gleamed in a pale stream on the white trunks of the trees, on the stone walls and the deep ditches.

Then in one desperate spurt the car made the few yards and came to a stop outside the only hotel, and refused to give another sign of life.

My husband marshalled us up the cobbled yard, still too angry to speak calmly, and uttering vague and impossible threats of vengeance against the crass stupidity of the poor young chauffeur. Clearly, it would have been better if Borys had been with us, and in the morning we found that we had a bit of grit in the carburettor.

That little place produced the most delicious supper; there were some half-dozen or so railwaymen, a buxom dame, our chauffeur and our four selves. We sat at a long deal table guiltless of a cloth, and with only the most elementary tools for feeding ourselves. With his usual tact Jean Aubry had now managed to restore my husband to a good temper. We were all tired and it was not long before I began my difficult journey up the winding outside staircase. Crutches were not easy to negotiate on that. The bedroom accommodation was somewhat unsatisfactory, and smelt rather damp. Joseph Conrad declined to occupy one of the single beds, of which there were two, one each side of a big, bare room. The intervening space was empty except for the usual strip of carpet by each of the beds. On one wall the ill-fitting door allowed a good current of air to circulate in refreshing eddies round the head of each of the beds, but the three windows in a row were tightly closed and each had a red sausage-like wad laid along the bottom.

My husband had collected all the rugs out of the car, he distrusted those beds, they looked and smelt damp. He turned the one over on the far side, sniffing in disgust, and then finally decided to share mine. There was nothing wrong with the springs anyway. The bed stood against the wall, and I am sure the picture of his thin figure standing erect between my recumbent form and the wall, draped in two of the coloured rugs, would have been droll in the extreme. He then let himself fall into his allotted space so suddenly as to cause me to bounce more than once. Then, after the lighted candle in the stick had been made to balance on the top bar of the wooden bedstead, he promptly fell asleep, without reading. I then removed the light to a place of greater safety and I, too, slept.

Another night on our way he decided to occupy the small bed in a dressing-room opening out of the big one, where I had retired directly we arrived in the early afternoon. This slip of a room contained also a bath—one of those abominations that fill as well as empty from the bottom. The deep bath was standing on a big leaden tray which covered half the floor space. An ideal arrangement, he declared: "I can have my bath and keep the lights burning as long as I like without disturbing you, my dear. You will have a good night."

He must have been over an hour getting that bath, bursting into snatches of his three bars from "Carmen" from time to time, until the repeated slam of a door a little way down the corridor induced him to consider that it was late, and the slamming might be intended as a protest against his vocal efforts.

It was about two hours later when a persistent sound roused me from my first sleep, and I sat up looking anxiously through the crack of the partly closed door that divided the two rooms. The light burnt in there perfectly steadily, but the strange noise continued. I was helpless to investigate, my crutches stood in the far corner of the room out of reach. I raised myself on my elbow and puzzled to account for the peculiar noise.

A few moments later and my husband let out a hearty "damn," a pause, then: "Why, it's raining hard." I heard a thud as he leaped out of bed and then sounds of great consternation before he flung the outer door open calling loudly for help, and then stumbled back to bed. "It's that damn bath, running over," this was in answer to my anxious enquiry.

Several women and girls in their night attire rushed in, and amidst all the fuss and chatter, which was very good-humoured while they mopped up the water and emptied the bath, he turned his back on them, and was asleep before the clearing up was accomplished. Still a good night was not possible under those circumstances. The next morning the array of maids who claimed to have belonged to the rescue party, I am convinced, was nearly double. They were duly rewarded, but he did say to me later in the morning: "I think I have been seeing double this morning." I agreed, but who or rather which were the double-doubles?

At Lyons Jean Aubry left us and we proceeded a party of four, including the chauffeur, to Marseilles. We stayed there the best part of three days, and my husband showed me two or three of the haunts of his youth of which he spent many months in that wonderful French town. He pointed out the place where he and the eight men, of divers nationality, had dined on the night when he, a boy of seventeen, had been given the contents of all their pockets, and sent into the rooms to gamble. His one gambling adventure, he paused and then continued reminiscently: "And, Jess, I won—that night I couldn't lose. But—if I had, we should all have had a cheap lodging for that one night at least."

Then the third evening we embarked on a desperately uncomfortable passage for Corsica. The cabin was small and smelly, there were not enough pillows, and my nurse, who was sick and desperately sorry for herself, lamented aloud. Joseph Conrad tried to procure a little champagne for us, but the only half-bottle, all there was on board, was already disposed of.

It was on this trip that a very nice young girl had come up to me and introduced herself as Miss Dulcie Jones, a patient of my dear friend Sir Robert Jones. And she was to be joined by a niece of another friend. We saw a good deal of the two while we were on the island.

I was thankful when we disembarked on the quay in Corsica. There were several small formalities to be gone through before we were allowed to start for the Grand Hotel in Ajaccio, here my poor husband's already sorely tried temper blazed forth in earnest. We had engaged our rooms by letter from England, and they had told a little white lie as regards the lift.

I suppose a good many people demand that convenience who could really manage without it, and the little deception is then overlooked. But in my case a lift was indeed a necessity. The Swiss proprietors were loud in their apologies and certainly did all in their power to make up for their " mistake," as they persisted in calling their very decided fib. But it was some time before Joseph Conrad could be appeased and consent to occupy the one ground floor suite. This had evidently been reserved for someone of importance, as we gathered from the scraps of disjointed conversation that floated from the bureau when the door opened from time to time. However, at last we were installed, and the unpacking completed. The suite was very complete, two bedrooms with a sitting-room between, and a bathroom at the far end of the corridor into which each room had a door.

Here it was that my husband renewed an acquaintance made many years before, at a lunch given in London by Sir Hugh Clifford. Almost the first person we met the day we arrived was Sir Maurice with his wife, Lady Cameron, who with an Irish artist had made their appearance in the hotel a few weeks before we came. The acquaintance was renewed with keen pleasure by both sides, and these dear people still remain very close friends, more than fourteen years afterwards. Except the Irish artist, Miss Alice Kinkead, who leaves a big gap in the little circle. But before this sad happening she spent many a week under our roof, and I grew exceedingly attached to her.

In a few days Miss Lillian Hallowes arrived to help with

the work, that was, as it turned out, never attempted. She used to declare that proofs would be found imprinted on her heart when she died. It may be so, she was a very efficient proof-reader, I believe. Then close on her heels J. B. Pinker and his wife and daughter arrived as our guests. That was to be the arrangement at least for the first fortnight.

In spite of my disability and the burden of my crutches I really enjoyed that two months in Corsica. J. B. Pinker was a very delightful companion, and his wife always ready to fall in with any plans we made for an outing. The young daughter speedily made friends for herself, and everyone seemed satisfied. Mr. Pinker had a knack of soothing my husband in difficult moods, who needed either sympathetic indulgence or tolerant disregard. Mr. Pinker's wonderful voice was a joy and a delight to us all, and his daughter was a very able accompanist.

There was a good deal of fun as well as exasperation when electric light failed in the hotel. Fun because we had no proper candlesticks, and the long candles had perforce to be stuck in the necks of the empty wine bottles. Exasperation because we all knew that the failure was due to the habit the Corsicans had of "failing" the light purposely, to show their power to make themselves unpleasant—when they wished.

One night my husband retired early from the dining-room, displeased with something on the menu, and we five sat laughing and talking over the rest of the meal. It was candle-light that night, which partly accounted for the disgust of the author. At last no reasonable pretence remained for lingering where we were, and we prepared to return to the sitting-room at the very end of the long passage. I believe the young daughter and my nurse would rather have joined the other guests in the salon. However, we each carried a light—that is except me—my crutches rendered that impossible, and also forced me to bring up the rear. J. B. Pinker walked first, the flickering light from his candle falling on his white head. His wonderful voice rose in a sacred chant and the waiters—all Swiss—fell into line with clasped hands or making the sign of the Cross. Very profane, no doubt, but inexpressibly funny because it was a sudden impulse. The Swiss were, of course, not Roman Catholics either, or they would not have entered into the fun.

Mr. Pinker, deadly serious and filling the place with his voice, proceeded right to the door of our private sitting-room. Suddenly my husband flung it open and said icily: "Yes, and I'm a Catholic, aren't I?"

The finish to what was intended only as fun was sudden. I passed on to my room without facing my lord and master, and left J. B. Pinker to weather the storm. For some time no sound broke the silence in the next room, then I heard the singer's voice murmuring insinuatingly, I could not catch what was said, but the effect was a peal of amused laughter from the "Catholic" and I knew the storm was over.

CHAPTER TWENTY

IT was not long after this that the Pinkers left us to return to England. We missed them a good deal and J. B. Pinker's kindly presence had made for a lot of the success of our Corsican visit. By this time I had once again discarded my crutches for the two sticks, but there the improvement ended. Joseph Conrad had relapsed into his usual rather invalidish condition and as usual insisted upon continuing a course of treatment that, from being a cure, became almost a disease. My nurse did the treatment and found it easier to humour him by continuing instead of seeking a doctor's further advice.

Our news from our boys was not very satisfactory. Borys had begun his work and as far as that went he seemed pretty hopeful, but his letters were rather disquieting generally. John, who had begun his first term at Tonbridge, had not settled down at all well. The boy had been living the life of a young animal and perfectly free. Most of his time had been spent in the trees and as he had undoubtedly the "luck of the wild," he found the rules and restrictions of public school life irksome in the extreme. He was disposed to be argumentative too, which did not make for his popularity with the masters. On one occasion he was reproved for neglecting his grammar, and he was heard to mutter that he "didn't see why he should have to learn grammar." The master mildly remarked: "But you can't write or speak correctly if you don't learn grammar." The boy turned upon him and demanded in respectful tones: "Have you ever read my father's books?" and when the master owned to having done that, John finished up by saying: "Well, he never learnt grammar." And this statement was perfectly true.

Also Joseph Conrad had, in the boy's hearing, criticized the system of education in English schools, declaring that system to be arbitrary, but he had suggested no mode of improvement.

We celebrated our silver wedding while we were in Corsica, and we were both greatly amused by the anxious letter I received from John just before the date, begging me very earnestly to marry the same man on the silver wedding day "because, you know, it's so dreadful to have to tell the boys that you have a new father."

We were greatly touched by the very real concern displayed by that artless letter, and hastened to reassure the child. By no stretch of imagination could either of us picture some other person as our life partners. We were as much one as a single person. I can claim the most intimate acquaintance with that complex mind of any person who knew him, and he would declare that he knew me through and through—with just one little reservation, but what that was he would never tell me.

Corsica was romantic enough to satisfy the most exacting

person, and we were a good deal amused at the efforts of several spinsters—of uncertain age—whose dream was to be kidnapped by the bandits. They would venture daringly close to the edges of the thickly-wooded slopes that hid the entrances to the bandits' fastness. But while we were there, at least, they appeared stale bait, and nothing happened. The chief bandit, then Romanetti, had but lately taken a new young wife and was not troubling about other ladies.

But even in those enlightened days, one evening we were to come quite close enough to the lawless and tragic consequence of a vendetta, fought to the death between three men on one side and five on the other. Each of them left sons to carry on the feud. The cause of the quarrel in this case had been a bitter one over some piece of land.

There was a dance in progress at the hotel that night, and my nurse was awaiting the doctor, her partner. When at last he appeared, the dancing couples at once stood still staring at the late arrival. His face, habitually pale, had that night a look of frozen horror and he was obviously greatly disturbed by the scene he had just left.

The men had fought to the death with knives, and the young doctor shuddered while he detailed the happenings to the people who clustered around him. The actual fight had been over when he arrived, but the picture he drew of the wailing women and frightened children put a very decided end to the dance for most of the visitors. As it happened there were only two other Corsicans besides the witness of the devastating tragedy present, and one of these was the doctor's mother.

It struck a curious note to all the rest of us to hear the Corsicans upheld the vendetta and the declaration that the French Government would never succeed in putting a stop to it. Even the sight of those bereaved women who would each wear their mourning for two years—and as likely as not there would be more bloodshed by that time, and they would continue to be clothed in those sombre garments for another two years—and so on.

We had all been rather surprised that the doctor, who avowed himself so true a Corsican, should have shown such evident distress recalling the scene, but none of us remarked upon it aloud.

I think that charming island must be one of the most exclusive countries there are. No stranger was welcome except on a visit, and there was no encouragement for anyone to settle there. The natives had a way of making any such thing extremely difficult. Tourists might come and they were allowed to spend their money, but there the matter ended.

Joseph Conrad spent several long hours in the house where

Napoleon was born which still stands intact, just as the tragic great figure left it so many years ago. There is also a group of statues near the water's edge of the man and his brothers. They are imposing because of the history connected with them.

Corsica, like Italy, has very wonderful side streets and alleyways and I am afraid I have never seen what most visitors can see because I have never been able to walk and explore as I should have loved to do. But narrow places between high stone walls or high houses give wonderful vistas as one drives past.

My husband struck up an acquaintance with the skipper of a small sailing ship lying close in shore, and I have the snapshot of these two devotees of the sea together, with J. B. Pinker on board. The main-boom makes a good background to their figures. There is also a photo of the two men sitting in front of a café. It was one day when the two sailors were in that café alone, and enjoying a yarn, the outcome of which would have been useful in days to come, and would have fitted into one of the books. There had been a heavy storm, which accounts for the two being inside the café instead of sitting outside.

I had been extremely sceptical over the chance of the very thing that happened, but then I could only judge things from the safe standpoint of an English waterside town. They were just about to put their glasses to their lips when the buzz of conversation stopped and the Corsican captain murmured " Hush," placing his hand on my husband's shoulder. " Don't move ! " he continued.

There was that in the tense silence that followed that kept the inevitable " damn," from passing my husband's lips, and the next moment he too got his thrill. Everybody in the place stood or sat silent and motionless, while the man who had entered a second before calmly closed the door behind him and leisurely, without glancing to either side, advanced to the wide counter. He laid a revolver in front of him and in a pleasing tone ordered the refreshment he needed. The proprietor was perfectly aware whom he was serving, and he knew too the consequences if one of his customers should unwittingly offer to leave the place, before the handsome stranger had been gone at least a quarter of an hour. I was impressed in my turn by the story, for I had been very much inclined to scoff.

Not many days afterwards we were stopped outside a little estaminet on a wild lonely road without any other sign of a human habitation in sight. Our chauffeur had removed a wheel to change a tyre, and we stood almost at the open door of the seemingly empty building. All our little party except Joseph Conrad, who stood talking to me over the side of the hood, had walked on out of sight. He had stayed because I was helpless to move, and I fancy he was disinclined to walk far, as usual. We intended to pick the others up later.

CAPTAIN DAVID BONE, JOSEPH CONRAD AND MR. MUIRHEAD BONE ON BOARD THE *TUSCANIA* IN 1923

JESSIE CONRAD KORZENIOWSKI IN "OSWALDS," 1923

It was a blazing hot day and there seemed no other living thing on the road as far as the eye could reach, except a few goats feeding, tethered together the other side of the thick undergrowth bordering the road. Presently I drew my husband's attention to a heavy cloud of dust that appeared to be steadily coming nearer and nearer. Then we heard the rhythmical beat of a horse's hoofs and in another second we made out the figure of a horseman in the haze of dust galloping towards us.

As he drew nearer the sun glinted on the barrel of the rifle he held slung across his saddle bow. We turned our heads and were amazed to see the road full of gendarmes, all with their carbines held ready to shoot. They issued silently from the doors of that apparently empty estaminet, and as noiselessly disappeared from our sight in the depths of the ditch where they were hidden by the thick growth of maquis. The figure on horseback drew steadily nearer and nearer, and the truth flashed upon us. "Good God, Jess, it is Romanetti," gasped a hoarse voice I scarcely recognized from the side of the car. "We stand a damn bad chance when they start to shoot."

The chauffeur slipped out of sight by the side of the car, and I gazed at my husband's set white face and slipped my hand into his. Another fraction of a second and out of nowhere,as it seemed, twice as many Corsicans appeared in the road. All the blue-grey figures of the gendarmes prudently vanished for the odds were dead against them. We still held each other's hands while the horseman drew abreast, passed the spot where we were and disappeared in the dust in the direction of his fastness in the hills. No further word passed between us till the chauffeur finished the changing of the wheel and hoarsely announced that he was ready to go on. But before we left that small hostel I had to ask for a drink of water; my tongue was too dry almost to perform its office.

Only a short time ago I read of the death of this redoubtable bandit who was betrayed and killed in ambush. I shuddered, recalling how closely we had come that bright sunshiny day to being involved in the shooting.

The roads in Corsica are wonderfully made, and all by the German prisoners during the war. The air is delightful, and the people friendly and very interesting. You have certainly a feeling, before you have been there long, that your interest had best be confined to the scenery, and any attempt to purchase any land in Corsica is rendered very difficult, if not absolutely impossible.

Next in interest for visitors after Napoleon's birthplace is, of course, the Château de Pozzo-di-Borgo. Carved on a big slab of granite that is pinkish in colour, there is the following inscription :—

"Jerome, Duke Pozzo-di-Borgo, and Charles, his son, have

built this edifice with the stones derived from the demolition of the Tuileries, reproducing one of the pavilions of that palace, burned in Paris in 1871, in order to conserve for the land of Corsica a precious souvenir of the land of France. The year of our Lord 1891."

The following extract is taken from Miss Hildegarde Hawthorne's *Corsica, the Surprising Island,* who continues: "On the Avenue of the Bois de Boulogne the château would be a fitting and magnificent thing. On this lone peak in Corsica it is an anachronism, a joke; yet it remains beautiful. And one can only thank the man who saved so much that is exquisite from destruction. According to report, however, it was not this amiable motive that impelled the duke to spend a fortune bringing part of the palace of the Tuileries to his Corsican hilltop, but an abiding hatred of the Bonaparte family."

The quarrel was a very old one, and much blood was spilt between the two families. But just what satisfaction the Duke Pozzo-di-Borgo got out of the building of that château, from the ruins of a French palace, it is difficult for any but a Corsican to understand. We made in all four journeys up to it during the two months we were on the Island. There is a wonderful view from the height and an element of danger in the drive up from Ajaccio. We nearly came to grief on one occasion. On our way down the zigzag path that winds down from the raised plateau, one of the horses, the near side one, lost his footing, rounding a sharp bend, and hung for a second or so in the harness. It was a moment of some anxiety and considerable danger. But the Corsican Jehu was equal to the occasion. He drew the off-side animal—fortunately this one was the heavier of the two horses and the harness held—well over to the right, and giving a sharp cut with the whip to the frightened, struggling horse, he jerked him back on the road, before we quite knew where we were. Neither of us spoke for the next two or three lengths of the sharp descent, and the man was busy calming his horses, who were pulling very hard and squealing loudly.

We looked at each other, and I noticed that the face beside me wore rather a twisted smile. "Don't look so scared, Jess, it's over now, but it was a dam' close shave." He turned to the driver and complimented him on the management of his horses. The Corsican showed his teeth in a gratified grin. Directly he had reached a level stretch, he ground his brake hard on, and jumped lightly to the road with the reins still in his hand. For a few seconds he stood patting the two horses, whose heaving flanks were streaming with sweat; their fright over, they stood perfectly quiet and hung their heads, exhausted.

The Corsican made a picturesque figure by the side of them,

smiling and gesticulating, and then turning, proceeded to gather a large armful of mimosa which he presented to me with much bowing, and remarked in pleased tones, "I shall with much happiness take Madame again to the château."

But I think that was the last time we went, as we left Corsica earlier than we had intended, on account of a railway strike in England. I had now discarded my crutches or "outriggers," as my sons called those cumbersome sticks.

CHAPTER TWENTY-ONE

THE homeward journey from Corsica was for the most part uneventful. The weather was hardly kind and there was some anxiety as to whether or not we should really reach Canterbury, on account of the railway strike. I have made the journey both to Caen and to Marseilles since, and I was gratified to find that I had retained so much knowledge of the route, the one we had taken in 1921. Each town we passed through on my lonely journey in 1929 recalled that earlier one when Joseph Conrad had been with me.

After our return to Canterbury it was difficult to settle down somehow. A great many people came and went, many strangers. Amongst them Perceval Gibbon was one of the most frequent, and as always most welcome guest. A number of American admirers and some few Poles.

When Jacob Epstein spent three weeks with us at Oswalds, making a bust of my husband, I patted myself on the back to think that I had succeeded in persuading Joseph Conrad to agree to the arrangement; for the sculptor and his wife and daughter, lodging in Bridge would be better than actually sleeping in the house. Epstein was with us only for meals. I had felt that the two artists, both great men in their different ways, would find this much easier than being always together.

These people were truly Bohemian, and I fear we, my husband and I, were still conventional and did not, perhaps, quite understand our guests. He had a very pleasant-speaking voice, and was, when he chose, extremely entertaining. He could tell a tale and enjoy it even when it was against himself. I remember once being greatly amused by the story he related.

One day when he was walking past the British Museum a dog ran out and barked at him, and a stranger, who happened to be passing at the same time, remarked audibly, " that dog must be an art critic."

He also told us that a lady had wished him to execute an original monument for the tomb of Oscar Wilde in Paris, and that she wanted something symbolic of a " fallen angel." I had some time later on a maid with me who much amused me by her remark. She had expressed her dislike for the art of Jacob Epstein and then asked, " what nationality is he, madame ? " When I told her " a Polish-American-Jew," she returned, " quite a League of Nations in himself."

Those three weeks were a trifle hectic, rather like steering a big craft through a mine-field. Both artists required very careful handling. If the sitting were to be prolonged or some weighty matter come up for discussion, it were well that I could be at hand to break into the conversation. At these times I might well be considered a nuisance by the sculptor—occasionally also by the author—who was often ready to enter the ring with some extra pugnacity. But I must own that, on the whole, the work proceeded with an ease I had hardly dared to hope for.

Mrs. Epstein would bring her needlework—at that time a nightdress, in some black figured stuff, and she remarked to me that black had the advantage of keeping clean all the summer. The great day was the last.

Mr. Epstein had been expressing his anxiety as to the condition —for work—in which his Italian plasterers might arrive from town. There might have been too frequent stoppages on the way—and the work for which they were required was delicate in the extreme.

I rather rushed things that Saturday night without giving quite the necessary amount of consideration to the matter in hand, when I suggested that the London taxi Epstein usually employed on such occasions should come direct to Oswalds and that the men should be fed—and watered—there. The arrangement met with the full approval of both artists, and a telegram of instructions was dispatched and the answer in the affirmative received early in the evening. Mr. Epstein arrived the next morning in a state of great excitement long before the taxi could possibly be expected. He fumed to and fro. It was one thing for the master of the house to fume—and Joseph Conrad soon had enough of Epstein's restlessness, and I suppose not unnaturally resented the opening and shutting of doors, and the prancing up and downstairs. The great sculptor would march up the front flight, which was covered with red felt, and down the back staircase leading to the garden, as soon as he heard the sound of any wheeled vehicle passing. A door alone divided one staircase from the other.

I had already begun to doubt the wisdom of my suggestion when my husband appeared by my side, and in a voice of concentrated fury, whispered a few home truths, as to my crass impetuosity of the night before. What he foretold—he had sometimes an uncanny habit of predicting exactly what would happen —came to pass.

That London taxi arrived pretty well up to time, and unloaded the rest of the sculptor's paraphernalia, such as plaster-of-Paris, and what not, the three Italians, Epstein's familiar devil, and a fat driver. The bust in clay was in a big room over the kitchen, and the fun began when the Italians began to fling the wet plaster at it in order to make the cast. Water poured into the kitchen between the floor planks, the maids after being amused at first became tearful as they got wet through. The preparing of the lunch was almost impossible, and no amount of old newspapers spread on the floor round the effigy were efficient in keeping the floor above dry. It was impossible to stop the work of making the cast because the wretched stuff dried too quickly. But mercifully it came to an end at last, and our scratch meal was eaten in different parts of the house. The place presented a most devastated appearance. The front staircase covered with big white footprints on its red surface. Three times a maid swept it down that morning, and at last in desperation Joseph Conrad locked the door between the two staircases, and the next moment, almost before he reached his study, Mr. Epstein was rattling and shaking the door in a fury, and declaring that he would not use the back staircase.

The final touches and the packing of the bust were concluded during the afternoon of that never-to-be-forgotten Sunday. And I was amply punished for my rash suggestion. Epstein and his helpers occupied the room with the bust, my husband and his secretary locked themselves in the study, Madame Epstein went to sleep in the drawing-room all the afternoon, and I was left to the tender mercies of Peggy-Jean. . . . "What a Sunday!"

Then a little after six we watched the overloaded taxi negotiating the drive, piled up with steps, stage, buckets of clay, and the precious cast packed into it. Then the Epstein family, five men and one woman and child, and the personal luggage made up the load, and brought the car well down on the springs. The last I saw of it as it turned the corner away from the house was a comical miscellany of small garments trimmed with embroidery, socks, etc., waving from the bursting sides of the trunks on the roof. I reeled against the door-post utterly exhausted, and almost reconciled to the idea of birth control—for other people at least. I appreciated something of what some children's nurses had to put up with in the course of their daily duties.

Soon after this J. B. Pinker started for what was destined to be his last trip to America. Poor man, he spent a few days with us in Oswalds before he sailed, and both Joseph Conrad and I were both quite shocked to see him so depressed over a journey that formerly he would have thought so little of. I remember going with him to the station when he left us, he scarcely spoke during the drive, and when he did it was only to say that his daughter would have to be quick and get the rest of her things ready, as she was going to accompany him. I tried to rally him by pointing out the pleasure he would get out of showing the young girl round, a proud father.

As if prophetically he turned at last to me and said as he was leaving the car: "Well, I will confess that I am going on this trip with a heart as heavy as lead" . . . he paused while I waited sympathetically. "I feel somehow that I shall never come back." A short time after he landed in New York his family got the first disquieting news and cables passed between his house and his doctor's every day, and then one evening, two days after we had been told that there was still some hope, the youngest son arrived at Oswalds with the news of his father's death.

I have wondered often whether those two young sons knew how much their kindly thought in breaking the news thus gently to my husband, was appreciated by us both. Joseph Conrad found it very hard to believe that death, impartial, as he had always declared it to be, should have taken his friend before him. I can still hear his incredulous voice, raised as if in protest, saying to me : " And he always promised to see me off, and do his best for you."

I recalled that indeed there had been made a solemn promise when Joseph Conrad began his war-time adventure. " You will promise to do your best for my wife and the boys, if I never return, my dear Pinker ? "

During the next few months there was a good deal of worry, and my husband worked slowly and was mostly dissatisfied with his work when done. We two, with John, paid a visit to Liverpool, staying with Sir Robert Jones, and making a very delightful little tour with him through a part of North Wales.

It should have been all enjoyment, if the efforts of our host had met with the just reward. Sir Robert and his daughter and his son-in-law were kindness itself, but Joseph Conrad had a weight of depression and anxiety upon him that he could not shake off, which made him, I fear, rather an irritating guest most of the time.

In the early writing days, these moods were usually the outcome of a period when he had been unable to work, but by this time there was no such urgent need for him to stay in his " torture chamber," as he called it, and I was disappointed that he could not shake himself free of his despondency.

He was little better when he returned, but continued restlessly unhappy and dissatisfied. After a time there was a suggestion that he should go to America. He had so many readers there and so many real friends over the water that there seemed a good reason for his visit. Particularly as the Doubledays, whom we had met several times, were anxious that he should be their guest in Oyster Bay.

For some months he toyed with the idea, talking over the project with his friends Richard Curle and Jean Aubry, amongst others. I said very little, I could not go with him, and I do not think many of his friends would have considered it advisable that I should, even had I been less lame. In the end it was decided that I should remain at Oswalds with my nurse-companion, with

Borys near enough to come to me if necessary, and John at school in Tonbridge. Richard Curle was to come to see me from time to time, and I had the best of all my personal friends in close attendance, Dr. Whitehead Reid, and his wife. The doctor was a tower of strength and I knew I could depend upon him absolutely, not only professionally.

Once the idea had taken firm hold in Joseph Conrad's mind there was no turning back. Almost he regarded the journey to America as an event ordained by fate. It was to cement the friendship between him and his publishers, and bring him into personal contact with his many admirers in America. Then the preparations began in grim earnest. He went himself to buy his "trousseau," as he insisted upon calling it. He bought, among other things, a new dress suit and that was certainly not before he needed it. In 1923 he had the same suit he had had ever since we were married, and by this time it was a true shade of bottle-green. It bore signs of wear by reason of its shiny surface, and one tear.—Fair wear and tear—without a doubt. The tear recalled a very distressing accident in the early days of our married life. He had been present at an informal concert in London, given at the house of a friend of John Galsworthy. This friend had three perfect little imps, children in ages ranging from seven to thirteen. This evening their "fun" took the form of putting nails into the chairs in the drawing-room. Perhaps the effect they desired to produce was something more dramatic than they succeeded in bringing about, but for Joseph Conrad it was quite sufficiently devastating. He sat down in the chair next to mine, there was a smothered "damn" and he hastily essayed to rise, the next sound was that of an unmistakable rending of cloth. An expression crossed his face of a pathetic horror, and he contented himself in the end by drawing his thin form closer to my side of the chair, clear of the nail. He remained perfectly still after that until the end of the concert, then, giving me a muttered injunction to keep close behind him, we joined the first movement to leave the crowded room. When we got back to the rooms where we were staying a large three-cornered rent showed in the back of the only pair of dress trousers he possessed.

The next morning I had to get them invisibly mended in time for him to attend a reception by M. Rodin, but the mending was indeed invisible, and remained so until 1923. I induced him to surrender the tail coat, crush hat and the waistcoat to our gardener for private theatricals; the nether garments the cook petitioned for—they would be so useful to her husband for funerals. Thus the suit fulfilled its complex destiny.

The trousseau for America was very complete, even excessive. Joseph Conrad bought a dozen of everything (except suits)—of these only six, including the dress suit. I had to make up his evening dress ties with press studs—his own ideas—fit links into innumerable shirts and pairs of cuffs. In fact do everything so that his dressing could be accomplished with the least amount of effort on his part. I made a separate little case for each shoe.

There was a curious air of determination over this journey that disturbed me somewhat, and the more hard and fixed those engagements, the more anxious I became. John was to come up from Tonbridge to see his father, and daily Joseph Conrad looked for a word that Borys would be in town then as well. One visit he was determined to make before he left, and that was to see his old friend G. F. W. Hope in Essex.

Two days before he was due to leave for Glasgow we left for London, and took up our quarters at the Curzon Hotel. Each time I went into our room the corded trunks seemed to hold an added significance, a something fixed and immovable like a fate. Quite a crowd of people coming and going all day kept my husband busy, and when at last we were alone he was too tired for much conversation. John arrived the day before his father was due to leave for Glasgow from where he was to sail for America. It was a load off my mind that he was to sail with Captain David Bone, who was then captain of the *Tuscania*, and whose brother, Muirhead Bone, was also to be a passenger. There is a photograph of the three men together.

There was another great relief and that was Richard Curle's letter to me to the effect that he would journey to Glasgow to see my husband on board for the great adventure.

The letter, or rather the extract, I include here shows that Joseph Conrad had no little interest in what he ate, even when he might have been a trifle sentimental at leaving me—the letter is addressed to Richard Curle. ". . . I see from your letter to Jessie that you mean, if you can, to see me off at Glasgow, I write to ask if you would have any objection to start from St. Pancras at 9.50 a.m. on Friday, arr. Glas. 7.5. p.m. I propose the Midland as the food on that line is eatable—but on the . . . it is *not*. Of course, if it is too early for you we might start at 12.15 arr. G. 9.25.

You are a dear fellow to stand by me so nobly. Methinks we might travel third on Midland and in fact spend most of our time in the restaurant car. What do you say ?

Ever yours,

J. CONRAD.

P.S.—B. (Borys) came for a few hours last Sunday. Everything's very satisfactory with him. Will you come to the Curzon on the 16th at 7.30 and dine ? "

Those two days at the Curzon came at last to an end, and the Thursday night, the last before my husband left for Glasgow, was crowded with engagements. One or two newspaper men turned up unexpectedly for interviews, and it was with a distinct feeling of relief that I saw the last one leave and Richard Curle enter. I felt then that I could relax my vigilance and get perhaps half an hour's rest before dinner. Almost I had risen to leave the lounge where we had been sitting, but at that moment a page entered with a registered and express letter which he passed to my husband. He gave one look at it and dismissed the boy with a curt command: " Give it to my wife, I won't have it. I told them not to forward any more dam' letters. Give it to Mrs. Conrad." He turned his back in a very decided fashion and the boy handed the envelope to me with his pencil for me to sign as it was a registered letter.

I turned it over and over in my fingers, somewhat puzzled, and made a movement towards the couch where my husband sat with two or three friends laughing and talking. He seemed to sense my approach without even turning his head. He waved his hand towards me and said in a testy tone: " I don't want to see it or know what it's about. It's forwarded from home, and I told them not to send on anything more. I told them . . ."

Still, for some reason I was reluctant to break the seal. The letter had been originally posted in London, and I could quite understand why my old faithful cook had forwarded it on, contrary to my husband's express instructions. Registered and express, she would consider it of great importance. I broke the seal and drew the short communication from the envelope. I glanced at the paper and as quickly crushed it in my fingers, and blindly made for the door. Almost I thought I could not get out of the room without one of the three men noticing my agitation and calling my husband's attention to it.

Once outside I tried to pull myself together, and get to my room somehow and think. I walked to the lift and mutely motioned that I wanted to go to my room. Then, trembling violently, I directed the porter to get me a little brandy and bring it to me upstairs. I stumbled into the room and locked the door after me.

That fateful piece of paper simply stated the bald fact that our son Borys had been married eight months and gave the date and the place. It was signed by his mother-in-law. Why have kept it secret?

I have heard it often argued that a man should have only himself to please, and nobody should choose his wife for him, and this I heartily endorse. But his father was a desperately unreasonable man. This concealment he could not be expected to understand or accept as a more prosaic Englishman would. Then it flashed into my mind that this was the reason, perhaps, that had kept the boy from coming to see his father before he left. He had waited too long, and funked it at the last. What should I do, he might even come yet ? I heard the footsteps coming towards the door and prayed it might be only the brandy I had ordered.

I could think of no way of breaking the news, which I knew would not be received well because of the secrecy. I had known ever since the boys began to grow up that their natural inclinations would be difficult for my husband to realize, and the knowledge that his son had been married for eight months—in secret—would need a good deal of getting used to, for Joseph Conrad to accept the fact. I knew that I myself had received a shock, something in the nature of a blow in the chest, but I could have recovered from it very soon. Not so my husband. It would have taken me many hours to even make him understand, and I dreaded the effect of such a piece of news for him on the eve of what he considered a big adventure.

I spent some three-quarters of an hour cogitating, and in the end I was not any nearer a solution of the difficulty. As I expected, a page was sent to tell me that they were waiting for dinner for me.

When I recall that night I wonder that my manner passed without his noticing anything strange. Everyone who entered that dining-room he looked up to see if by chance it might be Borys. His non-appearance seemed to cause him some disappointment. With John and me he was decidedly testy. It was an effort to swallow anything, and most of the dishes I sent away untouched. Presently one of the friends who were dining with us, who had evidently observed my want of appetite, leaned forward and patted my hand while he made some chaffing remark as to my being a "grass widow" for some two months or more. This broke the spell and also gave me my clue. My husband could easily be persuaded that I was fretting over his leaving me. The idea really pleased him. I decided then that if he did not refer to the letter I had better keep the news it contained to myself—for the present, even if I found no chance to tell him before he left. I felt convinced that either all these elaborate preparations would be thrown away—because he would not be able to go, or that he would brood over the boy's want of confidence when he got away to such an extent that he would not live to come back. This view may sound extravagant, but I knew my man so well I could not help the rather cynical reflection that two months added to eight would scarcely make a great difference to Borys, anyhow.

That was a terrible night. I lay awake watching my husband when I knew he slept and feigned sleep when I knew for certain that he was awake. The night seemed endless, and I was in dread of the morning. No other confession I might have had to make would have disturbed me to such an extent. I felt positively sick. Then, when the maid brought the early morning tea, I saw a buff-coloured envelope on the tray, and my heart was in my mouth. My husband noticed my agitation, and remarked irritably: "One would think you had never seen a telegram before." He seized the envelope and began reading aloud the message it contained.

To my intense relief, as I had decided to say nothing, the telegram only gave a pressure of work as the excuse for not coming to town from Manchester, and sent an affectionate farewell. The wording pleased Joseph Conrad, who immediately passed it on to me with the remark, made as if it had been me who had constantly commented upon the fact that he had not "seen fit to put himself to the trouble of coming to see him off": "There, my dear, you see what he says, pressure of work. I am very glad he did not neglect his work to come to London. You see for yourself he is very busy?" Then, the moment afterwards, under his breath: "But I wish I had seen him, I feel rather worried somehow. You know I feel sometimes that I do not know him, since the war, as if there was something . . . something . . . I daresay you know perfectly well what I mean, don't look so much like an owl." My expression might have been, and in fact I am pretty sure was, a bit strange. I had been thinking that the boy gave no indication of his altered status in the wire. Almost I laughed out loud, but I managed to restrain myself as John entered the room and I took notice of the instructions that I was to write and tell the "young sinner" that his father had left his love and would write to him from the ship.

The last few moments before he left with John for the station were tense and filled with anxious apprehension. I seemed to have loaded myself with a terrible responsibility by my decision. But it was too late now to alter my mind. I watched the taxi out of sight, and the last wave of the hand before they disappeared. Even then I dared not relax until John had gone back to school that afternoon.

I re-read that letter and had hard matter to keep myself sufficiently in hand not to call John's attention to my unusually restless manner. Somehow I must keep this disturbing piece of news to myself. I would not have anyone suppose that the mere fact that my son wished to get married would have met with any silly opposition from me, or from my husband—when he had accustomed himself to the idea, but I know this would have taken rather a long time. I, in fact we, had both met the girl who was now his wife; there was simply the secrecy, and that would have been a very real something to overlook.

My mind followed the train that bore the traveller on the first stage of his journey. At one time I almost decided to follow him by the next train to Glasgow, for no other reason but to ease my mind and conscience of this secret. I went as far as to find out exactly how long I should have to make up my mind, and whether John would have left for school before I had to start. Then in the midst of my indecision came a long letter from Borys declaring his intention to try and intercept his father in Glasgow and tell him himself.

This decided me not to attempt to follow, and instead I went to a solicitor friend and told him the whole case, asking him to procure for me a copy of the marriage certificate. I was beginning to feel the effects of the whole thing, and I dared not break down in London. I kept my appointment with my two great friends, and their advice, both medical and friendly, helped me very much indeed. They both, Sir Robert and Dr. Reid, understood my reasons for keeping the matter from Joseph Conrad until his return. I sent a very long telegram to Borys, warning him of what the consequences might be if he did succeed in reaching Glasgow in time to tell his father of his marriage. Then I returned to Canterbury, and took up my life alone with the burden of the secret, the first I had ever had from my husband in all our life together.

I first wrote to Borys, explaining my reasons for not telling his father, and forbidding him to do so until his return from America. I also pointed out that the fact that his father did not know of the marriage, made it impossible for me to receive his wife, as his wife, until his father had been told. This stipulation I felt had to be made, otherwise I might have been suspected of being disloyal to Joseph Conrad. For the next two months I did not see Borys. Each time he wrote he managed always to convey the idea that the blame of everything was mine.

In the two months that followed I devoted myself to the business of writing and answering the heap of letters, and during that time the very real friendship shown me by Dr. Whitehead Reid sustained and helped me much more than he knew. Once or twice something in my husband's letters showed that I had not been quite so successful as I thought, and he imagined that I had a grievance of some sort against him. He would write protesting that there was only one woman who could live in his thoughts, and declared that he was getting impatient to return to me.

The first letter I received from him from the other side speaks for itself, and I include it here because it gives such a wonderful picture of the very friendly reception accorded him from his American admirers. It shows also the great regard and tender care shown by Mr. and Mrs. Doubleday, who looked after the great author for the whole of his visit, and made things possible for that super-sensitive man who was now out of reach of my motherly care. I shall always have a very grateful and deep appreciation for their kindness. They even went so far as to bring him back to me themselves. And it was, as they would say in their country, "some journey." Mr. Doubleday amused me very much by asking for a formal receipt for Joseph Conrad.

I wrote across a two-penny stamp the following :

"Received with thanks, from Mr. and Mrs. Doubleday, one rejuvenated and regenerated husband. Jessie Conrad." (Adding the date.)

CHAPTER TWENTY-TWO

UPON consideration I will include this letter intact.

EFFENDI HILL. OYSTER BAY.
LONG ISLAND, NEW YORK,
4.5.23.

MY DEAREST CHICA,

You know from Doubleday's cable of my safe arrival in New York, also that I have arrived in this very place.

I will not attempt to describe to you my landing, because it is indescribable. To be aimed at by forty cameras held by forty men is a nerve shattering experience. Even D'day looked exhausted after we had escaped from that mob,—and the other mob of journalists.

Then a Polish deputation,—men and women (some of these quite pretty)—rushed me on the wharf and thrust enormous nosegays into my hands. Eric nobly carried two of them. Mrs. Doubleday took charge of another, I went along like a man in a dream, and took refuge in D's car.

Imagine, my dear, Powell was there too. Mrs. Doubleday has asked him to call, and he dined here yesterday and then played Beethoven and Chopin. Between whiles we talked of you. In fact, you have been very much to the fore in everybody's conversation.

To-morrow, Friday, I go to Garden City in the morning. In the evening there is a dinner-party for J. W. Davis (late ambassador to England) and Col. House to meet me. In an hour or so I expect Eric Pinker to arrive here for a quiet talk. From what I have seen he seems to be in good form. Certainly our prospects are excellent on the face of them. My reception by the press was quite remarkable in its friendliness. But I am feeling distinctly homesick. It comes over me strongly as I sit writing these words.

Doubleday insists on sending you a message in every week-end cable they despatch to Europe. It is very nice of him, and I am pleased to think you will hear of me pretty often. As to writing to you long reports of the daily proceedings, it is not to be thought of. It must be left till my return when I'll tell you all the wondrous tale.

I do long for a sight of your handwriting. Mrs. Doubleday has just knocked at the door of my bedroom (next to the billiard room) to say good night (she has been out), and asks me to remember her to you. She is really very good and tries to make me feel at home. The house is charming—large, luxurious ; and the garden quite pretty in the American way.

I close this by depositing many kisses on your dear face.

Tenderest love and hugs to the children—quite as if they were still little. Remember me to all the domestic staff of our faithful retainers."

And this extract, when he describes his great success at the reading of " Victory " at the house of Mrs. Curtis James. I could picture what a very great ordeal this reading was going to be. I could picture my husband so vividly standing up before all those people, and the fact that the watch I had given him should act as a stimulus and help to sustain him in the great effort, gave me a positive pang, a feeling of pleasure that in its intensity was almost a pain. I am taking the telling extracts from two letters.

He says he spoke for exactly an hour and a quarter. It could not have been the length of time, because he had talked for much longer than that on many occasions when he has had sympathetic friends to listen—and even they have not been that to start with. But the gathering on this occasion was composed of over fifty strangers, and there must have been a feeling of strain, let the audience be ever so kindly and sympathetic. And of course, the fact that he was reading in a language not his own. He was always terribly sensitive of his faulty pronounciation, right to the end of his life. I used to tease him by saying that he was only a "stupid British Subject," when he so often raised his hands and declared that we English people pronounced all words alike—we had no ear.

I was very touched by the following short extract from his letter written after the reading. " I may tell you that it was a most brilliant affair, and I would have given anything for you to have been there, seen all that crowd and all that splendour, the very top of the basket of the fashionable and literary circles. All last week there was desperate fighting and plotting in the N. York Society to get invitations. I had the lucky inspiration to refuse to accept any payment ; and my dear I had a perfect success. I gave a talk and pieces of reading out of ' Victory.' After the applause from the audience, which stood up when I appeared, had ceased, I had a moment of positive anguish. Then I took out the watch you had given me and laid it on the table, made one mighty effort and began to speak. That watch was the greatest comfort to me. Something of you. I timed myself by it all along. . . ."

The days on which no letter or message arrived seemed endless. As soon as I had satisfied myself that the weighty secret I held was still apparently a secret, I was greatly relieved. I began to feel the effects of the strain, but I could not see that I had been wrong in my determination to wait until he returned before telling him of Borys's marriage. I was very sorely tempted to confide in John, and I would have given worlds to have seen Borys and heard him say something that I could comfort myself with. But it was plain that my letter saying I could not receive his wife until his father knew also, had struck some note of resentment he did not, perhaps, understand, and I could not even appear to go back on my word. I wrote to him and I had letters in answer to the other news I passed on of his father, but that was all.

During those two months I saw a good deal of intimate friends, but to none I dared to speak of my worry and yet I would never dismiss it from my mind. On one occasion our fellow traveller on the trip to Poland came for a week-end, and John, because of the friendship that existed between Joseph Retinger and this boy, came home from school to meet him. Poor John looked in great surprise at me when Dr. Retinger made a request that I should allow the boy to go with him to Mexico when he returned in a few days to that country. I felt greatly exasperated because not many hours before this good man had explained at length that the doctors had given him less than six months to live. I was furious to think that a dying man should dare to dream of taking a young boy with him to such a hot-bed of strife as Mexico. However, the idea was so fantastic that I controlled my anger, and contented myself with mildly pointing out the futility of such a notion.

After this episode I felt more utterly alone than I had done before. Even the courtship that was proceeding under my very nose between my nurse and the young chauffeur, late autumn and early spring, failed to call forth more than a passing reflection on the strangeness of human fallacy. The project of this marriage presented many difficult situations and only my sense of humour prevented me from becoming somewhat incensed. This complication also was as yet unknown to Joseph Conrad, and there were times when I felt beset from all sides at once. I had no notion how my strange husband might regard the queer circumstances. It would, of course, depend entirely upon the mood he was in when the state of affairs should be revealed to him as to whether he retained the two in the household. There was nothing to do but wait and see.

She had lived in our house exactly the same length of time as the chauffeur had, and I for one could not see the attraction for either although, separately, I liked both—but then I was getting on in years and there was an air of frivolity about the whole thing, that robbed it of all, or nearly all, sentiment. She was a fiery temperament, and could be unaccountably rude when it so pleased her. She once treated me to a long tirade, in complaint of no less a person than Joseph Conrad, and then both boys. I had scarcely heeded the complaint at first, but at last I turned on her with the remark: "I have no doubt I owe you an apology for being the wife of one, and the mother of the other two people of whom you so strongly disapprove, but it is too late to alter it now."

The weeks flew past, and I rehearsed every form in which I might break the news of Borys's marriage to my husband on his return ; somehow I distrusted the idea of the young man undertaking the task himself—and I must confess in spite of my reluctance, I felt that I should be the better person to drop the bombshell. I fully intended to meet my husband in London, in spite of any opposition on his part, for fear the news reached him from some other source first. But the terms upon which he wrote urging me to send Borys to meet him and await him myself at Oswalds, provided some rather anxious deliberations. I used to say I had never promised to " love, honour and obey," but I do not think I had ever disobeyed a wish he had expressed before. The fact that I did so now would, I was perfectly aware, greatly displease him, and also prejudice my cause from the first. But what could I do ?

Joseph Conrad's letters came very frequently after his interesting evening at the house of Mrs. Curtis James, and I had news from many other people to whom he wrote from America. It was fortunate that I knew my husband so well. I might have had some very anxious hours had I not been so familiar with his habit of exaggeration, especially as regards his health. This extract from a letter he had sent to Richard Curle, for instance.

. . . " Am awfully rushed or else lying prostrate to recover, but in either case in no writing mood." He then refers to the great evening of his stay in America. " But I must drop you a line to say that the evening at Mrs. Curtis James' was a very fashionable affair—and what is more a great success. I gave a talk and readings from 'Victory.' One hour and a quarter, without an ovation at the end. They were most attentive. Laughs at the proper places and snuffles at the last when I read the whole chapter of Lena's death. It was a great social function . . . F. N. D. himself is impressed."

The reception in America had been most warm-hearted and friendly, and I had very great satisfaction and pride in the knowledge of the fact. It seemed somehow to make up a little for my loneliness and concentrated anxiety. The nearer the time came for me to meet my husband, the more restless I became. I have thought since that possibly my difficulty in getting about—under my own steam so to speak—may have exaggerated that feeling not a little. Just as a friend once said, he had fasted a whole week, and all the time had thought of nothing but food. I would wake in the night and ache with longing for movement. One night when Joseph Conrad was actually on his way home I woke with a feeling of such intense horror that it took me more than an hour to recover myself, or regain my composure.

My dream had been terribly vivid, and waking the impression still remained as an uncomfortable fact. I had seen my husband dripping wet and shivering with the cold, having been drowned, he had crept into bed by my side, and I found myself passing my hands down that side to see if I were indeed wet, when I awoke.

I could hardly possess myself in patience till his next telegram, which I did not receive until he reached France, two or three days later. Needless to say I kept this very disturbing experience to myself, but as an impression I know of nothing so real.

Before his actual return I had received a big batch of letters from American admirers which touched me profoundly. They were all loud in praise of my husband and his wonderful achievement in the world of letters in a foreign tongue. I told him jokingly that had I been in doubt as to the distinction of my "property"—this being my favourite expression—those letters would have made me realize his importance.

There is this tribute to Joseph Conrad by no less a person than Mr. Putnam, a publisher. He was driving with the Consul-General of Poland to the U.S.A. through the streets of Cracow, soon after Poland was again Poland. The Consul-General was none other than my husband's old school friend, Mr. Konstantin Buszczynski, who pointed out to his companion the house where the great author lived in his youth.

The house was a drab, uninteresting building with a narrow sidewalk in front. No. 9, Ulica Szpitalna (Hospital Street). "In that corner of the courtyard," the Consul-General continued, "under the archway, that strange boy told us the most extraordinary stories. They were always of the sea, of sailors and craft, and all the happenings were stories of far-away countries. It is strange, you must admit, that even then the sea was in his blood."

There is now a tablet placed on the house with a very suitable wording, and the one place I want to see once more before I die is Cracow, and the descendants of Konstantin Buszczynski I would see also once again. I still remember that day during my one and only visit to Cracow. The sight of the two school friends, meeting by chance in a public dining-room. I see my two boys' faces of concern as the two grown men rushed to embrace each other.

The strangeness of that situation called a flush of colour to the two young faces, almost as if they had been caught peeping at something they were not intended to see. For my part I turned away my face until that fervent greeting was over, and the boys and I introduced.

I came across a cutting this morning that I am moved to include here, because I feel that these pages would be incomplete without proper reference to my husband's own spoken tribute to the country that has in the past, and may, I hope, continue in the future, to reverence the name of Joseph Conrad.

He was asked just at the end of his visit, while becalmed, as the paper puts it, to give his opinion of America. I can picture his concern, and reading what he said in reply, I am bound to admire his tactful answer. Usually he would have "let fly" some expression of annoyance purely personal to himself, and most likely without any direct bearing on what he had been asked. But as I have said, his reply was tactful and sincere, and it appears to have pleased his interlocutor.

It was certainly understood that my husband had enjoyed his stay in U.S.A. "When I was coming over, people told me that I would find it different from anything I had ever seen before—and I have. Very. One would think that all cities would be alike, yet New York has a distinct individuality. I found it as people told me I would, only very much better. You are generally let down by an actuality, but it was the reverse with me in this case."

The cutting goes on to state that my husband had been interested in America since he was seventeen or eighteen years old, exploring the country through the pages of their most representative authors. "He knows them. I believe far better than he had admitted to any of us. A few casual remarks about his early reading of Washington Irving, his complete familiarity with Mark Twain and Edgar Allan Poe, Whitman and others, show a man who has been observing us through the printed page for many years. He knew what to expect in the general appearance of the country, its architecture, its spaciousness, but he says he found the buildings more artistic than he was led to expect, the people more gracious, and he speaks most glowingly of the generosity of the Americans with whom he has come in contact. In fact, Mr. Conrad's warmth towards us could very easily turn our heads. . . ."

The talk shifted after this to Joseph Conrad's last days at sea, and the good ship *Torrens*. This trip was made with the late John Galsworthy as passenger and Mr. Sanderson, who is head-master of the Elstree school. John Galsworthy was a barrister, and while at sea studied navigation (and here I would note that this fact must be the reason why someone declared that the great novelist Galsworthy sailed as super-cargo—a most erroneous idea), "while the schoolmaster spent hours learning the sailor's hornpipe from the bo'sun. Then someone mentioned *Typhoon*."

"Ah," said Joseph Conrad, "but that was one of my storm pieces. *The Nigger of the Narcissus* is the one on a sailing ship in a storm. Having done that I felt that I should do the steamship—*Typhoon*. (The Nan-Shan.)"

Later on he talked laughingly of the cheap editions he had been wont to buy of Mark Twain's masterpieces, and spoke reminiscently of reading these books when he was on the Congo.

" I recall a remark made to me once when I was paying a call on Arthur Symons. He had a friend sitting in his room who affected the appearance of Mark Twain. The white flannel suit, the white hair, in fact, the whole appearance was a direct copy of the great American author. I remarked upon the resemblance laughingly and with perfect good-humour the ' copy ' admitted the intentional likeness, but he insisted, ' you see the very name gives me that licence, " Mark Twain." ' "

This was unanswerable and showed what I always appreciate, a sense of humour, and after all, " imitation is the surest form of flattery," so they say. But it is a fact that before my husband went to America it was the one country to which I had no desire to go. His visit made me feel quite different and I would go to-morrow were it possible. It would seem to me that *if* I were well received it would somehow bring him again in close touch with the people of that nation. I felt that he would somehow have a better chance on his own, and I think that the idea might have been because he had become so dependent upon me as to be just a trifle laughable at times. He would demand to know, "Is there any sugar in this mint sauce —or is there any salt in that rice ? " before he had begun to eat. He never lowered his voice or made such a question in any way confidential, and his hostess would always feel a little confused. As to myself, as I had not tasted either it was impossible to answer the question.

We reached the Curzon Hotel early in the afternoon of his arrival at Southampton. We had very little dinner, and this very late, having waited until after nine, and then almost decided that he had been late getting ashore and must be staying the night in Southampton.

I had been looking through *The Times* trying to divert my mind and succeeding very badly. Several prolonged yawns from my nurse exasperated me greatly, but I still sought refuge in the newspaper. A sudden exclamation from my companion who was sitting by my side, recalled me to myself. I gazed towards the door, and there, motionless, stood Jossph Conrad, looking as if he had returned from another world, a lost soul, almost I fancied, with a catch in my breath, as if he sensed some untoward happening or disaster.

The next moment I shook myself free of that terrible sense of apprehension, and tried, to myself, to justify in some degree Borys' contention, probably his father would have done the same if the fancy had taken him. The lonely figure drew nearer, and his first words came in a tired tone of reproach : " Why didn't

Borys meet me at the station, I looked everywhere for him? Isn't he here?"

"I think he . . . is still very busy," I blurted out. "But I am here and John is coming up in the morning, his half term, you know. He seems to have grown so much older since you went away." He interrupted me with the question: "Yes, yes, he is a dear kid, I want to see him very much, but I still don't see why Borys . . ."

"Perhaps he will be here . . . to-morrow. I haven't heard from him for a few days. My last letter may have missed him . . . he may be moving about, you know. Would you like some dinner?" He shook his head, and turned irritably to the waiter who had come hopefully forward, and taken his parcel out of his hand.

"Look out, that's glass, be careful, dam'. What's the number of our room? No, no. I don't want any dinner. I shall go straight upstairs." He motioned again to the waiter and ordered irritably some tea and sandwiches. The man turned to do his bidding and my husband stood a few seconds motionless biting his lip, almost tearfully. I laid my hand on his arm and only then he seemed to remember that he had hardly greeted me.

"I am dead tired, Jess. I don't want to know anything whatever, or see any letters to-night. Come up and talk to me upstairs. I thought Borys was sure to be here, and that I must have missed him somehow at the station. You are certain I haven't, I suppose?"

I followed him from the room and smiled to myself as my nurse reappeared with her hat on. I knew she was going to seek her young man, and I only nodded when she said she should be with me in a few moments.

Once upstairs I tried to coax my husband's mind from the subject that evidently filled it to the exclusion of everything else. Such a reception as I had had was new to me. I knew somehow that he was aware that I was not quite in accord, and the knowledge made me more awkward than ever. I helped him to get ready for bed, and into his dressing-gown, and made no remark when he turned from the fire disclosing in the back of the £20 birthday dressing-gown I had given him just before he left, a large arch-shaped burn. The edges were singed, and the damage made him look a grotesque figure as he turned again from me.

Almost as if he could see out of the back of his head he flung round abruptly and said: "There's nothing to look so tragic about. It's burnt, that's plain, isn't it? I stood too close to the dam' electric fire in my cabin. You can take a piece from the back of the pockets and mend it when we get back. It's done, anyway, and pulling that face won't alter it."

No, it wouldn't alter it. Nothing could alter the news I would have to break to him—in the morning—it was clear that it must wait till then. As to his suggestion for repairing the damage! I tried to visualize the effect but the mental effort was beyond me. To change the subject I asked where he had left the Doubledays, and what the passage had been like; in fact, I asked a dozen questions, tumbling the words out, scarcely giving him time to answer any. He grew impatient at last and turned away a bit sulky—exactly as I had expected he would.

By this time my nurse had been in and said good night. He pulled himself together a bit, and apologized for not greeting her, when he first saw her. "I shall be better in the morning, my dear. Glad to get back home out of this. You won't catch me moving far away after this for a long time. Good night." He picked up the book he had been reading with such a decided air of dismissal that the lady faded away looking none too pleased, I somewhat flippantly thinking to myself that perhaps she would again call for my excuse for being the wife of one and the mother of the other two.

As on the night preceding his departure, I lay very quiet in my single bed watching the tired face that I had missed for a whole two months. The light fell full on it, but each time I cautiously moved with the intention of extinguishing that light, he shifted uneasily, and I knew that he was only feigning sleep. Perhaps because he did not wish to answer any more "silly questions," as he had said a short while before.

It must have been three in the morning before I completely got to sleep, and it seemed hardly a couple of hours later when I heard the movements of the hotel staff moving. Even then he obstinately refused to notice me till the maid appeared with the early tea. It was then that I took my courage in both hands, and made my fateful announcement in as natural a tone and with as little *impressement* as possible. I had the habit of calling him "boy" when I wished to be extra friendly. "Boy dear . . . Borys is married." . . . Joseph Conrad started up in bed, gripping my arm with cruel force. "Why do you tell me that, why don't you keep such news to yourself?"

He would listen to no explanation. He asked no questions, and for more than an hour made no further remarks, except his familiar dam'. He turned again to the book he had been reading, but I noticed that the pages remained unturned, and even his cigarette was allowed to go out. I felt desperately sorry for him, and yet for the life of me I could think of nothing to say. It had been in my mind that probably it was best that Borys was not at hand, at that moment. I don't think that if he had come in person to break his news would have made a very great difference at that first moment.

Presently my husband roused himself and leaping from his bed he went swiftly to the dressing-table and seized his hair brushes in both hands. This was such a familiar habit, that of brushing his hair when at all perturbed, that it seemed to lift some of the weight of oppression off my mind. I ventured upon some remark about a neighbour, but without heeding me he flung the brushes down and said in a terse voice: "I suppose you are certain of what you have told me?"

Somewhat surprised I answered at once, "Quite," and proceeded to explain the means I had taken to verify the news directly he had started for Glasgow. He interrupted me with scant ceremony. "I don't want to know anything more about it. It is done, and I have been treated like a blamed fool, dam'." He began brushing his hair again with the same energy, and then presently in an ominously quiet tone: "What address does he give?" But in the next moment he declared he did not wish to know. "I have accepted an invitation for us both for lunch to-day at Brown's Hotel, the Doubledays will expect us about one." He finished dressing and left the room, and I did not see him again until I was ready to start out for lunch. He refused to use our own car, and hailed a passing taxi.

We drove the short distance in silence, but immediately we arrived, and almost before I had time to greet the good people, he announced in a flat tone: "My son Borys is married. My wife knows all about it."

It was then that I felt thankful that I had written the letter to Borys saying I could not receive his wife until his father knew of his marriage. I was feeling very uneasy and apprehensive at the way my husband had taken the news. It was distinctly disconcerting, and I found it difficult to understand his attitude. Then I caught the words he was speaking from the other side of the room. "I have told my wife she should have kept such news to herself." Mr. Doubleday replied incredulously: "But that would hardly be possible. Let us hope they will be happy." . . . "Well, they won't, then. What has he got to keep a wife on? And let me tell you I don't like the way this has been done in secret. I wasn't to know then, why should I now?" . . .

Mrs. Doubleday was talking to me and generously trying to keep me from overhearing the conversation at the other side of the room. It was not a little heated on my husband's part—although the two men were not discussing the possibilities of my son's married happiness, but some remote business matter connected with the publication of a book of verse.

The lunch passed off after that without any further reference to our troubles, and we left soon after to return to our hotel. At the door eagerly looking out ahead we caught sight of the

"OSWALDS," BISHOPSBOURNE
Where Joseph Conrad died in August, 1924.

JOSEPH CONRAD AS A SHIP'S PROW, THE WORK OF MISS DORA CLARKE

Now in the Reading-room of the Seamen's Institute, New York.

dear boy John standing in the doorway. As soon as his father saw him he grabbed my arm with his usual nervous grip, and turned to me with a scowl that rather appalled me. "Does John know?" I shook my head. "And when did this dam' affair take place?"

I endeavoured to release his grip of my arm as I answered quietly: "The news was in the letter that arrived the day before you left, dear, and he had been married eight months before that."

He ground his teeth, a sure sign that he was desperately angry. "And why was I not told? Why am I told now? I've been treated like a fool."

I laid my hand on his knee. "That was my fault, dear. I was afraid to tell you. I was afraid you would not go, and all your plans were fixed—or," and I dropped my voice to a whisper, "you would never come back. Try to see, dear, what a dreadful choice I had to make, and make quickly. I knew you would be shocked, even as I was, but, dear, try to get used to it, they may be very happy together, and anyhow it is too late to alter things now."

He turned on me with fury, then muttered as he flung himself out of the car: "Yes . . . they may be, but they won't."

There was nothing further said on the subject. The meeting between the father and his younger son held all the elements of real tenderness and affection, that I felt must in a measure atone for the pain my news had evidently given him. He turned as John greeted me and assisted me to get out of the car, then wheeled abruptly round, put his hand through the boy's arm, and they disappeared together into the lounge. I crept to the lift and reached my room, trembling like a leaf. I had not thought I should feel the reaction so much. I stayed there till John came to fetch me for tea.

Two days later we left for Oswalds and home. John had gone back to Tonbridge after the one night, and I had had a brief respite during the time he had been with his father. The two were inseparable, and seeing this I kept as much in the background as possible. But the lull was brief, and as the train drew out of the station and the boy's last wave of the hand was lost to sight, Joseph Conrad returned to the subject of Borys as if the conversation had been only a moment or so before. Again he asked me: "May I ask if you are certain of . . . what you have told me . . . have you any proof?" I turned quickly towards him with the words: "Certainly, directly you had gone, and John had returned to school, I went to Robert Garnett and asked those solicitors to get me a copy of the certificate of marriage. It is true enough. I did that because if you had heard of it from anywhere I should have sent the certificate to you at once. I have no notion why it was kept a secret, and I have not seen either Borys or his wife since you left. I wrote to him telling him how you were when you left, and also how disappointed you had been not to see him in town, but I said that you were not to be told until your return. And I also said that I could not receive his wife until you did. I thought perhaps Borys——" My husband interrupted me with a mirthless laugh. "But you couldn't expect anything else. His duty was to his wife. I'm glad to see he had that amount of decency, anyway. Poor old Chica, you have had a bad time of it, I suppose. When did you hear last ?" And then before I could answer he flung out his hands and said: "Don't tell me, I don't want to know. Is there a child coming ?" I shook my head. "I cannot say, but I should say not."

CHAPTER TWENTY-THREE

I THINK I was never more glad to leave town than on this occasion. I could feel that the state of excitement under which my husband was labouring must have its inevitable consequences, an attack of gout. I doubted very much if he would keep up while Mr. and Mrs. Doubleday were with us for the short visit they were to make to Oswalds. My chief anxiety now was to get them quickly, and trust to chance.

Every time a fresh visitor had appeared in the hotel after John had left he had greeted with the terse announcement: "My son Borys is married, you know. My wife knows all about it," and invariably he would interrupt any explanation the friend asked for with his usual "dam'," and the ever repeated muttered question: "Why shouldn't I be told?" It mattered not at all who might be present, and I began to dread the enquiring glances that were turned towards me. I felt that it was rather unfair, and more than once the tears came into my eyes. Yet I could give no explanation to the most sympathetic, I was as completely in the dark as my husband.

We were only home some few days, less than a week, when our American friends arrived, and I signed the formal receipt for Mr. Doubleday who had jokingly asked for it. Somehow Joseph Conrad managed to keep up while they were in the house, but the day they departed he collapsed, as I had expected. Then I thought my receipt seemed a trifle ironical when I recalled the wording: "Received with thanks, one rejuvenated and regenerated husband."

The next few weeks were very trying, and Joseph Conrad kept his room, and at first refused to see a doctor. His hands were swollen, and painful, and furnished an excellent excuse for not using a pen, but his depression got deeper and deeper, and at last I called in Dr. Fox, who spent more than an hour with him. At the end of that time he had been allowed to give no medical advice whatever, and came to me in despair. Neither had my husband referred to the matter that was troubling him so greatly.

I begged him to return to my husband's room, and without any preamble he offered to go himself to Manchester and report on his return the true facts as to whether there was any truth in Borys's statement that illness was keeping him from coming to see his father.

The abruptness of the offer coming from the busy doctor touched Joseph Conrad very much, and in a moment he thanked him very much but declared his unwillingness to trouble him to such an extent. But he added: "My dear fellow, I do not feel equal to the journey myself and I don't want my wife to go. . . ." The doctor interrupted him with an exasperated "Good God, no, how could she go alone ? If she goes I go too, but it would be better for me to go alone. Anyway, think it over and let me know before the week-end." And the matter for the nonce rested at that.

Then several days after the week-end he was to write to Dr. Fox he called me to him, and after keeping me standing nearly a quarter of an hour before he would speak, he suddenly declared that his mind was made up and the matter rested entirely with me. Either he would receive the young couple and make no reproach whatever to the boy, or he would never see him again. Nothing would move him from this attitude, and he said further, with a laugh that had no hint of mirth in it : "You may tell him that I will make him an allowance of £200 a year." I began to speak then, urging my husband to wait before he made that offer. "He says, dear, that he got married in this fashion to show you that he could keep a wife, well, let him do it. Then you can always make him that offer when we see how he gets on." I might have spoken to the wind. "No, dam', he shall know my conditions at once. Two hundred pounds a year, paid quarterly, not a penny more or less. They will come here to lunch on Sunday week—I don't care how, but mind they are not late. I won't have my meals disturbed for anybody, I don't care what you say." He dismissed me with a wave of the hand, the least gouty one. And so the decision was to rest on me.

I turned at the door and looked back at him. He was lying with his hand over his face, looking worn and played-out, and yet I swear that at that moment I felt years older than the frail figure on the bed. I crept away, and half an hour afterwards sent up a dainty tea of which he ate every scrap, and sent word asking me if I had written the letter, which he refused to read.

The week that preceded that Sunday was rather like a prolonged nightmare to me. Joseph Conrad made no reference to the coming ordeal, but one might have wondered who could be coming, to judge by the preparations that had to be superintended personally by him. I watched him with curiosity not unmixed with awe. The manner in which he was staging this first visit of his daughter-in-law was exactly the same as that in which he had taken possession of his first English home. His hands were now once more free of bandages, and he had made one or two visits into Canterbury alone, each time returning with some extra provisions which I easily concluded were for the feast on the coming Sunday.

At last that morning came. Borys had wired the day before saying he and his wife would arrive for lunch at one. Anxiously I watched the clock hand tell the half-hour after one, two, nearly half-past. Joseph Conrad roamed up and down the hall, in and out of the study, standing glaring out of the window with his eyelid raised by one finger, a trick he had sometimes when particularly ruffled. Then when at last the car ran into the drive he turned and fled precipitately, banging the door of his study after him, and leaving me to greet the young people. I was forced to smile, although against my will. The cause of the delay was explained when John unfolded himself from the seat at the back, looking far the most concerned. It was evident that the boy's presence had been called in to cover some of their discomfiture. They had collected John in Tonbridge and brought him along. I don't believe he had any knowledge that his brother was married until then.

There were several awkward moments when my husband's hardly-acquired calm nearly deserted him. At one of the most tense moments Commander Luis del Ricci (Bartimeus) suddenly appeared, and saved the situation. Poor man, he sensed something unusual in the air, and many times I caught him looking from one to the other of us perplexed, but it was years later before I explained the situation to him. Joseph Conrad was at times inclined to be a little facetious, at others grimly sardonic that afternoon, and neither mood gave any preliminary indication, making my task of keeping the peace very difficult indeed. The young wife only was unaware of the strain, but both boys remarked upon it to me, John with understanding far beyond his years, but Borys with a certain resentment. I could not forbear giving him a somewhat sharp rebuke. I felt that he was getting off very lightly. Mine had been the most trying time of all, for I had suffered greatly, and suffered in silence.

Finally a little after six the three young people departed, John to be dropped at Tonbridge as they passed through on their way to London. His farewell to me was meant to be consoling: "Never mind, mum, I'll never get married." Fate ordained that I should be present at his wedding before he was more than twenty-one. . . . The clearest case of "Man proposes. . . ."

I can hardly claim to any feeling of relief after that first visit. I caught the far-away look on my husband's face as he stood at the hall window waving his hand, but without a ghost of a smile. He gripped my arm with the familiar nervous grip that meant so much before he retired hurriedly back into his study, where he remained sunk in gloomy reflection for the next two hours. I did not venture any remark when he appeared that evening, and was not very surprised when he turned away from the table without having touched what was placed before him. But I knew my man, and a little while afterwards I had prepared an appetising little dish, very small and light.

When the bait was taken I knew my efforts were appreciated.

I retired to my room and indulged in a good cry, which is supposed to be such a feminine relief in time of stress. But I got very little relief from it. I was glad the day was over, but what kind of impression remained in the mind of my husband I was not to know, in words at least. I tried very hard to make up to him for the smart of the want of confidence on the part of our son. He could not rouse himself, and accept the accomplished fact with any philosophy, but he did admit later on with one of his grim laughs, and as he flung away his cigarette barely lit, that he would not have liked the task of finding a wife for the boy. It had been quite enough to choose his own.

This extract from a letter written dated December 6th, 1923, shows, I think, the curious mood that was almost constant now, and I knew that he was feeling it impossible to capture a real writing vein of thought. He took very little interest in anything, and even his food scarcely interested him. I was almost in despair. The letter he had written to Mr. Doubleday was as follows :—

". . . This is in answer to your letter of Nov. 22 which reached me on the 3rd of this month. *Victory* (2 copies) and *Lord Jim* (2 copies) of the Concord Edition, arrived by the same mail, but did not reach this house till the day after. I honestly think it is a remarkable production, and I must say that I am pleased with every feature, the cloth, the paper and the Minute Man under the title, the title-page itself, the fount, the spacing of the lines which is just right, and the proportions of the margins. The jacket, too, is nice with its simple landscape. I must also mention the back which avoids being dead flat in a very pleasing manner. I am quite impressed by the consistent attention to detail which is visible in the finished product. Let me tell you, Effendi, that I feel that I have never had such a birthday present in my life. . . ."

If I had been helping him I don't think this letter would have been posted, indeed hardly written. He would have said of anyone else that they had been juggling with the words. His approbation could have been expressed in a quarter of the space. But it may have been that he was simply trying to arrange the words in his mind, and then felt too tired to re-read what he had dictated.

I had been teasing him because only the month before all the manuscripts I had been at such pains to preserve, and which later on we had sold to Mr. John Quinn, had been re-sold in New York for no less a sum than £24,000. We had received £2000, but Joseph Conrad was sportsman enough to be pleased at the sale "taking place during the lifetime of an author," as he wrote to his friend and publisher, Mr. F. N. Doubleday.

In that letter he asks: "Was the atmosphere of that sale-room vibrating with excitement or, on the contrary, still with awe? Did Quinn enjoy his triumph lying low like Brer Rabbit, or did he enjoy his glory in public and give graciously his hand to kiss to the multitude of inferior collectors who never, never, never dreamt of such a coup? . . ."

He goes on to say: " The reverberation in the press here was very great indeed; and the result is that lots of people, who had never heard of me before, now know my name, and thousands of others, who could not have read through a page of mine without falling into convulsions, are proclaiming me a very great author. And there are a good many also whom nothing will persuade that the whole thing was not a put-up job, and that I haven't got my share of the plunder. . . ."

It was because of what was being said in our English Press that I disobeyed my husband and wrote a short article to the *Daily Mail*, and it was in print that he first saw it. Because it so evidently cleared away an erroneous impression I was forgiven, and even patted on the back.

If this sale impressed him, how much more would that sale of the first editions, in which he had written a few words on each fly-leaf and signed for his great friend, Richard Curle, have stirred his pride in his achievements. He was fond of pointing out this friend's almost uncanny ability in knowing what would bring money out of things that to the ordinary mortal such a possibility was closely hidden. He was flattered to be requested to sign those books, and I have known him spend hours thinking of some rare phrases, or telling sentences. But such an amount as £8000 because of those " strokes of his pen," these words are his own, he would have laughed at the notion. " Yes, my dear," he would have said, " and only a few more strokes and even Dick would have been mistaken. It would have been overdone."

This friend has spared no pains to make the inheritance my husband left behind worthy of his constant care and efforts. I for one would wish to express my gratitude for those efforts. He disagrees with me that it was Joseph Conrad's cherished dream to return to Poland to end his days, but it is true nevertheless. We had talked over that project many times during those last months. Directly John had embarked upon a successful career we, the old folks, were to divide up what of the home we could not take with us between the boys, and return to his beloved land. It was a dream—and a dream that was never realized. But the fact that he indulged in it has led me to send all the family papers in Polish for safe keeping to lie with those of his father in the Library in Cracow. Either of his descendants can go to see them, if there should arise any need, otherwise they will remain safe, and in good company.

There are still a few things to say of the last months, those in his last year of our life together. Months that were very like a deep twilight, grey and chill, a portent of what was to come. I would find it somewhat difficult exactly to explain my meaning, unless it was that being in such complete concord with him, I felt the hold he kept on his interests getting less firm, and the reins, so to speak, slipping, slipping from his grasp.

In this way I was somewhat prepared for the end—that is to say, I was becoming apprehensive. I found myself preparing—in my mind—for some kind of catastrophe, some disaster, no amount of forethought could avert. This must have been the reason that urged me to get taken back from the Nursing Home only that short time before the end—twelve days only, to be exact.

Borys had been married nearly two years before it became necessary to assist in the small trousseau. Here again my husband preserved an unaccountable secrecy. I had told him that I was providing the outfit, and very great pleasure I had in fashioning those small garments. It brought to my mind a question my son had asked when he was a small child. As usual Joseph Conrad's fit of gout impressed the small boy very much, and one day he came to me with the question, making very round eyes as he said: " Mama dear, when I'm a man, shall I have a little boy, and," he dropped his voice in awe, " shall I have the liver and the dout ? " Well, there was now every prospect of " the little boy," but I fervently hoped the other part of his question might never come true.

The great author kept his own intentions a strict secret. He had promised Borys to pay the expenses of the new arrival, but apparently had set no limit. In due course those expenses were declared to be in the close neighbourhood of £70. Once again I was the sufferer, I was wigged unmercifully and asked to compare the difference of cost between the first grandson's entry into the world, and that of our own two boys. I felt a bit flippant and recalled John's remark when I said to him once: " Oh, John, you cost me ever so much more than your brother did " and the young rascal answered, at once: " Well, Mum, that was only the difference in the doctor's bill." He was only about five years old at the time.

My husband's reproaches seemed decidedly unfair, but as usual there was nothing to be gained by any discussion, he would not admit that he had been unwise not to set a limit to the offer he had made, and declared I had no right to haul him over the coals for not having told me before. Only then I remarked quietly: " Well, hadn't you better suggest that the next grandchild should be cheaper ? " At this he laughed loudly, forgot his annoyance and finished the discussion with his familiar little " dam'."

From that time he delighted in devising little surprises for the young couple, although he seldom allowed me to participate in them.

I always maintained that it was ever so much easier to be generous than just, and I still think I was right. Joseph Conrad's lavish generosity was partly due to the indolence of ill-health, and a super-sensitiveness. He could not bear the sight of pain. He continued to be an ostrich, he was for ever putting his head in the sand and refusing to face facts. And he had a propensity for putting things off, delay at any price. On one occasion he had declared that his second son's birth could quite easily have been delayed some days—had I really wished to please him.

My pleasure in the small grandchild would have made me greedy if I had not remembered that my claim on him was only a secondary one. As it is the most likely crime I should commit would be baby-stealing. In the moments of the greatest physical pain, a baby to cuddle would have had a much greater effect than any sleeping-draught. And as to physical pain, I am fully qualified to speak, I am sure.

As it was I had to content myself with rather rare visits from the young parents. The baby early displayed quite remarkable intelligence and curiously enough he has inherited many marked characteristics from his grandfather, although he was only six months old when that grandfather died. For instance, it seems absurd to say it, but it is perfectly true, as a tiny baby if he should be lamenting as small children will, and you took him to a book-shelf he would begin to croon and forget his woes. It was almost uncanny. At the age of six I was reading aloud to him and he began to play with the dog. For the sake of my dignity I said reproachfully: "Oh, Phil, grandma is reading to you." He turned with a positively angelic smile and said: "It doesn't disturb me, grandma dear, your reading to me while I am playing with the dog."

The months between Joseph Conrad's return from America and his death, about fifteen months all told, seemed crowded with incidents, and we made many new friends. I don't think a single American came over who was connected with literature who did not come to see us. And there were many foreigners, Frenchmen and Poles, who found their way to Oswalds to do homage or renew some old acquaintance. Of all those visitors Don Roberto (Mr. Cunninghame Graham), Hugh Walpole, Richard Curle and Jean Aubry, were perhaps the most frequent. Mrs. Grace Willard and her daughter Catherine came often and Perceval Gibbon. We seldom saw F. M. H (Ford Madox Hueffer), but on the one outstanding occasion when he appeared—as was his wont—many years ago at the same time as the telegram announcing the intended visit, my husband said in a very decided tone: "You call him Mr. Hueffer." But I pointed out that I had always before addressed him as Ford, and I would rather not run the risk of a possible slip, and nothing could be more likely if I called him Mr. Hueffer.

One day stands out in my recollection very clearly. We were expecting Miss Catherine Willard for lunch, she was at that time playing at the old "Vic" and Joseph Conrad as usual decided to go himself to the station to meet her. There was a lull as to ailments at that moment, we were both able to get about the house. I watched our car on its way through the park, and had returned to the kitchen to complete some small preparations for the lunch when we heard the sound of wheels coming into the drive. There had been no time for the notion that this could be our own car returning, and in a flash I at once knew who this would be.

About this time John was nearly seventeen, and not very happy at school, and not at all sure what he wanted to become. After a long talk with our friend M. Jean Aubry it was decided to place the boy in the home of a Pastor in Le Havre to learn the language. To this end Joseph Conrad was to go over to see M. Bost and make the necessary arrangements for the boy's stay. I succeeded at last in persuading him to let me go with them, but I was not at all prepared for the tirade I had perforce to listen to. He nearly spoilt all the fun for me by declaring that his objection to my being of the party was that I could not help myself much if anything happened in the way of a collision, and I was too heavy to make it an easy task for me to be rescued under the worst circumstances. I had to laugh. It struck me as so droll, rather like his anxiety and subsequent insistence many years before, and when I was very lame, that I should try to wedge myself through a narrow window frame, to be used to the drill in case of fire. A contingency I could only hope would never happen.

After John's first visit home my husband expressed himself as very well pleased with the result of the experiment, and began to make all kinds of plans, amongst which were plans for finding a little house, one without any garden. This because I had raised some very decided objection to his notion of giving to the gardener 50 per cent of all he could sell out of the garden produce, flowers, fruit or vegetables. This, too, in addition to his cottage, wages and the usual perquisites of a gardener.

He came home one day with the information that he had found the very place. "The garden is about the size of a pocket-handkerchief, my dear. No garden to worry over there." He was mightily pleased with his find, and I was taken to see it. It was so unsuitable that I never for a moment considered the idea seriously,

Imagine a man, practically an invalid, removing himself and his wife, who was even more dependent on the good doctor's constant care, to a house on the bleakest part of the North Foreland, in the teeth of every wind that blew. A long distance from the nearest railway station. Some thirty miles from either his doctor or mine—and a garden the size of his pocket handkerchief. " You won't be able to grow even an onion," he chuckled. I certainly could not, but I remained calm and collected, going into the case very carefully and preserving my good humour with some difficulty.

" Well," I said at last, putting my calculations before him on the sheet of paper. " Have you thought that it will be necessary to keep someone constantly plying between that house and the nearest shops ? You will have to go a few miles to the telegraph office, as far to buy the onion you pretend to despise." I got no farther, with a gesture of disgusted exasperation he flung himself back on the seat of the car and fairly snarled an order to the man to get back home at once.

After this I noticed that his health seemed to seriously decline, he was at times sunk in the deepest despondency, and many days passed when he would hardly rouse himself to speak. I have a very real feeling of gratitude to Richard Curle, who came often in those days and invariably succeeded in rousing the invalid for a few hours any way. It became a habit for this friend to arrive about half-past nine or ten, have his supper which I would have ready for him downstairs, and then go to my husband's room and talk with him until the small hours.

Writing by this time was hard work, and as usual " contrarywise " as they say in *Alice in Wonderland*, as if to increase the magnitude of the undertaking, he would attempt to write with his pen while he dictated.

The book *Suspense* advanced slowly, and the only relaxation he would consider was scouring the country-side for the house that he was bent upon finding. It was while I was making another visit to the Nursing Home that he and his secretary found a house that he only delayed taking until I could go to give the casting vote. This delay would of necessity bring the time of our tenancy of Oswalds to an end. We had already given the required notice to expire in September.

The novel *Suspense* got itself written very slowly, and it was very plain to my anxious watching that the energy was out of everything for him. From my bedroom in the room above I could hear his voice strained to the top pitch. It was useless to attempt to get him to do only one or the other, either write or dictate. The more nervous he got at the prospect before me, the more he used his strength in this trying fashion.

My nurse and the young chauffeur were married by this time, my anxiety as to the way in which he would receive that piece of news was as it turned out quite unnecessary. When I told him of the romance he laughed long and heartily. Then as he wiped the tears from his eyes he flung his arms out widely and started pacing the room with rapid steps. I waited, I was wondering whether he would decide that the man or both had better depart. I could see a great many difficulties ahead if the present situation continued. But my husband proved himself again most unusual. He paused at last in his rapid pacing and leaned his head on his arms on the mantelpiece, which was a high one, letting his forehead rest on them. For some moments he remained perfectly quiet, then he came over to where I sat and said lightly: "Well, let's hope they will be happy. They are both good people in their own way, and it's quite plain that this romance has gone too far to be stopped whether I like it or not. I tell you what, Jess, we'll give them her bedroom furniture for a wedding present." Then a moment afterwards he chuckled aloud. "Oh dear, but hers is a single bed—dam'. But I'll tell you what, I'll have that one and let them have my big double one. Now, don't make mountains out of mole-hills, my dear. I shall be perfectly comfortable on that, and 'long Charley, and his good little wife' can have mine." This bedstead was the identical one that had once displayed so pathetically its naked springs in the early days of my own married life. Perhaps I had some more than common affection for the iron and brass affair. He had apparently forgotten there was, or could be, any sentimental value to me in the piece of furniture. In the end I said nothing against it, and left the room to do his bidding, and send the bride-elect to him in his study.

The single bed proved very unsuitable for Joseph Conrad, because, apart from its legitimate purpose as a resting place, his bed had to be hospitable to a heap of books, all open and face downwards, maps, bed-rest, and more than once a wooden Spratt's dog-biscuit box he had ordered his man to place at the foot of his bed to brace his feet against. I seem to see him now, looking desperately uncomfortable. He had not trimmed his beard for some few days, being gouty, he crouched between the erect bed-rest and the Spratt's biscuit box. Numerous books lay around him, and he was restlessly pulling the silk threads out of an old Italian bedspread, two or three small tables stood around within reach, and from the many ash-trays on them thin spiral columns of cigarette-smoke rose. Sitting in that crumpled condition in the haze of smoke he had the appearance of a pathetically thin and angular idol. Only there was nothing restful or holy in his frequent outbursts of concentrated fury each time one of his books fell to the ground or slid behind the wooden box out of his reach. I could not help regretting his big roomy double bed, and I determined that before I left for the Nursing Home I would somehow manage to procure him another—he had refused to use my room while I was away. I was somewhat disconcerted although I was deeply touched at his refusal, or rather at the way it was expressed. He pursed up his lips and looked absolutely tearful for a few moments when I suggested that mine was a double bed. "Oh no, I simply couldn't bear it; besides, it's so cold in your room. Windows wide open night and day. I should catch my death of cold."

I did not think it of any use pointing out that the windows would close, and that there was a fireplace in the room. He refused to leave his own room, putting forward every possible and impossible objection. In the end I bought him a bedstead while he had gone to town to lunch at the Polish Embassy. But of this later.

I was still awaiting the fixing of the date for a further painful interview with the surgeons, and feeling very depressed because of the impossibility of rousing my husband to anything like a reasonable frame of mind, when we heard of two young Polish girls, one of his nearest connection, being in England. I was greatly relieved when they accepted the invitation to come to Oswalds for a few days. Here was a diversion, anyhow. They amply fulfilled my wishes, and Joseph Conrad took an immense interest in the young people. John was at home for his holiday, and fell immediately under their spell.

The brief visit ended all too soon, and the day of their departure came. Overnight it had been decided that John should escort them to town, lunch them and take them to some form of entertainment. I cannot help a smile at the recollection of that morning. About half an hour before they were due to start for the station, the boy sought his father in his room. Joseph Conrad must have forgotten what the expenses must be for such an expedition. He handed John a £1 note and that was that. Tactfully and with a philosophy far beyond his eighteen years, the boy took the note without comment, and came to me, suggesting the obvious thing, in the face of his small capital: "Don't you think I had better make some excuse and see the girls into the train? You see, I can't do more than get their tickets out of this, can I?"

The boy's face expressed his keen disappointment but, as usual, he was perfectly reasonable. I knew that my husband had miscalculated or forgotten what the arrangement had been. I handed John another £5, and he left for his first day as cavalier with the two charming countrywomen of his father. They had been gone rather more than an hour when I heard from the other side of the door that divided his room from mine, the familiar expression, "dam'," and then a prolonged chuckling laugh. "Did John come to you for anything before he left with the girls?"

He had just remembered himself, and was wondering what had happened, evidently. I knew him so well and I answered him in the same spirit as he had hailed me. "Well, yes, dear, he was afraid he had not quite enough to carry out his programme." Another loud chuckle interluded with his favourite "dam'." "I suppose you gave him what he wanted, poor kid. Let me know and I will return it to you."

CHAPTER TWENTY-FOUR

THIS last chapter contains the most poignant hours of human suffering and sorrow, and leaves me a sorrowing widow instead of a wife once happy in the knowledge that everything, every happening, great or small is referred to her. Every life that is spent in close contact with another, if it lasts beyond the purely sentimental stage, must contain a fair share of trouble, some hint of discord. Especially if each is to retain their own individuality—and only in this way can a couple hope to continue life together in mutual respect and esteem.

I am no believer in a wife being completely absorbed by her husband, still less in the husband being absorbed by the wife. Marriage would be so much more enduring and happy if both the contracting parties would be prepared to give and take. The very discussion of ways and means, hopes and fears, would make for mutual happiness. A selfish wife will take instant advantage of an over-indulgent husband, and a really timid and colourless wife will lose all attraction for her husband once she has lost her own individuality. Domestic adoration is foolish, but appreciation, just and considered, is the best foundation possible for life together.

I had learned during the time we had lived together to value beyond everything Joseph Conrad's truly lovable nature, to admire his genius and to be tolerant of his nervous sensitiveness. Possibly had I been incapable of understanding his exotic nature, we might never have lived in such complete harmony. I think I can say this without the fear of being contradicted or thought unduly egotistic. He has said himself, many times, that he could never have lived with anyone else, and other people who have known him have said the same. Then, too, I have felt no little apprehension as to our life when his sons were of an age to display their individuality. It was one thing for me to devote myself entirely to my husband, to have surrendered most of my desires to him, I mean in the way of outside pleasures, and most friendships—household goods, etc.—but already the question of another will had begun to make itself felt. The manner in which he had received the news of Borys's marriage had been sufficient. The idea he put forward that as soon as John was embarked upon a career of his own, we, he and I, should pull up our roots in England and retire to his own country, had this in its favour, if little else. He had to be the supreme being in his own home, and there he would continue to be so. When I knew my first baby was coming, reference to the same thing I have made in the early part of these pages—I wondered how I should continue my life. Which would be God and which Mammon? My husband or my child?

The days preceding my next visit to the Nursing Home where I spent a bad seven or eight weeks, came about in the June of 1924. And the day before my husband went to town to lunch with the Polish Minister, now Ambassador. He had complained very much of the single bed he had exchanged with my nurse, and left imperative instructions that the springs should be tightened, and the whole thing put into a more comfortable condition—while he was away. He had gone up only for the day.

This proved an impossible task. The bedstead, as far as the springs went, was done for. In desperation I wrote to a firm in Canterbury asking that a roomy bedstead should be sent out without delay. They obligingly sent the best they had according to my requirements, and I rested that afternoon in the belief that I had overcome the difficulty and secured comfort for my husband while I should be away from home. Without doubt, if he had not been able to make a grievance of my choice, he would have had to find something else. His nerves were on edge, and he was unable to resist the desire to create a scene.

But with all my previous knowledge of the dear fellow's strangeness, I was unprepared for the storm that burst that night on my devoted head. He literally raved at me, and in the end retired to the despised couch exhausted. In vain I tried to explain that if my purchase was so much to his disapproval it could be changed in the morning. He said I had bought for him a catafalque, and in the end retired to his room without first kissing me good night for the first time in our married life. And that night I spent in tears—foolish, I have no doubt—but the thought of what was before me on the morrow and the failure of my well-meant efforts for his comfort, proved too much for me.

No mention was made of the matter the next morning, and he had certainly forgotten his displeasure, and was disposed to be rather more tenderly affectionate than usual. I resolutely put aside all feeling of resentment, and responded to his improved mood wholeheartedly. The day wore on and early in the afternoon dear Sir Robert Jones arrived to spend the night before the operation with Joseph Conrad. He tried to persuade my husband to rest, and let him escort me alone to the Nursing Home but in the end both Sir Robert and the author came into Canterbury, and for the best part of the short drive the two maintained a lively discussion on some trivial matter connected with local sanitation if I remember rightly.

The operation the next day differed very little from the previous entertainments. My room in the Home was downstairs on the same floor as the theatre, and it was arranged by my own request that I should walk from my room to the theatre. When all was ready, Dr. Reid came for me, dressed for the part and looking wonderfully like a "Sheik," with his mask hanging at the back of his head.

Perhaps the injection had increased my idea of the ridiculous, any way I was struck by the tall erect figure of the dear man, and my own short statue provided the resemblance to the quotation from "Lear's Nonsense," I took the proffered arm with the flippant remark: "Mr. Daddy Long-legs, and Mrs. Floppy-fly." My progress was painful and slow in spite of the firm support.

After the operation was over and surgeons had gone their separate ways, I had nothing more exciting to do than to lie and worry myself as to how things were going in my absence, in every case I had discovered that after all I was not quite indispensable. A reflection that is as well not to indulge in while one is feeling blue, in the first days after such a trial. I was not surprised that my husband had soon succumbed to an attack of gout—as I thought at first—but as time went on the truth became clearer that this was not an ordinary attack. We wrote notes to each other as usual, but I had not seen him after the second day, and I felt somewhat more anxious than formerly. Then came a batch of not less than twenty-eight letters with the request that I should answer them as I thought best. The task at that moment took all my energy, and my mind wandered rather frequently from the matter in hand. At first this distressed me a good deal, but my good friend, Dr. Reid, pointed out that I was not quite clear of the effects of the anæsthetic, and the effort of using my brain was bound to tell upon me for a time.

The two or three visits Joseph Conrad made me were short and hardly cheerful. He arrived each time worn out by the short drive, and his emotions. He was disgusted that I was not making quicker progress, and he was in a state of more than usual nervous exasperation. He seldom tried to be in the least entertaining, and was usually asleep in the big chair a few moments after he arrived, and remained mute and silent till the car arrived to take him back home again. "I want you back home again, Jess, quickly," he would repeat insistently.

He wrote to the hospital giving the most minute instructions for my transport. No less than four men were to be sent with the ambulance and he insisted upon being there in person. His rage exhausted him when he found that only the customary two attendants were sent, and he raved up and down the road, hindering the men whose time was short to start with.

Dr. Reid and another doctor with the two ambulance men at last got the stretcher under way. Even under these trying circumstances I laughed outright when my good friend whispered: "Do you mind going feet first?" My answer amused them all. "Not if you don't upset the flowers."

That was a home-going with a vengeance, my second in an ambulance, but this time there seemed more formality and ceremony. It was as it turned out only just twelve days before that tragic Sunday morning, August 3rd, 1924. Just the day after John's eighteenth birthday.

I was forced to remain upstairs but I was thankful to be again at home and Joseph Conrad and I were together almost continually. I was able to help him by typewriting the last thing he wrote, and which, in fact, was still unfinished when he died. *Legens*, Richard Curle, as usually resourceful, had suggested this article for the daily paper. He could see that it was not possible to proceed at the moment with the novel, *Suspense*, and had given my husband the idea of this short thing to occupy his mind.

Between the writing and my copying we used to play either dominoes or bezique together every evening, and the Friday evening brought Richard Curle down for the week-end. As was usual now, this friend was met at the station about ten, arriving upstairs and a greeting first to Joseph Conrad and then to me, and then the visitor descended to the dining-room where a lonely supper was served to him. After which he rejoined my husband and the two would talk until the small hours, the sound of their voices reaching me in my room next door. Not infrequently I would be hailed from time to time to bear witness to this or that or give some opinion as to some project for the next day. That particular evening the visit seemed to do more toward cheering the invalid than anything that had preceded it. He had to be told that on the next day the young people were expected with the little grandson, Philip, also John was returning from a visit to keep his birthday. A good laugh echoed from time to time, and no hint of evil or breath of tragedy came to me, alone in the next room.

The next morning the two friends, after some hours spent looking over the article, went out together to inspect the new house that my husband had discovered. I had a kind of sneaking hope that "Dick," as we affectionately called him, would somehow manage to put Joseph Conrad off the place. It seemed such utter madness to me to think of getting out of reach of our good friends, Dr. Reid and Dr. Fox, while my husband's health continued so indifferent —and in the face of my complete helplessness. I could not move with an open wound still in my knee, and there was no immediate prospect of my being able to either approve or disapprove of a new home.

I was left sitting on my long chair with a few pages to copy but before I had more than begun my task the car was back again and Joseph Conrad was calling my nurse and complaining of severe pains in his chest. I managed to get to him on my crutches as soon as he was in bed, but his distress and apprehension as to the harm I might do to the wound induced me to yield to his wish, and return to my chair. Dr. Fox was summoned from Ashford, some fifteen miles away, in a hurry. He reassured us all, telling us that it was due to indigestion, and that although Joseph Conrad was in a very nervous condition there was nothing to be at all alarmed about.

The hours passed, the pain continued, and the nervousness increased. At three o'clock the sad news came that dear Lady Colvin had passed over to join the shades. I have never been quite certain that my husband ever understood that she was dead for he made no comment. He called to me as the telegraph boy rode out of the drive, asking: "Is that wire from Sir Sidney? How is dear Francis? Is she better?" My answer: "No, dear, not better," brought forth no answer and another hour or so passed slowly.

Richard Curle had been sitting with me, and neither of us seemed to dare to pass any opinion as to the condition of the sufferer in the next room. There seemed every cause for alarm in spite of the good doctor's assurance to the contrary.

At five the car arrived with the three young people, and the small grandson. Joseph Conrad was all impatience for the child to be taken to him at once. It was like a breathless rush, I never felt the burden of my helpless immobility more. A little after six we called for the doctor once more. He was out, and so was my dear friend Dr. Reid, who had promised to attend for his colleague if necessary.

The terrible oppression increased, and it was not possible to think of anything to ease it. Both his sons were full of anxiety and apprehension, but it was the more mature advice of Richard Curle that decided me to call in another doctor from Canterbury.

My nurse assured me that the pulse was strong still, and that it was very evidently the state of terrific nervousness that was the chief cause of my husband's distress. The strange doctor came, and stayed an hour in the room with his patient, and then came to me with precisely the same opinion his usual medical adviser had given me earlier in the day. There was no cause for alarm. He did suggest that my husband should have his teeth removed as soon as he had recovered from this attack, but that was all.

That night passed somehow. Neither Joseph Conrad nor I slept, and all night I listened helplessly to the sounds from that room next door. The low tones of the faithful man Foot who spent the night in attendance, and the gasping requests for this and that, never giving the man time to execute one order before demanding something else. Long before morning I, who was so well accustomed to every shade and intonation of that voice, had determined that directly it was light I would ask one of the two doctors to send a male nurse in. The patient was completely out of hand and although I had known him quite as bad many times before, as I could not get to him myself there was grave need for some authoritative handling before he exhausted himself and his attendant completely.

Curiously enough it was a little after six when he had Borys called, and directed him to fetch him a male nurse. An hour or so afterwards he called to me through the closed door, quite as was his wont. "You Jess, I am better this morning," a short sharp laugh, with a catch in his breath, then a cheerful hail: "I can always get a rise out of you."

It was all much as I had known it many times before and even then my anxiety, all our anxiety, seemed to have been unnecessary. I breathed a fervent "thank God" and called a cheery good morning. There was a sound of movement, and I distinctly heard him praising the man for his attention, then directing him to place a chair near the fire and go and liven himself up by washing his face and hands.

The moments passed, I heard the familiar tattoo of his fingers on the arm of the chair, a short cough and renewed tapping. Then a gasping "Here . . . you," then a confused shuffling sound almost as if a ghost had fallen to the floor, then silence.

They rushed into his room in answer to the pealing of my bell, and found him still on his hands and knees as he had slipped dead from his chair. I had heard his last words, and by the irony of fate I could not move to go to him. My crutches were against the wall the far side of the room out of reach. It was the fulfilment of the premonition that had haunted me for weeks, the dread that had led me to agitate for the permission to return from the Nursing Home only twelve days before.

In breathless silence I heard the steps coming and going past my door. I knew I had not been forgotten and I knew also that the end had come even before Dr. Reid entered my room and gently closed the door behind him, before he advanced to the side of my bed.

His quiet tones as he bade me realize that my husband was very ill in the next room, and the solemn bend of the head in assent when I asked, or rather asserted: "He is dead."

What he did that day for me I can never forget, and my gratitude is, and always must be the more complete because this dear friend himself is a memory only now. But while he lived I never felt friendless. It was his part in these awful moments to break the news and sustain with the wonderful wealth of sympathy he could give, that part of his own personality that made that sympathy such a living quality. He uttered no mere platitudes, which, after all, were cold comfort. Sudden death is and must always be a tragedy, but a much more merciful end for those who pass out than a long lingering death.

When I was once more alone, quite calm, and with only the burden of my tremendous responsibility facing me with the grim truth, and the sudden stillness, like a breathless pause borne in upon my consciousness from the room next door, it seemed to me I had known that this end was near, was inevitable and now complete.

My mind is rather confused as to the immediate happenings directly afterwards. I heard many cars come and go, caught the sound of hushed and sad voices inside the house, and the muffled sounds from beyond that closed door that hid the dear form from my gaze. The man with whom I had lived for nearly thirty years, in the closest of human ties. Then came the thought that I seemed to have failed him at the end, even although it had been no fault of mine.

The day passed and night came once more. There beyond that closed door lay all that remained of perhaps the strangest being one could ever know. In death he seemed to have retired completely from his fellows. I too shared in the impression that there was still something I did not know and now could never know.

The tragic Sunday was the day preceding the August Bank Holiday, and that fact made it more difficult to make the necessary arrangements. Here again, Dr. Reid was a tower of strength. He and his wife, to whom I give my deep and sincere gratitude, met the friends we were expecting for lunch on that Sunday, and whom there was no means of preventing from arriving at the station, according to plan—yes, these were met and lunched by these good friends. A fact I did not know at the time.

That Sunday night I could not sleep and I could not bear the light extinguished. I fancied as I lay awake that I could still hear the restless tapping of the dead fingers on the wooden table, or the tinkle of his watch-chain running through his fingers, with nervous regularity against the top of the bedside table. Fancied I heard the familiar "damn" or the rustle of the book being turned from time to time. All these sounds I had lived with. I recalled the many times I had cut the pages of the magazine so that I should not hear the impatient tearing of the top of the pages. It was to come to me no more, and the only sound that broke the stillness that night was the hoot of an owl, or the cry of some other nocturnal bird.

He had passed on and left me with my two sons, with some true tried friends, and enough memories to keep me company if I lived to be a hundred. Each trivial happening crowded into my mind during those lonely hours, taking precedence, in a curious way, of matters much more important. He had been to me as much a son as husband. He claimed my care and indulgence in the same manner as the smallest infant would have done. And yet, at the same time, there was that sense of pride in the great achievement, admiration for the volume of work done under difficulties that were unique. In a tongue that was to the end absolutely foreign to him.

Who can speak with such sympathy and understanding of those difficulties as his wife, now his widow? My personal pride is threefold. First of all my care of the artist in words, that had to be constant and unremitting, in every sense of the word, watchful that his mood should not be ruthlessly invaded or disturbed by outside influences. This, at least, was often no light task. Secondly, the care of his material well-being, his home and his children. For the first half of his writing life I was also his secretary, and each book became like another infant. And lastly, I have the privilege and the immense satisfaction of being considered as the guardian of his memory, and of the inheritance of fame that comes to his sons, and through them to their children in turn.

Already I have three grandsons, Philip, Richard and Peter The first the son of Borys, and the other two of John. It is to be my pride to watch them grow into manhood, and in the fervent hope that some part of their grandsire's mantle of fame may descend upon these children I intend to dedicate this book of recollections to them, and to make use of the motto that appears on the front page of *Youth*, which is the one book that is dedicated to me.

I do not think either of my sons have as yet realized the magnitude of the task I set myself, ten years ago. A task that without being considered in any way conceited, I claim to have been enabled to do. I still receive letters from the far corners of the world asking for a small scrap of handwriting for some admirer to treasure—together with a few words from myself, some mention of a characteristic phrase. Two of the most familiar sayings of Joseph Conrad come into my mind at this moment, and seem rather fitting to be included here. The first is " Nothing succeeds like success," and " The world is to the young."

Both are undoubtedly true, and are because of their entire truth, something more than mere platitudes. The success of this book will certainly revive the works of the man who inspires these pages. And the fact that the world is to the young may be some sort of good fairy-godmother's prophecy for the small boys—who in a sense inherit these recollections.

No! it has been no light task, and has left no leisure for the self-indulgence of grief, or forgetfulness. There have been many times when I have had to lay the task aside or lose my self-control. In every instance Joseph Conrad has been a presence, so vividly clear that I have found myself recalling a familiar gesture, or tone, with every word I have written. And at the end the memory is as clear as it was ten years, even twenty or thirty years ago. But the words that appeal to me the most of all that have ever been written are contained in the wonderful tribute paid by Mr. Cunninghame Graham to his dead friend.

. . . "The voyage was over and the great spirit rested from its toil safe in the English earth he had dreamed of as a child in far Ukrainia. A gleam of sun lit up the red brick houses of the town. It fell upon the towers of the cathedral, turning it into a glowing beacon pointing to the sky. The trees moved gently in the breeze, and in the fields the ripening corn was undulating softly, just as the waves waft in on an atoll in the Pacific, with a slight swishing sound. All was well chosen for his resting-place, so we left him with his sails all duly furled, ropes Flemished down, and with the anchor holding truly in the kind Kentish earth, until the Judgment Day. The gulls will bring him tidings as they fly over his grave with their wild voices if he should weary for the sea, and the salt smell of it." . . .

These words from the monument erected to his father far away in Cracow are a fitting note at the end of these recollections. . . . "I will arise, Lord, when Thou callest me, but suffer me to rest for I am very weary." . . .

INDEX

G

H

I

J

K

L

M

N

O

P

Q

R

S

T

U

V

W

Z

HANDLIST OF CURLE'S WRITINGS ABOUT CONRAD

A HANDLIST

of the Various Books, Pamphlets,
Prefaces, Notes, Articles,
Reviews and Letters

Written About

JOSEPH CONRAD

By Richard Curle

1911-1931

COMPILED, WITH AN INTRODUCTION AND ANNOTATIONS,
BY RICHARD CURLE

INTRODUCTION

The compilation of this handlist was urged upon me in a mood of humorous enthusiasm by my friend, Professor Herbert West, of Dartmouth College, Hanover, New Hampshire. I must admit, even so, that I do not quite understand yet why I should have gone to all this trouble, for from the very first it never occurred to me that such a booklet could be of the faintest real interest to anybody but myself, or of the slightest real value to anybody at all. Theoretically, I suppose, it might be useful to students, but the type of student who wants to read everything that one man has written about another is a myth. At least, I trust he is: it would be too depressing to think otherwise.

It is true that much that I have written about Conrad has never been reprinted, but it is also true that most of it is not worth reprinting. My two main books on Conrad contain a quite sufficient mass of my opinions on his work and of my reminiscenses of his personality; though if I were to rewrite the earlier book I hope my criticism would be more mature and if I were to rewrite the other one I could probably add to my recollections. But there they are. The printed word has a terrible, if only relative, immortality; and it is but too apparent, as the French say, that while unspoken words are our slaves, spoken words are our masters.

All this does not sound very encouraging, but it is just as well to be frank. Let us make no mistake: this brochure is simply a curiosity. It has amused me to compile it, this record of twenty years of admiration, and it may feed a mild vanity to see it in print— though, heaven knows, that sensation has long since lost its finer magic! And yet any vanity is more than offset by an emotion of regret. So much that I have written on Conrad would never have been written had he remained alive—and he would have been only 75 this year—that I heartily wish the booklet had been an impossibility.

I believe that this list of my writings about Conrad is virtually complete, but, of course, it does not include interviews, broadcast talks, reports on my lectures, reviews of my books, and all those other connected links which would round off our association so far as print and publicity are concerned. But I might mention, however, that I had a good deal to do with the production of Mons. G. Jean Aubry's official biography of Conrad, *Joseph Conrad: Life and Letters.* As one of Conrad's trustees and executors I helped to select him for the task, and I read the work through both in manuscript and in proof and offered a great number of recommendations. And I also slightly assisted Mr. T. J. Wise in his *Bibliography of the Writings of Joseph Conrad (1895-1920)*. Indeed, with his usual generosity he wished to associate my name with his on the title-page, though assuredly I did not do enough to earn that honour.

Conrad showed his friendship for me in many ways. He dedicated *The Arrow of Gold* to me; he wrote a 17-page preface to my work, *Into the East: Notes on Burma and Malaya;* and he even suggested that we should collaborate in a book and that I should finish any novel left uncompleted by him. Whether he meant these suggestions seriously I doubt, for he often voiced the vague and momentary fancies that floated through his mind, but, in any case, it would never have done. That is obvious. And yet I did help him to end up one of the briefest of his essays—an essay so brief and unimportant, indeed, that it was not even reprinted in his posthumous *Last Essays.* However, such as it is, the ultimate sentences were written by me and approved by Conrad. I like to think of that small fact: it seems to complete the cycle of our friendship and to give at least the semblance of an excuse for this catalogue.

R. C.

BOOKS

1.

JOSEPH CONRAD: A STUDY

Kegan Paul, Trench, Trubner & Co., London, 1914; Doubleday, Page & Co., Garden City, New York, 1914. A work of about 250 pages. It contains a frontispiece of Conrad taken from a photograph. The eleven chapters are headed as follows: "Conrad, His Critics and His Contemporaries"; "Conrad's Biography and Autobiographical Works"; Conrad's Novels and Stories"; "Conrad's Atmosphere"; "Conrad as Psychologist"; "Conrad's Men"; "Conrad's Women"; "Conrad's Irony and Sardonic Humour"; "Conrad's Prose"; "Conrad as Artist"; "Conrad's Position in Literature".

The English edition appears in two bindings, one in light blue cloth, gilt top, and gilt on the back and front, and the other in green cloth, plain top, and gilt only on the front. This second form is obviously a remainder binding. In America the book seems only to have been issued in one form.

My effort throughout this pioneer work—for it was the first book ever devoted to Conrad—was to make him known, so far as lay in my power, by a study of his creative energy, strengthened by quotations from his work. The latest book I was able to deal with was *Chance* and the volume is in need both of revision and of bringing up to date.

My remembrance is that, taken by and large, the reviews were extremely unfavourable, although Conrad himself thought rather well of the work. A number of his letters referring to it may be found in *Conrad to a Friend: 150 Selected Letters from Joseph Conrad to Richard Curle.* I will quote here from a couple of these: "I have read and have been touched deeply in places by the sympathetic understanding of my work you display all along." . . . . "Well, I must say that the book is receiving a magnificent acknowledgment of its existence anyhow. That you are attacked causes me great pain, but there can be in it for you no sense of defeat. I have told you that you would have brick-bats thrown at you. You jostle too many people's idols for my sake . . . . After the flouts and jeers, which you can't deny you have to a certain extent provoked, there comes always a note of genuine respect for the singleness of purpose, the transparent rectitude of your 'pioneer' (as the *Times* points out) achievement." Despite such remarks, however, the book was a dismal failure.

2.

THE LAST TWELVE YEARS OF JOSEPH CONRAD

Sampson Low, Marston & Co., London, 1928; Doubleday, Doran & Co., Garden City, New York, 1928. The English edition is about 240 pages long; the American edition about 220. The work contains 8 illustrations. The twelve chapters are headed as follows: "Conrad as a Friend"; "The Personality of Conrad"; "Conrad's Talk"; "How Conrad Worked"; "Conrad's Attitude to His Own Books"; "Conrad's Ideas on Art"; "Conrad at Home"; "Conrad in Prosperity"; "Stray Recollections of Conrad"; "Conrad and England"; "Conrad's Fame in America"; "Conrad's Last Day".

I endeavoured in this book to portray Conrad, the man, as I knew him from day to day. I ransacked my memory at the time, but every now and then fresh recollections rise before me and sometimes I feel inclined to write a supplementary pamphlet in which I would relate other revealing incidents and so build up my picture still further.

Although this work, like the previous one, had a very small sale both in England and in America, yet the reviews were on the whole favourable. In both countries the book was issued in a style similar to the companion volume of letters, entitled *Conrad to a Friend: 150 Selected Letters from Joseph Conrad to Richard Curle,* but neither volume helped the sale of the other.

PAMPHLETS

1.

JOSEPH CONRAD IN THE EAST

London, 1922. An 8-page pamphlet, of which the first two pages are taken up by the title and the certificate of issue and the last page is blank. Reprinted from the type of an article in *The Blue Peter* of September-October, 1922. The certificate of issue reads, "21 copies privately printed for the author, July, 1922."

In this little pamphlet, which is divided into two chapters, I gave many unknown facts about Conrad's Eastern wanderings.

2.

JOSEPH CONRAD: THE HISTORY OF HIS BOOKS

J. M. Dent & Sons, London, 1924. This 8-page pamphlet, within wrappers, reprinted in part from an article in *The Times Literary Supplement,* August 30, 1923, was produced by Messrs. Dent as an advertisement for their collected edition of Conrad.

It tries to do exactly what its title describes—tell, in short space, the history of Conrad's different books.

3.

JOSEPH CONRAD'S LAST DAY

London, 1924. This 36-page pamphlet, within wrappers, was produced in an edition of 100 copies privately printed for the author. It is, to a large extent, a reprint of an article which appeared in *John O'London's Weekly*, September 20 and 27, 1924, and elsewhere in America and South Africa.

This essay, which gives a detailed description of Conrad's last hours, during which I was much with him, was written a few days after his death and while the tragic recollection of his loss was strong upon me. Much of the material was used later in the final chapter of *The Last Twelve Years of Joseph Conrad.*

4.

THE PERSONALITY OF JOSEPH CONRAD

London, 1925. This 13-page pamphlet, within wrappers, privately printed for the author in an edition of 100 copies, first appeared as an article in *The Edinburgh Review,* January, 1925, and was reprinted from the types of the Review. The contents were later used to a large degree in the second chapter of *The Last Twelve Years of Joseph Conrad.*

In this essay I sought to portray the complex, enchanting personality of Conrad.

5.

A HANDLIST OF THE VARIOUS BOOKS, PAMPHLETS, PREFACES, NOTES, ARTICLES, REVIEWS AND LETTERS WRITTEN ABOUT JOSEPH CONRAD BY RICHARD CURLE, 1911-31

Brookville, Pennsylvania, 1932. I scarcely know whether it be permitted to catalogue a work within its own covers; but if so, then the preface and notes to this little compilation, of which 250 copies have been printed, speak for themselves.

NOTE: In 1928 a Conrad collector kindly commissioned me, at my own suggestion, to write a pamphlet on his collection—probably the finest in the world—of the various early editions of *The Nigger of the Narcissus.* It was set up in proof in New York, but the collector then expressed dissatisfaction with its appearance and said he was going to have it set up again—this time in Paris. But I incline to think that this was never done, as I have heard nothing more about it.

PREFACES, ARTICLES, REVIEWS, ETC.

(Where any variety of nom de plume or pseudonym was used I do not insert "Anonymous." Where there is no mention of any author and no "Anonymous" I employed my own name).

1.

UNDER WESTERN EYES

Long review, headed "Mr. Conrad's New Novel", in *The Manchester Guardian,* October 11, 1911. This is, I presume, my first printed criticism of Conrad.

2.

SOME REMINISCENCES

Long review, headed "Mr. Conrad's Reminiscences", in *The Manchester Guardian,* February 2, 1912.

3.

'TWIXT LAND AND SEA

Review in *The English Review,* November, 1912.

4

"JOSEPH CONRAD"

Article of 11 pages in *Rythm,* November, 1912. It was this article, written largely to express my admiration for *Nostromo,* that first got me in touch with Conrad. It was shown to him by Edward Garnett. Conrad wrote to me on November 6, 1912: "I need have been an ungrateful churl not to be moved by your article for the *Rythm.* A mere sympathetic attempt would have been something to be thankful for—but you have very definitely achieved an analysis which (whatever others may think of it) I hold as very valuable both in matter and in tone. A great friend of mine (Edward Garnett) said to me the other day: 'This is the first thing worth reading which has been written about you in the way of general appreciation.' " What Conrad said to Garnett may be quoted from a letter Garnett wrote to me on October 17th: "Conrad is delighted with your criticism. He writes: 'Would Curle care to see me? That criticism is *something* and no mistake. I am exceedingly pleased. Give him my friendly greeting . . . I shall ask him down here soon. Send me his address and just tell me whether he can leave London on weekdays.' "

5.

"THE ART OF JOSEPH CONRAD"

Everyman, November 22, 1912, 1 page.

6.

'TWIXT LAND AND SEA

Long review in *Everyman,* December 27, 1912.

7.

CHANCE

Long review in *The English Review,* February, 1914.

8.

CHANCE

Long review in *The Bookman,* London, February, 1914.

9.

"JOSEPH CONRAD—A STUDY"

The Bookman, New York, August-September-October, 1914, 25½ pages. These three articles were reprinted, in an expanded form, as the first three chapters of my book, *Joseph Conrad: A Study.*

10.

"MR. JOSEPH CONRAD AND VICTORY"

The Fortnightly Review, October, 1915, 9 pages. A study of his genius in the light of his new novel, *Victory.*

11.

THE RESCUE

Long review in *The New Statesman,* July 3rd, 1920. My recollection is that Conrad was extremely pleased with this review and I fancy that in one of his printed letters there are words to that effect.

12.

"EARLY CONRAD FIRST EDITIONS", BY AN OCCASIONAL CONTRIBUTOR

The Bookman's Journal, July 15, 1921.

13.

"NEW DISCOVERIES IN THE BIBLIOGRAPHY OF CHANCE", BY A CONRAD COLLECTOR

The Bookman's Journal, December, 1921.

14.

"THE BIBLIOGRAPHY OF CHANCE", A LETTER BY THE WRITER OF THE ARTICLE

The Bookman's Journal, January, 1922.

15.

"THE FIRST U. S. EDITION OF CHANCE"

The Bookman's Journal, February, 1922. (Presumably anonymous).

16.

"CONRAD AT HOME", BY A FRIEND

The Daily Mail, April 7, 1922.

17.

AT SEA WITH JOSEPH CONRAD, BY CAPTAIN SUTHERLAND

The Daily Mail, June 28, 1922. Review under the heading, "Book About Conrad." Conrad was pleased with my rather contemptuous review of what he called, if I remember, "preposterous bosh". (Anonymous).

18.

"JOSEPH CONRAD IN THE EAST"

The Blue Peter, September-October, 1922, 5 pages. This article was later produced as a pamphlet, printed from the type of the magazine with new pagination, etc., in an edition of 21 copies.

19.

WISDOM AND BEAUTY FROM CONRAD

Very long review in *The Times Literary Supplement,* March 1, 1923, headed "Conrad in Extract". (Anonymous).

20.

"THE HISTORY OF MR. CONRAD'S BOOKS", FROM A CORRESPONDENT

The Times Literary Supplement, August 30, 1923, about 3 columns. This long article also appeared in *The New York Times Book Review,* August 26, 1923, under the title, "Conrad's Treasure Chest of Experience", and was reprinted in part in my pamphlet, *Joseph Conrad: The History of His Books.* (Anonymous in London; probably signed in New York).

21.

"THE STORY OF LORD JIM"

The Times Literary Supplement, September 13, 1923. This brief letter was in response to a column letter from Sir Frank Swettenham arising out of my article in *The Times Literary Supplement,* August 30, 1923. It was followed by another letter from Sir Frank and also by one from Alfred Holt and Company, the Liverpool shipowners. (Anonymous).

22.

THE ROVER

Review, under the heading "Conrad Looks at Nelson", in *The Daily Mail,* December 3, 1923. (Probably anonymous).

23.

THE ROVER

Long review in *The Blue Peter,* January, 1924.

24 & 25.

ACCOUNT OF CONRAD'S LAST ILLNESS AND DEATH; AND OBITUARY

Conrad died at Oswalds, Bishopsbourne, near Canterbury, on the morning of August 3, 1924. I was there at the time. On the afternoon of that day I returned to London and wrote an account of his last hours, which was published in *The Daily Mail,* August 4, together with a rather detailed biography of his life which I had prepared long before. (Both anonymous).

26.

"RESOLUTION: A MORAL FROM JOSEPH CONRAD." UNDER THE PSEUDONYM, JOHN BLUNT

The Daily Mail, August 5, 1924.

27.

"JOSEPH CONRAD AND THE DAILY MAIL", BY A FRIEND

The Daily Mail, August 14, 1924. An account of the various reviews and articles he had written for this paper.

28.

LEGENDS

The Daily Mail, August 15, 1924. Conrad was at work on this article when he died. When published in *The Daily Mail* I wrote a preface to it. (Anonymous).

29.

"THE LAST OF CONRAD"

John O'London's Weekly, September 20 and 27, 1924, 6 columns. This article describes the death of Conrad and was written only a few days after that event. It was reprinted in *The Mentor,* New York, March, 1925, and also in the Johannesburg *Star.* Revised and enlarged, it was subsequently issued in a privately printed pamphlet, limited to 100 copies, which itself was used as the basis of my final chapter in *The Last Twelve Years of Joseph Conrad.*

30.

THE NATURE OF A CRIME

The Daily Mail, September 30, 1924. Review, headed "Conrad and Hueffer". Probably written by me. (Anonymous).

31.

LAUGHING ANNE AND ONE DAY MORE

The Daily Mail, October 22, 1924. Review under the heading, "Two Plays by Conrad". Almost certainly written by me. (Anonymous).

32.

"THE PERSONALITY OF JOSEPH CONRAD"

The Edinburgh Review, January, 1925, 13 pages. This article, reprinted from the type of *The Edinburgh Review,* with alterations as to pagination and with a title-page and wrappers, was also issued in a private pamphlet of 100 copies. Much of it was used in the second chapter of *The Last Twelve Years of Joseph Conrad.*

33.

A CATALOGUE OF BOOKS, MANUSCRIPTS, AND CORRECTED TYPESCRIPTS FROM THE LIBRARY OF THE LATE JOSEPH CONRAD

Hodgson & Co., London, 1925. This sale took place on March 13, 1925. I wrote a 1-page preface for it.

34.

NOTES BY JOSEPH CONRAD WRITTEN IN A SET OF HIS FIRST EDITIONS IN THE POSSESSION OF RICHARD CURLE, WITH AN INTRODUCTION AND EXPLANATORY COMMENTS

London, 1925. This privately printed booklet of rather more than 40 pages was limited to 100 signed and numbered copies. Mrs. Conrad wrote a preface to it. My introduction consists of 4½ pages and I also wrote footnotes to the entries.

Conrad was in the habit of writing special notes for me in his first editions, and 50 of these are reproduced here. T. J. Wise had previously made use of a few of them in his *Bibliography* of Conrad, and others were reproduced in the Catalogue of *The Richard Curle Conrad Collection,* sold by the American Art Association in 1927, and in the fifth chapter of *The Last Twelve Years of Joseph Conrad.*

35.

"CONRAD'S SUSPENSE"

The New York Sun, May 8, 1925.

A letter on the subject of the propriety of not allowing anybody to finish *Suspense.*

36.

SUSPENSE

J. M. Dent & Sons, London, 1925. For this uncompleted and posthumous novel by Conrad I wrote a 2½-page introduction. This did not appear in the first American edition, but it does appear in subsequent American editions.

37.

SUSPENSE

The Daily Mail, September 16, 1925. Review headed "Conrad's 'Last' ". Probably written by me. (Anonymous).

38.

NOSTROMO—MEMORIAL EDITION OF CONRAD

Doubleday, Page & Co., Garden City, New York, 1925. For this edition of Conrad's complete works, produced the year after his death, the publishers asked various well-known authors or friends of Conrad to write introductions to the individual books. My introduction, which fills 4 pages, was to *Nostromo.*

39.

"CONRAD TODAY"

The Daily Mail, December 28, 1925. A review of the Medallion Edition of his works, signed R. H. P. C.

40.

THE NIGGER OF THE NARCISSUS

The World's Great Books in Outline, Part VI, January 12, 1926. A summary by me, with commentary and quotations, of this novel, together with a 1-page introduction entitled, "A Note on Joseph Conrad".

41.

JOSEPH CONRAD'S DIARY OF HIS JOURNEY TO THE CONGO IN 1890

London, 1926. This privately printed booklet of about 35 pages was produced in an issue of 100 copies. My introduction occupies 9 pages and I also transcribed the manuscript and wrote a number of footnotes. It was first published in *The Blue Peter,* and the booklet, just as it is, was reprinted in Conrad's posthumous volume, *Last Essays.*

42.

LAST ESSAYS

J. M. Dent & Sons, London, 1926; Doubleday, Page & Co., Garden City, New York, 1926. I assembled the material for this posthumous volume and wrote a 7-page introduction to it. The "Congo Diary", with my preface and notes, was published at the end of the book.

43.

LAST ESSAYS

The Daily Mail, March 3, 1926. Review headed "Conrad Essays". Probably written by me. (Anonymous).

44.

"SOME INTIMATE RECOLLECTIONS OF JOSEPH CONRAD"

The Blue Peter, April, 1926, 1½ pages.

45.

"OBJECTION AND REPROOF"

A letter in *The New York Times Book Review,* May 9, 1926. This letter refutes a statement by Joseph Pennell to the effect that Conrad was a Jew.

46.

JOSEPH CONRAD AS I KNEW HIM, BY JESSIE CONRAD

William Heinemann Ltd., London, 1926; Doubleday, Page & Co., Garden City, New York, 1926. For this volume of personal reminiscenses of Conrad by his wife I wrote an introduction of 1½ pages.

47.

"MY CONRAD COLLECTION"

The Mermaid, Detroit, October, 1926. A 7-page article regarding my Conrad collection, half of the first page being an introductory description by the editor about myself and my collection. This little article, revised, was used by me as the Preface to my Conrad sale catalogue.

48.

"THE REAL CONRAD"

The Herald-Tribune, October 23, 1926. Long article.

49.

THE RICHARD CURLE CONRAD COLLECTION

American Art Association, New York, 1927. For this sale catalogue I wrote an introduction of 2½ pages and, indeed, compiled most of the entries. The catalogue, with its many facsimiles and its elaborate descriptions of what was probably at the time the most interesting of all Conrad collections, must always be of value to students and collectors of Conrad.

The sale took place on April 28, 1927, and was an enormous success. Some time before he died Conrad suddenly said to me—the subject had not been even remotely touched upon between us—that I ought to sell my collection of his works; and therefore, when it did become necessary for me to sell the major portion of it, I was able to do so with the certain knowledge that he would have highly approved.

50.

CONRAD'S LIFE AND LETTERS

Long review in *The Weekly Dispatch,* headed "Conrad as Critic of His Own Books", October 23, 1927.

51.

CONRAD'S LIFE AND LETTERS

Long review in *The Daily Mail,* October 27, 1927. (Anonymous).

52.

CONRAD'S LIFE AND LETTERS

Very long review in *The New Statesman,* November 5, 1927.

53.

"CONRAD VILLAGE UNVEILS PORCH AS MEMORIAL"

The Herald-Tribune, November 13, 1927. An article describing the unveiling by R. B. Cunninghame Graham of the porch to the village hall at Bishopsbourne—the village in Kent where Conrad spent his last five years—subscribed to as a memorial by friends and admirers in England and the United States. I used the substance of a few paragraphs in the tenth chapter of *The Last Twelve Years of Joseph Conrad.*

54.

THE EDWARD GARNETT COLLECTION OF INSCRIBED BOOKS AND AUTOGRAPH MATERIAL BY JOSEPH CONRAD AND W. H. HUDSON

American Art Association, New York, 1928. For this catalogue I wrote a 1-page introduction to oblige my friend, Edward Garnett. The prices at the sale, which took place on April 24 and 25, were on the whole very satisfactory.

55.

A CONRAD LIBRARY COLLECTED BY THOMAS J. WISE

London, 1928. For this privately printed catalogue of one of the finest Conrad libraries in the world I wrote a 2-page introduction.

56.

LETTERS: JOSEPH CONRAD TO RICHARD CURLE. EDITED WITH AN INTRODUCTION AND NOTES BY R. C

Crosby Gaige, New York, 1928. This work, which consists of 150 letters from Conrad to myself, was limited to an edition of 850 copies on all-rag paper and 9 copies on green paper (a hideous book). The copies on all-rag paper were bound in green boards with a white linen back and green and gold label, whereas the copies on green paper—why they should have chosen such a colour I cannot conceive!—were bound in black cloth, gold-lettered on the spine. It was printed by William Edwin Rudge and the typography was by Bruce Rogers. This same book was produced twice more in the same year by different publishers and under a different title. (See next entry).

My preface covers 3 pages and I wrote many footnotes to the letters themselves. When this book was already printed I came to the conclusion that some of Conrad's remarks about other people might be better omitted, and therefore the sheets had to be unstitched and several pages reprinted. I understand, however, that about 8 sets of the original sheets were pasted on to plain paper and bound up in a different style.

56a.

CONRAD TO A FRIEND: 150 SELECTED LETTERS FROM JOSEPH CONRAD TO RICHARD CURLE. EDITED WITH AN INTRODUCTION AND NOTES BY R. C.

Sampson Low, Marston & Co., London, 1928; Doubleday, Doran & Co., Garden City, New York, 1928. This is essentially the same book as the one mentioned above: it is the ordinary trade edition, in the different types and bindings of England and the United States, for both countries. But my recollection is that the text of the introduction, the notes, and the letters themselves vary in all three editions, though I must leave it to some industrious enthusiast, if such a one there be, to clear up the differences.

57.

"CONRAD AND EXPLORATION"

The Herald-Tribune, September 10, 1928. A letter in amplification of a leading article of the day before stating that a set of Conrad was to be carried in the ship's library of the "City of New York", which took part in the Byrd Antarctic expedition.

58.

"JOSEPH CONRAD AS A LETTER WRITER"

The Herald-Tribune, Books, September 30, 1928. This lengthy article was given the place of honour in *Books*.

59.

A CONRAD MEMORIAL LIBRARY, THE COLLECTION OF GEORGE T. KEATING

Doubleday, Doran & Co., Garden City, New York, 1929. For this magnificently produced catalogue of a famous Conrad collection I wrote the introduction to *The Arrow of Gold.* It fills 4 pages, appearing on pages 273-7.

60.

A CONRAD MEMORIAL LIBRARY, THE COLLECTION OF GEORGE T. KEATING

A long review, headed "Man and Author", in *The Saturday Review of Literature,* November 2, 1929.

61.

A CONRAD MEMORIAL LIBRARY, THE COLLECTION OF GEORGE T. KEATING

A long review, headed "In Memory of Conrad", in *The Daily Telegraph,* November 6, 1929.

62.

"CONRAD AND THE YOUNGER GENERATION"

The Nineteenth Century and After, January, 1930, 10 pages. In this article I tried to follow the trend of the latest criticism about Conrad and to explain why it was that while a certain group of younger critics was repelled by his work, other young people were being increasingly attracted to it.

63.

TWO ESSAYS ON CONRAD, BY JOHN GALSWORTHY

Freelands, Mentor, Kentucky, 1930. For this privately printed booklet, of which 93 copies were printed to the order of W. T. H. Howe, I wrote an account of the friendship of Conrad and Galsworthy under the heading, "The Story of a Remarkable Friendship." I understand that Galsworthy was pleased with it. It runs to 12 pages.

64.

THE POLISH HERITAGE OF JOSEPH CONRAD, BY GUSTAV MORF

The Herald-Tribune, Books, March 1, 1931. A review, under the heading, "Conrad's Race".

65.

THE POLISH HERITAGE OF JOSEPH CONRAD, BY GUSTAV MORF

The Saturday Review of Literature, June 6, 1931. A review, under the heading, "Conrad and Poland".

66.

"RECOLLECTIONS OF CONRAD AND CUNNINGHAME GRAHAM"

These few hundred words about the friendship between Conrad and R. B. Cunninghame Graham are to appear in Professor West's forthcoming study of Cunninghame Graham's life and work. I mention this little article here, although both unimportant and yet to be printed, because, as I have already written my reminiscences of Conrad and Galsworthy, I would like to include this brief reminiscence of Conrad's association with another of his oldest and closest friends.